Knowledge Economies

This book makes a strong and coherent contribution to the discussion of the knowledge economy and of innovation, offering a range of theoretical insights from different disciplinary perspectives. The role of knowledge, knowledge development, and knowledge diffusion is discussed not only at the micro level of individuals and firms, but also at the level of groups of firms and sectors, as well as at the level of the economy at large.

Dolfsma analyses knowledge development and diffusion as a thoroughly social process, depending on communicative structures to support cooperation. The author combines insights from economics and management with perspectives from sociology (network theory), anthropology (gift exchange), social psychology, science studies and information theory (scientometrics), using empirical analyses to demonstrate where knowledge impacts the dynamics of an economy.

This book will be of great interest to students and researchers engaged with the economics of innovation and knowledge as well as policy makers interested in knowledge development and transfer.

Wilfred Dolfsma, economist and philosopher, holds a PhD in economics and is currently employed at the University of Groningen School of Economics and Business as professor of innovation. In addition, he is corresponding editor of the *Review of Social Economy*.

Routledge Studies in Global Competition
Edited by John Cantwell, Rutgers, the State University of New Jersey, USA and David Mowery, University of California, Berkeley, USA

Knowledge Economies

Organization, location and innovation

Wilfred Dolfsma

Routledge
Taylor & Francis Group

LONDON AND NEW YORK

First published 2008
by Routledge
2 Park Square, Milton Park, Abingdon, Oxon, OX14 4RN

Simultaneously published in the USA and Canada
by Routledge
605 Third Avenue, New York, NY 10017

*Routledge is an imprint of the Taylor & Francis Group,
an informa business*

Typeset in 10/12pt Times New Roman by Graphicraft Limited,
Hong Kong

British Library Cataloguing in Publication Data
A catalogue record for this book is available
from the British Library

Library of Congress Cataloging-in-Publication Data
Dolfsma, Wilfred.
  Knowledge economies : innovation, organization and location /
Wilfred Dolfsma.
    p. cm. — (Routledge studies in global competition)
  Includes bibliographical references and index.
  ISBN 978–0–415–41665–8 (hb) — ISBN 978–0–203–92969–8 (eb)
1. Intellectual capital. 2. Organizational learning. 3. Knowledge
management. 4. Communication in organizations. 5. Communities of
practice. I. Title.
  HD53.D65 2008
  330—dc22

                                                        2007037730

ISBN 13: 978–0–415–56953–8 (pbk)
ISBN 13: 978–0–415–41665–8 (hbk)

To Marnix and Jorinde who, together, know that knowledge is about facts, interpretation, and social context.

Contents

Tables

Figures

Preface

Developing new knowledge is necessarily a cooperative effort. That is one of the main themes of this book. It applies reflectively as well, and, as I hope that new knowledge is offered in this book, it is inevitable that it is very much the result of joint efforts. I have been in the very fortunate position, in the past years in which this book has come to fruition, to have worked with people who have helped me better understand the role of knowledge in the economy and in economic and social theory. There are widening circles of people that I would like to identify as contributing to my work, I just hope that I have been able to contribute as much to each of them as they have to me. In light of Mauss' (1954 [2000]) insight that there is a need for people in a given community not just to give, but also to receive, and finaly to reciprocate, I can only express deep gratitude to the people who have given whom I will mention momentarily.

Some people I owe deep gratitude to can readily be identified through work that is included here. In combining knowledge and insights when working on a project it is possible that novel insights and knowledge may develop. I am sure that this has happened in the projects on which this book draws, at least for me personally. Consequently, it pleases me to thank Rick Aalbers, Rene van der Eijk, Albert Jolink, Otto Koppius, Loet Leydesdorff, Gerben van der Panne, Pat Welch for their inspiring, provoking and fruitful cooperation.

Others have read and discussed individual pieces critically and constructively. I would like to thank Mark Blaug, John Davis, Sheila Dow, Hinnerk Gnutzmann, Jeroen Hinloopen, Ferdinand Jaspers, Peter Leeson, Killian McCarthy, Robert McMaster, Bert Mosselmans, Arie Rip, Franz Schaper, Rudi Verburg, Ulrich Witt, and Fia Wunderink. While these contributions constitute the kind of intellectual gifts without which academia would grind to a shrieking halt, contributions such as they have made I cherish. Reflecting on my personal intellectual trajectory on the role of knowledge in the economy and in economics, I should go back to the times when I was graduating from economics and philosophy over 15 years ago. Since then Jack Vromen, John Groenewegen, Alfred Kleinknecht, Luc Soete, and perhaps also George Waardenburg and Gernot Grabher provided stimulus. Certainly Arjo Klamer did. My institutional odyssey reflects this too; from Erasmus University (economics of culture), University of Twente (philosophy of science and technology), University of Bonn (economic geography), Delft University of

Technology (economics of innovation), RSM Erasmus University (business school), to UNU-MERIT, and the Utrecht School of Economics. I have learned from colleagues and friends in each place.

Participants in seminars at the Max Planck Institute, Jena, at a 2004 ECIS seminar at Eindhoven University, at a 2006 CIRCLE, Lund University workshop, at UNU-MERIT at Aberdeen University School of Business, at the 2005 EAEPE Conference, at the 2004 Sunbelt Conference, at the 2004 ISS Conference, at the 2005 EGOS Conference, at the 1996 and 2006 AFEE meetings and the 2005 World Summit on the Information Society should all be thanked and I do so eagerly.

All of this came to a head during a sabbatical I spent at the Netherlands Institute for Advanced Studies in the Social Sciences in the Humanities and the Social Sciences (NIAS) in the academic year of 2005/2006, at that wonderful location in the Wassenaar dunes. Perhaps the changes in the way NIAS worked and how it facilitated its visiting scholars during that year – seen as revolutionary by its staff – have brought out the angle on the theme of this book: cooperation is necessary for new knowledge to develop and diffuse. Cooperation between individuals from a different disciplinary background was certainly stimulated to the best possible extent. Seminars organized, five minute talks, wonderful lunches and a great library service guaranteed that. Cooperation with more likeminded people, with whom one has an extended cooperation, however, requires that they may not only be enticed to come over to Wassenaar, but also that they can sometimes be called. It is with great relief that I learned soon after I arrived at NIAS that landlines would be installed in each office! While this, of course, is a joke, some element of each joke is always to be taken seriously. In thanking everybody who has made my stay at NIAS such a wonderful experience, I would still like to single out Jos Hooghuis, Wouter Hugenholz, Rita Buis, Eline van der Ploeg, and dean Wim Blockmans.

Publishers and journals are important, albeit sometimes anonymous players in the academic scene. Some of the material presented in this book was published before, in articles in the Journal of Economic Issues (2006, AFEE), the Journal of Economic and Social Geography (2003, Blackwell), Research Policy (2005, 2006, Elsevier) and the Review of Social Economy (2001, Routledge). I acknowledge the efforts that publishers, associations, referees, and editors have made to uphold quality, and to make sure that a setting was created and maintained where relevant and fruitful discussions could be staged.

1   Introduction

How to analyze the knowledge economy? How, in other words, to understand the changing and extending role of knowledge in the economy? Depending on how one defines 'knowledge economy', economies the globe 'round should always have been referred to as knowledge economies (Leydesdorff 2006). As the pace of innovation increases and knowledge assets[1] are increasingly recognized as important input in production processes that need to be recognized explicitly and can even be output that even for-profit organizations seek to develop for their own sake, as economic processes increasingly require intended or unintended self-organizing coordination between parties, and where the prospects of firms may be more related to their prospects for future profits based on newly developed goods than on current sales, one may well claim that currently most economically developed economies today can be characterized as a knowledge economy.

I argue that one necessarily needs to use a range of theoretical insights, at multiple aggregation levels, and from different perspectives to start to approach this question. The role of knowledge, knowledge development, and knowledge diffusion is discussed at the micro level of individuals and firms, but also at the level of groups of firms and sectors, as well as at the level of the economy at large.

The development of new knowledge is the result of individuals cooperating in groups, sometimes within a single organization, sometimes across the boundaries of an organization in a disciplinary field. Knowledge development thus, certainly ex post, can be recognized to follow specific trajectories. The trajectories align with routines and institutions that guide the search for, and further development of, knowledge. Knowledge or technological trajectories do not prevent one from explaining novelty, but rather explains how new insights can emerge, and with whom.

Trajectories are kept alive by people cooperating, working together to further knowledge. Cooperation may be motivated quite differently; people rarely have unmixed motives. Cooperation can be, and has been, studied by looking at the structures for cooperation – social networks. Specific patterns have been found to hold across a differing set of organizations. This sheds important light on the issues at hand. What is left out of this equation is the content of the relations depicted in these network structures. Specifically, in the context of trying to develop new knowledge – where the outcome hoped for may not materialize, the usefulness of what is found cannot be predicted, the input each party gives may not always be monitored, and breach of trust can largely go unpunished

– there is a need not just to analyze the structures of social interactions, but the content too. How do relations get started, how may relations be drawn upon, when can they come to an end? Social capital, and the trust that supposedly ensues, is too easily ascribed to a social network. In line with what former president of the American Economic Association, Kenneth Boulding, suggests, one may look at gift exchange as the theoretically more encompassing framework for such interactions. It is a theoretical framework that offers a richer perspective as communication and interpretation or framing enters the picture too.

Child and Faulkner (1998) may be the only ones to have hinted at the micro foundations for relations between firms – such as high-tech firms, or firms in a specific region – going through specific individuals. Managers of firms are an obvious link. Formal and informal relations between others can also constitute relations that cross firm boundaries. In anticipating the effects of such relations, firms decide where best to locate. This shows in the geographical patterns of economic activity as well as in macro analyses of communication structures that constitute preconditions for knowledge transfer. The latter is included here as well, measured in terms of entropy indicating the extent to which uncertainty in a knowledge economy is (locally) reduced due to (the possibility) of expectations being aligned by communication. Communication both requires and may create, if parties are willing, a shared frame of reference.

All too readily, economists have tended to ignore issues of interpretation and framing, sticking rather to a view that is most readily summarized in Figure 1.1;

Figure 1.1 The standard economic view of knowledge and learning
Source: DaDA, courtesy of © Gilia van Dijk filmprodukties, 1994.

the knowledge people have consists of explicit information that can be easily inspected. Somebody's knowledge is like books one carries around on one's head. Chapter two discusses this at more length, and argues how this view must be altered if a degree of realism is sought.

If the dynamics of a knowledge economy should be conceived of differently, if communication and miscommunication are of import, and if the concept of knowledge itself must be reconceptualized at least by economists, should then the way in that one is to evaluate relevant phenomena also be altered? In a final chapter to this monograph, I argue that indeed the usual Paretean welfare economics should be complemented by the kind of dynamic considerations of communication that play out in the longer term that are hinted at by Schumpeter. In particular, institutional changes to the system of Intellectual Property Rights (IPRs), central institutions in a knowledge economy, are scrutinized.

Obviously, then, insights from economics and management are presented, but these are combined in a coherent manner with insights from sociology (particularly network theory), social psychology, science studies and information theory (scientometrics). These are the most salient perspectives to be discerned from the manuscript. In addition, for these various aggregation levels, empirical analyses are presented that indicate just how, and where, knowledge impacts the dynamics of the economy. As a result, the monograph you now have in your hands can easily be distinguished from its 'competitors'. It fills a void in the literature. Even though it is interdisciplinary in spirit, it offers a coherent analysis, theoretically as well as empirically, of the topic. Others either offer an analysis from a specific perspective (Cooke 2002; Rooney *et al.* 2005; Foss 2005), seem to lack coherence even though they might have other strengths (Rooney *et al.* 2005; Dolfsma and Soete 2006), or do not offer the unique combination of theoretical discussion and empirical analysis (Rooney *et al.* 2005). Some hardly offer empirical material (Foss 2005 includes 'critical essays'), or are rather reflective (Thrift 2005).

While I primarily write this book as an economist, one will find that insights from management, philosophy, (economic) sociology and network analysis, economic geography and public policy are actively drawn on and integrated into the framework. Graduate, as well as undergraduate, students should be able to understand its argument, and fellow scholars may find useful insights here as well. The phenomenon discussed is clearly tropical, and the angles taken appreciable, so policy makers may also find it informative. I have certainly tried to cater to this group also.

2 Knowledge and learning

'The Caterpillar {said} sternly "Explain yourself!" "I can't explain myself, I'm afraid, sir," said Alice "because I'm not myself, you see." '
                                    Lewis Carroll – *Alice's Adventures in Wonderland*

'Knowledge' takes a central place in the economy, but is a rather undertheorized concept in the economics literature. The metaphor pervasively used in economics to understand knowledge is that of 'capital'. Taking capital as a metaphor of knowledge introduces problems, as becomes apparent when economics addresses issues of learning and technological development. Instead, it is argued that economists could learn from what philosophers as well as psychologists have said about how to understand knowledge. In the fields of technology studies and the history of economics, such views have had some impact.

2.1 INTRODUCTION

The newly emerging reality of our economies today is that they are knowledge economies (OECD 1996b). This is recognized in diverse strands of thought in the economics discipline after the puzzling findings in the Growth Accounting literature (e.g. Denison 1967). Romer (1987, 1993) has been developing ideas about how knowledge impacts on economic growth, better known as New Growth Theory. The work of Baumol (2002) relates to this. Studying a dynamic, knowledge-based economy requires that a conceptual understanding of knowledge is developed to be used in economics. This chapter, therefore, first finds fault with some conceptualizations that have some currency in economics, then looks more closely at some of the features of the concept of knowledge, such as are relevant, and subsequently discusses the merits of the views of knowledge expounded here.

2.2 KNOWLEDGE IN ECONOMICS: CAPITAL

According to Nobel Laureate in economics Friedrich Hayek, the concept of 'knowledge' is central to economic theory (1937, 1945). Many strands in economics have, however, largely neglected the discussions on the subject of the nature of knowledge – epistemics is largely ignored. The view on knowledge, whether implicitly subscribed to or explicitly taken, has important consequences for the development of economic theory. The opposite is also true – a scholar's epistemic position relates to the kind of economic theory adopted. Because the concept of knowledge is such an elusive one, economists, in search of a way of grasping it, have tried to come to grips with it by employing the known concept of capital in a way that stretches its original use.[1] I draw on ideas proposed by philosophers and psychologists who have studied the concept of 'knowledge' to make the case that knowledge is not usefully treated as if it were capital.

To most economists, the metaphor of capital seems most useful in dealing with 'knowledge'. Such comparisons of knowledge with capital are the cornerstone of human capital theory, as developed by Becker and others. A consequence for economic theory of perceiving of knowledge as if it were capital is that the phenomena of technology and technological change present theoretical difficulties.

In order to find a description of what is generally taken as capital by economists, one can perhaps best go back to one of the founding fathers of the science. Marshall (1920) is one of the most influential among them, and, moreover, quite explicit with regard to what is to be regarded as capital. 'Capital' is a collection of goods external to the economic agent that can be sold for money and from which (hence) an income can be derived (Marshall 1920: 71). In this regard, Marshall is following the lead of Adam Smith in his *Wealth of Nations* (1776: see for instance paragraphs II.i.1 and II.i.17). Capital is something tangible to these early economists, although Machlup (1984: 403) does not hold that capital is necessarily tangible. Nevertheless, if one is to inquire about the way the concept of capital is used today, the positions taken by these authors still seem to hold their own. Hennings (1987) has provided a lucid overview of the way in which the concept of capital is used in economic theory from the day of its inception, to present times. In this article, it is argued that capital is considered in the history of the development of the concept to be something tangible, external to the economic agent, that can, moreover, be measured or valued in terms of money.

Figure 1.1 is one frame from an animation picture called DaDA. The knowledge that people in the imaginary world of this motion picture have is measured by the number of books that each of them carries on his head. Furthermore, by consulting the books, one can easily determine the nature and amount of knowledge somebody has acquired. This is the idea of learning as the linear and unidirectional accumulation of knowledge that inspires human capital theorists. It does not resemble the way of conceiving of knowledge that is generally adhered to in philosophy and psychology, as I will indicate below.

Several authors, working in diverse fields of the social sciences, have drawn on ideas propounded in economic theory to build theories to explain human behavior. An important concept used in this regard is the concept of 'capital' in lieu of the concept of 'knowledge'. Where the term 'human', 'social', 'organizational' or 'cultural' is placed in front of it, there seems to me, in particular, to be some misperception as to what use can be made of the concept of capital. I here refer to such authors as Stigler and Becker (1977), Becker and Murphy (1988), Becker (1996), North (1990), Denzau and North (1994), Coleman (1998) and Bourdieu (1984). Becker's work (1996) and the work of North (Denzau and North 1994) will be focused on primarily here because of the explicit way in which they address the issue of knowledge and learning, and because of the prominence of the authors and these specifics works. Authors use a metaphor in order to come to grips with an elusive concept and thus strengthen or simply make an argument. McCloskey (1983) has argued forcefully that metaphors are essential to (neoclassical economic) theories and arguments, but that they often remain implicit. Vroon and Draaisma (1985) take the argument further, saying that a particular metaphor *directs* human thinking and the development of theories. I will now compare the concept of capital with that of knowledge.

The earliest explicit argument, to my knowledge, for treating human knowledge as if it were capital and actually attempting to find more than simply indicative measures for it, is expressed by Walsh (1935). In the present time, human capital theory has become so 'successful', that some scholars claim it was 'discovered' much earlier. Brahmananda (1988), for instance, claims that Jevons should be credited. Jevons was certainly not the only, or the first, to have remarked that education can increase a person's productive capacities.[2] As it turns out, Smith made similar allusions (1776: Book II, Ch. I, 17), as did Sir William Perry in the late seventeenth century (Kiker 1966). However, as far as I am aware, Walsh was the first to follow the logic of the capital metaphor for knowledge to its end and make calculations. He observes that the more advanced and prolonged the education, the more exclusively vocational its purpose the more probable it is that the guiding principle will be that of ordinary economic gain. *If this is true*, it would seem clear that the abilities acquired through strictly professional education *resemble* capital very closely (1935: 257, emphasis added).

Note that he does not equate human knowledge with capital here, although he applies the same methods in both cases. Even more, he restricts the treatment of knowledge in terms of capital to specific ways of acquiring knowledge, or to specific types of knowledge. Elsewhere in the article, Walsh is less cautious in his statements and speaks of '*other* forms of capital' when referring to machines and the like (1935: 284, emphasis added). The general line of reasoning is clear, however, that when the motive of monetary gain is used to assess whether or not to spend money on an education which may yield future monetary benefits, (neoclassical) capital theory should be applied. Stigler and Becker (1977: 83) take one more step in equating knowledge with capital, although they restrict the knowledge they refer to as 'specific' knowledge.

As McCloskey has rightly pointed out, the concept of capital was turned into a metaphor when Becker *cum suis* introduced 'human capital into the rhetoric (conceptual apparatus) of economics, and the field of economics treating human skills was at a stroke *unified* with the field of treating investment in machines' (1983: 504, emphasis added). While this unification was perhaps illuminating for businessmen in emphasizing the importance of the 'human factor' in production, it is mystifying in economic theory. It led to calculations similar to those of ROI (Return On Investment) and Present Value of investment in education (see Stigler and Becker 1977: 79). Calculations such as these can be useful if their importance is not overemphasized. Much more, however, is involved in education and child-rearing than the acquisition of capabilities useful, or valuable, in the market place. It is the latter that is stressed when talking about the ROI and Present Value of human capital, often to the neglect of the former.

Most salient in this way of employing the metaphor of capital are Becker and Stigler (1977). In the case of the appreciation and consumption of music, for instance, *exposure* to it will lead to the accumulation of a 'capital for the appreciation of music' (ibid.: 78). From this an 'income' is, or can be drawn, although Becker and Stigler do not explicitly use the word 'income' in this particular case. Boulding (1977: 4) and Becker and Murphy (1988) are, however, more explicit on this count. This income will accrue to the person in the form of reduced shadow prices of listening to music in the future. From the stock of cultural or consumption capital runs a flow of 'interest' which will (partly) compensate for the cost of listening to music (ibid.: 79). More recently, prominent neoclassical economists have been influenced in their thinking by the capital metaphor in their attempts to conceptualize knowledge, cognition and learning. Becker (1996) has been explicit, North, in his often referred to 1990 book, less so, however in later work North has been more elaborate (Denzau and North 1994). These recent studies present interesting and new arguments. I will show, however, that using the metaphor of capital to conceptualize knowledge analytically, does not provide much mileage.

Central to Becker's approach is what he calls the 'extended utility function' (1996: 5):

$$u = u(xt, yt, zt, Pt, St) \hspace{4cm} \text{(Eq. 2.1)}$$

where x, y and z stand for 'different goods' and P and S stand for Personal and Social Capital, respectively. According to Becker, this function allows one to explain both individual learning, and the effects of social relations on persons. Becker says: 'the utility function itself is independent of time, so that it is a stable function over time of the goods consumed and also of the capital goods'. This puzzling statement is clarified later on the same page:

> utility does not depend directly on goods and consumer capital stocks, but only on household-produced 'commodities', such as health, social standing and reputation, and pleasures of the senses. The production of these commodities in turn depends on goods, consumer capital, abilities, and other variables.
>
> (Becker 1996: 5)

In terms of utility functions, what this means is that their shape remains the same throughout a person's life, although somebody may attain higher levels of satisfaction in terms of more fundamental 'goods' by investing in his or her social and personal capital. 'A person's personal and social capital form part of this total stock of human capital' (Becker 1996: 4). Learning takes an effort that is like an investment and creates human capital. Economic agents are thought to have a production function internal to themselves for transforming goods into 'higher order' commodities.

Now preferences for *particular* goods are no longer fixed and given, but the extended preferences are. Of course, Becker asserts that this is what he had been saying all along (ibid.: 6), and technically he is right. In their *De Gustibus Non Est Disputandum*, Stigler and Becker (1977: 77) do not speak of particular goods either. These more basic things are 'health, social standing and reputation, and pleasures of the senses' (Becker 1996: 5). What this view boils down to, is that people know from the start what kind of person they want to be. We are concerned with the broad picture, of course, not with details. So, Bill Clinton always wanted to be president, and Keith Haring always a painter. Behind Becker's cold analytical front stage, however, there is an oddly romantic back stage. His view of individuals is the romantic idea that an individual remains an utterly independent and autonomous person.

The most serious problem, however, relates to how Becker perceives of information. Not only is this the most serious problem, it is also a crucial part of Becker's argument, and neoclassical arguments in general. Information speaks for itself, data needs no interpretation. The key word here is 'interpretation'. Different interpretations of a situation can only occur in the Bayesian world that Becker adopts when people are faced with uncertainty. Uncertainty is subsequently translated into incomplete information. As soon as more information is gathered, differences of interpretation disappear in Becker's view (cf. Dow 1998). Conceptions of Bayesian learning rest on the assumption that 'the laws of logic and probability theory represent the laws of rational reasoning and that humans actually follow these laws' (Ortmann and Gigerenzer 1997: 700).

Becker's treatment of 'culture' is somewhat awkward in this regard. Culture implies differences, differences of interpretation that do not reduce to a lack of information, differences that persist despite the fact that people have the same knowledge. When in the USA a woman and a man, for instance, walk hand in hand, one can reasonably infer that they are intimately related. They may be in love. When in India a woman and a man walk hand in hand, they are frowned upon. A woman and a man who are in love with each other do not walk hand in hand in India; only two or more women *or* two or more men who are friends walk hand in hand in public. By dealing with culture as though it were a kind of capital with an extremely low depreciation rate (Becker 1996: 16), differences such as these remain puzzling.

A social or institutional economist could analyze these differences in terms of the different institutions or norms that exist in the different societies.[3] Such an economist would study the emergence, change, and consequences of institutions closely, taking notice of the rich and overwhelming quantitative and qualitative empirical material that bears on the issue. Not so Becker. To him, institutions are created by individuals who stand to gain from them. Since he acknowledges that, in reality, people have imperfect foresight and are not omnipotent, he takes a position that in philosophy is known as 'rule-utilitarianism'. Not every single action can be utility maximizing because of human fallibility, but people create 'optimally imperfect' rules of thumb. The human intellect is then just another constraint, besides budget and time constraints. This is how habits are formed and addictions have started (see also Baumol and Quandt 1964).

When talking about identical people, whose differing interpretations of their environment have no place in this framework, the result would be that everybody adopts the same rule of thumb, were it not for the accumulation of personal and social capital. Were personal and social capital not to interfere, habits would create institutions. If habits were optimally imperfect for one person, others would adopt the same habit, either by themselves or by imitation. As Alchian's (1950) evolutionary argument would have it, to make the case complete, the most efficient solution would prevail. People who are not efficient would not survive; all must and will imitate efficient rules of thumb. Thus, an individual habit grows into an institution among people of similar personal and social capital.

If, however, personal habits and social institutions (culture) are merely perceived as some kind of capital, however low their depreciation rate may be, how do we explain the persistence of habits and institutions that are obviously detrimental to the very existence of a person or a social group? How do we explain that people take overdoses of drugs that kill them, and how do we explain that groups of people make large sacrifices for their ideals? Since information is clear-cut, people in their right mind cannot make such mistakes. Becker, naturally, has also confronted this issue.

People might (temporarily) have a distorted perception. Becker indeed does talk of 'distorted perceptions', but he stresses that:

> . . . they may receive excessive attention at the expense of more significant weaknesses in standard models of rational choice for explaining behavior in real, as opposed to experimental, situations. These models typically assume that preferences do not directly depend on either past experiences or social interactions . . . To highlight these neglected constraints, the book does not emphasize cognitive imperfections, but rather the influence of personal and social capital on choices.
>
> (Becker 1996: 22)

Hence, these phenomena can safely be included in a *ceteris paribus* clause.

Becker, nevertheless, has yielded to his many critics by giving a different reason for what he is doing. Instead of (implicitly) relying on Milton Friedman's methodological argument (1953), which he previously would do, he makes an empirical claim that his problem is the more important one. He thus seems to acknowledge, contrary to what Friedman has advocated, that it is important to have realistic assumptions on which to rest your theoretical framework. At least he is explicit about it.

Yet, the implicit assumption that information does not need interpretation seems unrealistic. Cultural differences cannot be explained from this perspective. Similarly, treating social relations, culture and human knowledge as if they were capital, each with its particular depreciation rate, is unrealistic and raises a number of problems. For one, because tacit knowledge cannot be measured, it complicates the picture tremendously. The factor of time, and consequently that of change, also creates problems. If it can be addressed at all, and I doubt this, it can only be done for gradual changes in time within the economy. Sudden changes would remain baffling from this perspective.

The capital metaphor not only makes one think of the knowledge acquiring process as a uni-directional one, where past knowledge is automatically incorporated into present knowledge, it can also accommodate differences in the perspectives people take only by invoking 'noise'. Information in this view is open to just one interpretation – additional information will take away the ambiguity noise creates. With reference to Figure 2.1, differences between learning paths A and B cannot be accounted for.[4] At at the individual level and nor at super-individual levels, should one not strictly adhere to the prescripts of methodological individualism as North (1990) has come around to doing.

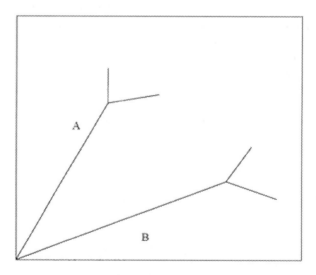

Figure 2.1 Differing paths – learning and interpretation
Source: Dolfsma (2002).

A Bayesian learning perspective incorporates the idea of information needing no interpretation before being added to the stock of knowledge already in place. It nicely allows for modelling. Denzau and North (1994) are uncomfortable about this assumption. Their suggestion for how to solve the problem is to allow for 'punctuated equilibria' in learning. Learning can sometimes be discontinuous, and involve periods of stagnation and spurts. Learning will still develop in one direction in Denzau and North's view, however, and punctuated equilibria presumably are only temporary breaks in the progression of knowledge towards true knowledge (cf Dolfsma 2002b).

2.3 KNOWLEDGE

Because of the 'intimations of an indeterminate range', as Polanyi (1966) phrases it, knowledge on a specific topic may not be measurable. A Return on Investment may not be computed: 'the sort of knowledge with which I have been concerned is knowledge of the kind which by its nature cannot enter into statistics' (Hayek 1945: 52–54). Knowledge is not a homogenous good (cf. Neale 1984). By learning, information becomes part of a larger framework of knowledge. Within that framework, a distinction cannot always be made between different kinds of knowledge. It is often impossible to separate where exactly knowledge of one subject ends, and where knowledge of another begins. To use the concept of capital to understand knowledge requires that such clear distinctions be possible, allowing one to identify relevant stocks and flows.[5]

Further, how can equating knowledge with capital account for changes in a person's views, interpretation, knowledge and preferences? Is there a 'capital for change' conceptually to be included in the framework? This is not likely to be the case, since no active involvement of the agent in assumed capital is accumulated when *exposed* to something. In a recent article Arrow (1994) argues in this vein. Knowledge is gained, according to Arrow, either by observing nature, or learning from other individuals (intended or unintended). His discussion strongly suggests a rather automatic and unproblematic accumulation of knowledge.

By contrast, I would argue for the inclusion of a concept of volition to account for changes of views, knowledge, interpretations and preferences (Biddle 1990). In some sense an active involvement of the economic agent has to be assumed. It requires at least some effort to construct the framework of knowledge that Polanyi (1983), Ryle (1949) and others speak off. Active involvement of the economic agent introduces unpredictabilities, uncertainties (Hodgson 1997). Uncertainty has no place in the capital view of knowledge. Risk only plays a role in the form of 'noise', but genuine uncertainty does not feature in economic theory (Knight 1921). In addition, adopting an epistemological view along the lines suggested below, entails not only that differences in the type of information is discussed, but it also entails that one is able to discuss the possibility of economic agents being different from each other. A concept of a person's identity is, however, not present in neoclassical economics, and, moreover, cannot be incorporated into the framework (Davis 1995, 2003). Finally, and almost trivially, the fact that in some eras and places, monetary gain is one of the motives for a particular group of people to try to acquire knowledge does not mean that the phenomenon can best be understood in terms of capital, emphasizing self-interest as a primary or even the sole source of motivation.

Besides the fact that the human mind is incapable of encompassing all information that is relevant, the mind is constructed in such a way that it is impossible for humans to put into words or text all the knowledge that they possess on a particular subject. A certain part of knowledge has to be tacit (Polanyi 1983 and Ryle 1966). Here, I use the term tacitness, often used by Polanyi, to refer to a phenomenon that has also been called knowing-how as compared to knowing-that by Ryle. Knowledge-how, the total of unconscious and conscious knowledge, encompasses more than knowledge-that. Knowledge-that may be described as conscious knowledge, as the knowledge that can be articulated. Knowing is used to indicate both practical as well as theoretical knowledge. Economists try to deny a tacit element exists in the total of a man's knowledge. To quote Ryle, they try to 'reassimilate knowing *how* to knowing *that*' (Ryle 1966: 29). Nelson (1959: 299) is a telling example. He asserts that 'knowledge is of two roughly separable sorts: facts or data observed in reproducible experiments and theories or relationships between facts'. In implying that certain types of knowledge can successfully be distinguished from others, Stigler and Becker (1977: 83) implicitly assume all knowledge to be knowledge-that. In fact, Ryle makes the plausible assertion that knowing-how is more extensive than knowing-that (ibid.: 41) and that knowing that by no means entails or naturally flows into knowing-how (1966: 56). The distinction, unfamiliar to many economists, between knowing-how and knowing-that is useful in thinking about the knowledge an economic agent has at any particular moment.[6]

Polanyi has developed a theory of knowledge acquisition that should also be of interest to economists. Polanyi (1983: 7) argues that (tacit) knowledge is acquired in a process he calls 'subception'. Any piece of information to be transplanted from one person to another is 'recepted' (ibid.: 5) by this other person and integrated, or subsumed, into a larger framework of knowledge in which meaning is given to this new piece of information (ibid.: 19). To the extent that information is subsumed (and it has to be subsumed if it is to have any meaning) into a larger framework of knowledge, it is interiorized (ibid.: 29), as it were, to become a part of the body (cf. Douglas 1986: 13). From this, it follows that man cannot always accurately state what it is that he knows about a certain topic. Such knowledge is typically 'fraught with further intimations of an indeterminate range' (Polanyi 1983: 23). Where knowledge relevant to the particular subject becomes irrelevant, is difficult to ascertain. The reason that knowing-how is more encompassing than knowing-that is this difficulty of separating relevant from irrelevant knowledge. Veblen (1961: 74) goes even further than this in asserting that man is 'a coherent structure of propensities and habits'.

The supposition that there will ever come a time when the economic agent is in possession of all the relevant knowledge, as Lucas (1987) assumes, cannot hold for two reasons. Separating 'relevant knowledge' from 'irrelevant knowledge' requires, firstly, a conception of the totality of knowledge. Without having some idea of the totality of knowledge, no distinction can be made as to what is, and what is not 'relevant' (see Dolfsma 1994). Humans, having limited brain capacity, cannot conceive of the totality of knowledge. The philosopher Whitehead (1968: 43) says that knowledge about something can only be complete from a limited perspective. He explains by saying that 'to feel completion apart from any sense of growth, is in fact to fail in understanding' (ibid.: 48). This argument is similar, although not the same, as the objection against Bayesian learning theory made by, among others, Hargreaves Heap (1993) and Elster (1986). Secondly, to remain in possession of knowledge on a certain subject, in a certain degree, requires that no changes in one's environment occur, or that changes in one's environment are not faster than changes in knowledge (learning). These are unlikely conditions in a rapidly changing world.

The ideas of Polanyi (1983) and Ryle (1966) may be seen to be complementary and make a useful contribution to an understanding of knowledge and a possible conceptualization of it by economists. At any point in time, what knowledge is tacit depends on the framework in which the particular piece of knowledge is included, and on the ability of the particular agent to formulate his or her knowledge in a way that can be understood by other agents. The framework in turn is a product of past learning processes in which pieces of knowledge are fitted into the framework present at that particular point in time, thereby altering the framework itself. The totality of knowledge, which is partly tacit, is the intermediate result of a perpetually ongoing process of acquiring knowledge (Ryle 1966: 42; Dolfsma 2002b). The importance of the element of time needs to be highlighted, an element that is usually not incorporated in economic theory (Clark and Juma 1990). Hence, while Ryle (1966) stresses the static view of the state of knowledge at any point in time, Polanyi (1983) lays more stress on the dynamic process responsible for reaching a particular position. Polanyi (1983) thus provides a reason for regarding knowing-how as much more extensive than knowing-that, for it is in the process of acquiring knowledge that the framework of knowledge is constructed. A framework may have interconnections that change over time. Ryle's (1966: 45) 'inquiry . . . into {human} capacities, skills, habits, liabilities and bents' also points to a very important and often disregarded phenomenon of the human intellect: that knowledge may be acquired without (continuous) intellectual effort. Knowledge can also be acquired in a rather passive way. It is difficult to understand and conceptualize knowledge. The conceptualizatons of Ryle (1966) and Polanyi (1983) is in line with the work of psychologist Albert Bandura (1977, 1986). In the process of learning, knowledge changes (grows). Bandura's work in social psychology has been successful empirically in explaining how people learn.[7]

Technology

How may one conceive of technology in light of this? The common position for economists to take when thinking of technology can be illustrated by giving a few examples. Nelson (1981b) equates technology with 'well articulated blueprints', Schmitz (1985) equates it with 'machines and labour', and Teitel and Westphal (1984) with 'productivity, total factor productivity'. These positions are understandable in the light of the discussion by Hennings (1987). One may, however, conceive of techno-logy more along the lines of what Hayek has suggested (De Vlieghere 1994): All the knowledge – tacit and articulable – that is used by an economic entity (agent, firm, organization, etc.) to produce something. This is indeed a very broad definition and it needs to be explained. The concept includes more than physical capital (machines) or blueprints readily available and implementable off a shelf. However, not all pos-sible knowledge is included (as Neale 1984 does), since it restricts itself to know-ledge that is *actually used* to produce something for which there is a need (cf. Hayek 1941: 72). Technology is only 'one type of knowledge' (Machlup 1980: 10).

To what kind of knowledge does my argument refer? Let me confine myself to the case of a firm. Knowledge individuals need to function in a normal way in the firm involved. For convenience let us call it 'operational knowledge'. Veblen (1961: 71) referred to machines as 'productive goods', observing that 'these productive goods are facts of human knowledge, skill and predilection; that is to say, they are, substantially, prevalent habits of thought, and it is as such that they enter into the process of industrial development'. Next to this, technology includes the machines and tools with which labourers work to produce output. These machines are prod-ucts of other production units (firms) where knowledge was used to produce them. Knowledge incorporated in machines and tools may be called 'contained knowledge'. De Vlieghere (1994) has called it 'embodied knowledge' – though this may induce an association with the term 'embodied technology' current in the discussions of macro-economists building models of the economy. A third constituent of technology is the organizational set-up of the economic unit. Rip and Kemp (1998) provide an excellent and extensive discussion of the conceptualization of technology and tech-nological change in the field of Science Studies that is close to what is proposed here. The knowledge every person involved in the production process uses, also needs to be called technology because without such knowledge people would not be in a position to work with machines/contained knowledge. Part of that knowledge cannot be articulated, that provides a good reason for an emphasis on 'learning-by-doing' and similar phenomena (e.g. Bell 1984). Thinking of technology in terms of knowledge helps to explain why shipping technologically advanced machines to the economically less developed countries of the world has not had the expected results. For similar reasons the organizational aspects of economic units are included. Without an adequate organizational set-up, the opportunities for division of labour cannot be realized. Some elements should not be considered technology. One prominent example is inventions that have not yet been used in a production process. Inven-tions are only relevant for my definition of technology to the extent that they are (procured and subsequently) used in a production process. Should they be used, but not used to produce an output, they might better be called consumption. Inventions not (yet) used to produce something may be called 'potential technology'. According to Sen 'while goods and services are valuable, they are not valuable in themselves. Their value rests on what they can do for peop le, or rather, what people can do with these goods and services' (Sen 1984: 510). The same line of reasoning holds for technology: it is only valuable to the extent that it is used in a production process.

2.4 KNOWLEDGE IN A SOCIAL AND ECONOMIC CONTEXT

To paraphrase Isaac Newton, knowledge is developed by people who could see further because they stand on the shoulders of giants. This, of course, is a well-established observation about the cumulative nature of development of knowledge but, at the same time, was a derisive remark against Newton's opponent in a discussion about the nature of gravity in a letter in 1776 to Robert Hooke. Hooke was a short man who walked bent forward. Knowledge develops as much in a social context as it is cumulative. There are at least two other characteristics of knowledge that entail, in assessing welfare effects, one needs a perspective that takes into account dynamic processes by which knowledge develops. The development of knowledge involves tacit dimensions, and requires coding and decoding. These four characteristics are at work at the individual, the organizational,[8] the regional[9] as well as at the societal level. Knowledge development essentially involves individuals too and I will discuss this at some length. As the welfare perspective introduced below takes social welfare of a community (society) as a touch-stone, the implications of the characteristics of knowledge development for the dynamics at the societal level are also discussed.

In a recent book, Joel Mokyr (2002) has argued that the industrial revolutions need to be explained by the development, but mostly by the use, of new knowledge. He also makes a number of noteworthy observations about the role of knowledge for economic development. One of these is that there have been striking macro inventions before the first Industrial Revolution in England. None of these inventions gave rise to sustained economic growth, however. Figure 2.2

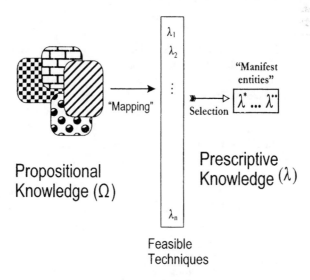

Figure 2.2 Propositional and prescriptive knowledge
Source: Mokyr (2002).

shows a framework that Mokyr suggests to understand the role of knowledge in the economy and society. Propositional knowledge is knowledge about 'how to manipulate nature' (Mokyr 2002); this includes more than what one would now call academic knowledge. Savants posses this type of knowledge. Prescriptive knowledge contains concrete directions about how to solve a particular problem; it is useful knowledge possessed by fabricants. Developments in both types of knowledge may stimulate one another. Mokyr explains this by pointing out that the knowledge base of economies (propositional knowledge) earlier was too limited, the knowledge available was not 'tight' enough to convince people to invest in the creation of new products or processes based on prepositional knowledge.

A second observation is that it can be considered a coincidence, in a way, that around 1780 England was the first country where sustained economic growth, based on the use of newly developed knowledge, could be observed. England was by no means the most technologically advanced country, and indeed it used knowledge developed in countries such as France extensively. Mokyr points to the institutions of English society that lowered the costs of communication about new knowledge. The result was that knowledge was much more readily exchanged among savants, fabricants, and between these two groups. Thus, new knowledge was more easily created, and existing knowledge was put to good use faster, even if the knowledge would be of a tacit nature (Cowan *et al.* 2000).

Communication then, according to Mokyr's argument, will both broaden, and tighten, the knowledge base of prepositional knowledge, stimulate the development of techniques (prescriptive knowledge) that find an immediate application in society and stimulate economic activity.

Knowledge may affect a firm's processes in other ways too. Knowledge can be recognized as immaterial assets in a firm's financial accounts, acknowledging its importance as a productive factor. Introducing knowledge in a firm's financial accounts allows it to use it as collateral in capital markets. Rules implemented in Europe in 2005, following the American example, clarify this hitherto murky situation (Lev 2001). Intellectual property (knowledge made exclusive) also plays an increasingly important role in strategic manoeuvring between firms (Lev 2001; Shapiro and Varian 1999; Granstrand 1999). Intellectual Property Rights (IPRs) may make a firm an inevitable player in a network, and it may allow a firm to exclude others from a network. This does not only hold for IPRs, but also for trade secrets and tacit knowledge, as long as access or use of such knowledge can be restricted. Economists have argued that agents need incentives to be persuaded to develop new knowledge. If such incentives – primarily in the case of a system of IPR laws – would not exist, there would be an undersupply of new knowledge and basic knowledge in particular (Nelson 1959). This argument is made in the case of both patents and copyrights (Landes and Posner 1989). Without incentives, agents would not develop new knowledge, or would not make it publicly available. Nevertheless, it is known that firms do engage in fundamental research and have good reasons for doing so (Rosenberg 1990), even when they know they cannot receive a patent to legally prevent others from commercially exploiting their knowledge. In addition, not all firms find it worthwhile to apply for a patent (Arundel 2001; Nelson *et al.* 1987). Increasingly, the arguments legitimising a system of IPRs have shifted to emphasizing the need for these institutions to offer protection so that investments in production facilities can be recouped before copycats, whose costs are therefore lower, enter the market (Hettinger 1989).

2.5 CONCLUDING REMARKS

The metaphor generally used in economics to understand 'knowledge' is that of 'capital'. By contrasting this idea with views put forth by such scholars as Polanyi (1983) and Ryle (1966) regarding how people learn and how knowledge may alternatively be conceptualized, I show this to be an unrealistic, and for some purposes, incorrect way of understanding knowledge. This has consequences for economic theory. Since 'knowledge' is such a central concept in economics, as Mirowski (1995) and others have argued, the consequences are potentially profound. One is the characterization of technology by economists. In academic discourse, one should be more cautious and more explicit about how one perceives knowledge than in general discourse, or in policy circles. Analytically, conceiving of knowledge as if it were capital can be misleading and provides little conceptual mileage. The idea of knowledge underlying many discussions among economists about technology and technological development, for instance, is misleading and potentially economically disastrous. The views on knowledge developed here inform the discussions in the following chapters.

3 Creating knowledge

Transfer, exchange and gifts*

The concept of social capital is often alluded to when an explanation for the nature and workings of relations within, and between, companies is sought especially in relation to knowledge creation and diffusion. The concept has been the focus of attention for quite a while now which, so far, has not crystallized. How is social capital created, how is it put to use, and how is it maintained? The concept of social capital remains a black box as the mechanisms that constitute it remain underdeveloped *and* that it is a black hole as many empirical phenomena are attributed to its presence. I suggest that using and developing the literature on gift exchange provides a firm theoretical basis for understanding the concept of social capital.

3.1 INTRODUCTION

Social capital resides in members of a group, and in their relations. It may extend to (parts of) a company, and may extend beyond the company. Understanding social capital is relevant for understanding what is going on within and between companies. How does social capital emerge, how is it maintained, and how is it used? The vast literature on social capital has only begun to address these questions.

Over the years, the concept of social capital has gathered attention at an extraordinary rate. Fine (2000) states that social theory is currently being rewritten through the lens of social capital. The idea that relationships and social networks are a valuable asset, in that they can facilitate action, is the common denominator. As such, much of the attention of scholars has focused on the tangible benefits social capital can provide and has, as such, been put to the test in a wide variety of contexts (e.g. Adler and Kwon 2002; Field 2004; Fine 2000; Portes and Sensenbrenner 1993; Woolcock 1998) demonstrating its relevance in those contexts. Despite its popularity, social capital has not yet crystallized and, conceptually, is still hampered by the lack of a common definition regarding the concept and its elements (Adam and Roncevic 2003). Furthermore, much attention in the literature has been directed to identifying social capital and less so to issues of how social capital is created, how it is put to use and how it is maintained.

---

* With Rene van der Eijk, Albert Jolink.

These processes are not self-evident; the benefits of social capital do not materialize at will and not every individual is likely to benefit to the same extent.

The focus of this chapter is, therefore, on relations between individuals in a community, and the cooperation between them. These relations will be studied by reviewing the economic and management literature on social capital, supplemented by the literature in sociology and anthropology on gift exchange. This latter literature focuses, on the one hand, on gift exchange as a potential instrumental exchange of resources, services or information. On the other hand, in line with Homans (1951), the literature reveals that relatively frequent gift exchange generates cohesion and commitment to exchange relations (Lawler *et al.* 2000), where people are more likely to invest in mutual relationships under such circumstances (Mauss 1954; Bourdieu 1977; Larsen and Watson 2001). From this literature, social capital emerges as a consequence of exchange relations, capturing the procedural aspects of social relationships. The literature on gifts suggests mechanisms for reciprocity, equity, interpretation/meaning and the strength of a relationship, that may be tied up with the existing literature on social capital.

Social capital, as a concept, has so far remained a black box in the sense that the mechanisms that constitute it remain underdeveloped *and* that it is a black hole in the sense that many empirical phenomena are attributed to its presence. The literature on gift exchange suggests ways of opening the black box by exploring mechanisms and proposing that creation, use and maintenance of social capital is to be understood as a corollary of gift exchange.

3.2 SOCIAL CAPITAL

The concept of social capital was mainly developed in the late 1980s. Although the first use of the term has been credited to Hanifan in 1916 (Dika and Singh 2002; Fine 2000), Bourdieu (1986), Coleman (1988) and Putnam (1993) are considered to be the founding fathers of the concept. Their approach and conceptualization of social capital differs substantially resulting mainly from the respective points of departure or perspectives. One of the contentious points for discussion is whether social capital is an egocentric or a sociocentric concept – does it reside in individuals or in the relations between them (Adam and Roncevic 2003; Adler and Kwon 2002)? Most authors agree with Coleman that social capital deals with aspects of social structure that enable social action; social relationships can act as a resource for social action (Coleman 1988; Burt 1992; Bourdieu 1986). Tentatively, one may describe social capital as the sum of actual or potential resources embedded within, available through, and derived from the social structure that facilitates exchange and social interaction. As a function of the configuration and content of the network of more or less durable social relations, one can access social capital either directly or indirectly. Social capital thus emerges as the intended, instrumental *or* unintentional result of social interaction or exchange.

Adler and Kwon (2002) have argued that social capital has a number of characteristics. Firstly, social capital can be invested in, for instance one can expand or deepen one's network of external contacts thus enlarging the stock of social capital (Bourdieu 1977, 1986); secondly, it is appropriate in the sense that an actor's network can be used for different purposes by the focal actor and not by others (Coleman 1988; Bourdieu 1986); thirdly, social capital requires maintenance as social ties may weaken due to relational atrophy (Cheal 1988), and lastly, social capital resides in individuals as well as in mutual ties. As a result, if one party defects on, or terminates, the relationship, social capital vanishes. Social capital in some ways resembles a 'collective good' (e.g. Coleman 1988). Although one can 'own' social capital, it is not one's private property since it resides in the ties between individuals. However, unlike a pure 'collective good', one can exclude others, or be excluded by others, from social capital's benefits.

Nahapiet and Ghosal (1998) claim that social capital can have three dimensions – structural, relational and cognitive dimension. The structural dimension describes the totality of the impersonal configuration of linkages between actors (Nahapiet and Ghosal 1998; Scott 1991; Wasserman and Faust 1994). According to Coleman (1988), social capital is accumulated history in the form of a social structure appropriate to productive use by an actor in the pursuit of his interests. Among the most important facets of the structural dimension that can be identified is the presence or absence of network ties between actors (Scott 1991; Wasserman and Faust 1994). The significance of an actor's social capital is not exclusively determined by the number of direct and indirect ties and the respective resources that the individuals have at their disposal. The structural embeddedness or configurations of ties that make up an individual's exchange network play a role as well. Thus the configurations of the focal actor's exchange network affect the quality of someone's exchange network and therefore his social capital. Networks – defined as specific types of relations linking sets of people, objects or events (Knoke and Kuklinski 1982) – may however be just one example of the structural dimension of social capital.

Secondly, the relational dimension focuses on the specific content of an individual's ties: how individuals value their contacts, over and above the quantity of ties. The emphasis is on the embeddedness of relations which is determined largely by a history of interactions (Granovetter 1992, p. 35).

Thirdly, the cognitive dimension of social capital deals with that aspect of the social infrastructure that represents shared meanings and interpretations. As Foley and Edwards (1997) have argued:

> social capital cannot be conceived in purely structural terms because even in its structural sense it carries a cultural freight ('expectations, obligations, trust') that is nested in structure but not simply reducible to structure. Second, what is equally clear about the cultural component of social capital is that it is appropriated by individuals but is not simply an attribute of individuals (. . .) It is precisely this socio cultural component of social capital that provides the context with which it acquires meaning and becomes available to individuals and groups in a way that can facilitate an individual or collective action not otherwise possible.
>
> (Foley and Edwards 1997, p. 670)

The cultural dimension then represents a resource in that it provides shared understanding among parties (Nahapiet and Ghosal 1998; Cicourel 1973). If one were to take a sociocentric position, one would obviously be more inclined to emphasize this cognitive dimension.

Coleman (1988) emphasizes that social capital constitutes an aspect of the social structure and is capable of facilitating the actions of individuals within that structure. These actions relate to the (potential) benefits of social capital, identified and categorized by Sandefur and Laumann (1998) – information, influence and solidarity. These benefits allow actors to achieve ends that would be impossible to achieve without social capital, or only by means of (significant) additional costs.

A substantial amount of research, in difference areas, has focused on the (mostly positive) consequences of social capital (see Adler & Kwon 2002; Jackman and Miller 1998; Field 2004; Fine 2000; Portes and Sensenbrenner 1993; Woolcock 1998). Significantly less has been written about the way social capital is created and maintained, which is at stake here. Or, as Ulmann-Margalit (1978) argues, an explanation is incomplete if the How-question is not addressed in addition to the Why-question.

3.3 SOCIAL CAPITAL & GIFT EXCHANGE

The literature on social capital, trust, and collaboration identifies a number of sources of cooperation, most of which can be categorized in two categories (e.g. Shapiro 1987; Nooteboom 2002). On the one hand, impersonal sources, such as sanctions by an external authority, social norms and values, are discussed (Bradach and Eccles 1989; Dore 1983; Granovetter 1985; Zucker 1986). Personal sources, as a source of social capital and trust are, on the other hand, discussed in this literature as well. In part motivated by self interest, current and ongoing cooperation can bring benefit to the focal actor (Abreu 1988; Axelrod 1984; Frank 1988; Heide and Miner 1992; Hill 1990; Kreps *et al.* 1982; Parkhe 1993; Telser 1980). A focal actor's reputation (Weigelt and Camerer 1988; Kreps 1990; Coleman 1988), or the hostages taken by the focal actor (Williamson 1985), can be a basis for it to trust the partner to cooperate. Some others refer to such sources of social capital as closed networks, shared ideology, culture and social norms and values without further elaboration (Coleman 1988; Ferrary 2003; Field 2004; Laumann and Pappi 1976; Portes 1998; Putnam 1993, Sandefur and Laumann 1998). In part, the latter have altruistic motivations such as relations of affect as well as by routines or individual habits. Where impersonal sources of cooperation from the point of view of an individual actor can be regarded as a given, and can only to be altered indirectly, personal sources, arising in specific personalized interactions, can be influenced. Entering gift exchange relations provides the actor with the means to create and maintain relations of trust where social capital might be said to reside. In the literature, the purported effects of a presence of social capital is mostly discussed. Social capital appears to emerge from a black box, and is enigmatically invoked to explain a plethora of phenomena

– mostly good, but sometimes bad. In that respect, social capital is in many cases perceived as a black hole. By suggesting a way in that the creation, maintenance, but also demise, of trust and social capital can be understood, one may be able to open the black box.

Some authors have hinted at other sources for social capital, leaving it until later to elaborate. Putnam (1993) points at norms, trust and network ties as sources of the creation and maintenance of social capital. For Coleman (1988), social capital results from properties of social structures, most notably network closure and multiplex ties, but this seems to raise an even greater amount of questions. According to Portes (1998), the motives of recipients and donors are sources of social capital. She distinguishes between consummatory motives that consummate, referring to an internalized norm resulting from socialization during childhood and/or from a shared faith, and instrumental motives, referring to access to resources. The viability of instrumental motives in the creation of social capital results from the creation of mutual obligations and enforceable trust. Bourdieu (1986) also emphasizes the instrumental nature of social capital construction.

Bourdieu (1986) and Coleman (1988) argue that social capital can be formed purposefully as well as unintentionally. Social capital may result from instrumental behaviour. Bourdieu emphasizes the role of social obligation, trust and the advantages of connections in social capital (Smart 1993). Bourdieu underlines the fact that connections and obligations are not givens, but are the product of investment strategies – consciously or unconsciously – aimed at establishing or reproducing social relationships that are directly usable in the short or long term (Bourdieu 1977; 1986). Thus, self-interested and otherwise purposive actors may strategically enter into certain kinds of relationships (Coleman 1990, 1994; Field 2004; Portes 1998; Sandefur and Laumann 1998). Social capital may also be a by-product of a broad spectrum of activities, and many investments in social capital are not intentionally made as such. Social capital may emerge and vanish as a by-product of activities engaged in for reasons other than the accumulation of social capital (Coleman 1988, 1990; Field 2004; Sandefur and Laumann 1998; Paldam and Svendsen 2000). In addition, its value is often as much for the broader public as for those individuals who actually belong to, and have invested in, the relations (Coleman 1988; Field 2004).

Gift exchange is a notion developed predominantly in the anthropological literature as a concept which allows social scientists to understand how relations emerge, how they are maintained and how they may be drawn on. As Portes (1998, p. 5) has pointed out: 'Resources obtained through social capital have, from the point of view of the recipient, the character of a gift'. The notion of gift in this literature is thus more encompassing than the one understood in ordinary day life. Here, gifts are equated with *charitable* gifts – a significant economic phenomenon (The Economist 2006). Coleman (1994) cites examples of individuals' intentional creation of obligations by, for instance, performing unsolicited favours and giving gifts to others. These obligations become a basis for future exchange. Coleman in particular argues that they are a kind of 'entitlement' to future social support.

Gift exchange and emergence of social capital

Boulding (1981) surmises that gift exchange is the quintessential form of exchange. The vast literature on gift exchange points out that it plays a vital role in the construction of social networks (Cheal 1988; Larsen and Watson 2001; Gouldner 1960); gifts may be used to initiate, maintain, or sever relationships with individuals or groups (Belk 1979; Sherry 1983; Larsen and Watson 2001; Cheal 1996; Darr 2003; Mauss 1954; Gouldner 1960). Frequent gift or favour exchange leads to positive emotions and uncertainty reduction which, in turn, generates cohesion and commitment to exchange relations (Lawler *et al.* 2000).

In contrast to popular belief, gifts may be exchanged for both instrumental as well as for more purely altruistic reasons. Classical anthropologists such as Mauss (1954) and Malinowski (1996) have argued persuasively that, indeed, the exchange of gifts is motivated by self-interest in many cases. Even when altruistic motives play a role, these tend not to be unrelated to the motive of self-interest. By drawing on the well-established research on gifts, one is able to incorporate all of the dimensions that are attributed to social capital, as well as clarify how social capital is established and maintained.

The literature on gift exchange points out that it may both be a form of ***instrumental*** behaviour often taking place in a context of quasi-enforced reciprocity, but the obligations resulting from gift exchange may also be an ***unintentional by-product*** (Blau 1964, Bourdieu 1977, Heath 1976; Homans 1974; Mauss 1954). Rose-Ackerman (1998) points out that gifts, presented to people and institutions in a position where they might benefit the giver, actually come close to being prices (or, depending on the situation, even bribes) – if the appropriate ritual is not adopted (Smart 1993).

Gift giving may be a strategic, self-motivated action meant to create an obligation in the exchange partner to reciprocate (Bourdieu 1977; Humphrey and Hugh-Jones 1992; Darr 2003). The generosity and voluntarism observed in gift giving may be an illusion and only be altruism in appearance (Blau 1964; Mauss 1954). Ostensibly, there is not necessarily an expectation of equivalent or formal return ([Beals 1970] quoted in Sherry 1983), but in reality the purposive focal actor – consciously or unconsciously (Komter 1996; McGrath and Englis 1996; Levi-Strauss 1996) – takes into account past and, or, future outcomes for oneself, and is at least partly motivated by the expectation of some return-gift, whether direct (such as power over others) or indirect (such as social approval) (Blau 1964). As Zucker (1986) argues, creation of trust is *implicit* in the expectation of a counter-gift in gift exchange; it should not become explicit, however (Bourdieu 1992, Darr 2003). It is, nevertheless, this equity over the longer-term that makes the exchange mutually beneficial and therefore its existence and continuance is reasonable (Cook and Emerson 1984). Enforcement is self-regulating, since, between equals, if one partner fails to reciprocate, the other actor is likely to discontinue the exchange (Nye 1979).

Because gift exchange is generally unbalanced when viewed at one particular point in time, a longitudinal perspective more accurately reveals the nature of gift giving. A deferred return obligates one individual to another, and creates 'social debt'. Significant time may pass between the gift and the counter-gift. Gift exchange is carried out without a legal contract (Ferrary 2003), but instead informal existence of interpersonal relationships and trust makes it possible to leave the particulars of the exchange unspecified (Uehara 1990; Zucker 1986). If the obligations could in fact be enforced and imposed on third parties one would be talking about market transactions.

Gift exchange is a distinct form of exchange that is characterized by a set of **three principles** that Marcel Mauss (1954) has been very adamant about. As part of a community, anybody is obliged to give, receive[1] and reciprocate (cf. Dore 1983; Gouldner 1960; Levi-Strauss 1996; Malinowski 1996; Sahlins 1972; Schwartz 1996; Simmel 1996). The imperative nature of this three-fold obligation derives from its cultural embeddedness (Sherry 1983). These obligations are certainly social in that they are enforced by the community. In addition, they may have moral overtones. As a result, donors and recipients feel psychologically obliged to act according to the principles (cf. Schein 1965). In a situation where this psychological contract is violated, one will question the reciprocal goodwill of the other. Acceptance of the gift is, to a certain extent, acceptance of the giver and the relationship between the parties (Larsen and Watson 2001; Carrier 1991). It is also an acceptance of the perception the giver has of the receiver. It is for this reason that a gift that is perceived as improper by the receiver may be rejected, may fail to initiate a relation, and may harm an existing relation. Refusal of the initial gift marks the refusal to initiate the dynamic of exchange, thus to refuse a gift is to refuse a relationship and one's role in that relation (Ferrary 2003; Mauss 1954). Reciprocity is open to discretion as to the value and form of the counter gift; the currency with which the obligation is repaid can be different from the form with which they were incurred. Schwartz (1996) states that it is even prohibited to make an equal-return 'payment' (homeomorphic reciprocity) in gift exchange, as that is tantamount to returning the offered gift to the donor and discontinuing the relationship. Gift exchange is diachronous since reciprocity is open to discretion with regard to time; a gift is not reciprocated by immediate compensation, but instead by a deferred form of compensation (Mauss 1954; Bourdieu 1977; Ferrary 2003; Deckop *et al.* 2003). The 'objective' value of the counter-gift may be ostensibly lower then the original gift if circumstances permit this. If the party who is originally at the receiving end is evidently not in a position to return gifts of approximately equal value he need not do so, he may not have enough resources, but there may be other reasons for the scales being 'objectively' out of balance, even permanently (Komter 1996). Material value of gifts exchanged can be compensated for by obvious inculcation of immaterial value – such as time, effort and creativity – in the counter-gift. The instrumental nature of gift exchange can also be apparent when a dependent party who is evidently less well endowed gives to a more central party, being better endowed, in the expectation to receive in return, but certainly not something of equal value. The instrumental reason for giving in the first place is to be able to establish a relation that will be beneficial in the long run, possibly by being able to tap into the other relations that the receiving party maintains (Ferrary 2003). Thus, the exact nature or moment of the counter-gift is necessarily not specified beforehand – gifts are 'silent' as it were (Bourdieu 1977; Gouldner 1960; Mauss 1954; Deckop *et al.* 2003). Many scholars emphasize that the returngift should ultimately be of roughly equivalent value, however this equivalence refers to equivalence as defined by the actors involved, including their inter-subjective understanding of the value of the gifts actually exchanged, given an understanding of people's positions and endowments. 'Objectively', even in the long run, the exchange might not be equal in value (Gouldner 1960). One could thus propose that Social Capital emerges by people exchanging small but increasing more significant gifts not *ostensibly* motivated by the counter-gift anticipated.

Maintenance of social capital

Virtually any *resource* – material or immaterial, tangible or intangible, of high or low value – can be transformed into a gift or favour (Blau 1964; Heath 1976; Homans 1974; Sherry 1983). Gifts may be flowers, a box of chocolates, an invitation, a handshake or joke, a suggestion or tip one knows to be relevant, for the received attention, knowledge and ideas. A gift may even take the form of money, if and when given with the proper ritual such as a gift-wrapping (Zelizer 1997; Khalil 2004). The more obviously valuable a first gift is, for instance, the more the giver is likely to signal to the receiver (or givee) that the gift is actually a bribe or price.

The alteration from a resource to a gift is realized by observing and keeping in mind the social relationships, the proper occasions and decorum, and using the signals and rituals that should accompany gift giving as established in a community (Deal and Kennedy 1982). Relations start with gift giving, as they convey the message that one intends to relate to the other; gift giving conveys that one has a specific perception of the other as someone who would appreciate the gift offered, and is willing and able to offer a counter-gift the original giver would also appreciate. A first gift is in fact an offer to become a member of an existing, what one could call, *Social Capital Community*, or, alternatively, a request to be allowed to join the Social Capital Community of the receiving party. A Social Capital Community can be as small as a group of two persons. Given the possibility to offend the receiver by giving a gift, the original gift with which a relation starts is not likely to be idiosyncratic. The more a first gift signals a specific perception of the receiver and his context, the bigger the chances of offence are as the giver might have wrongly perceived the situation. Gift exchange allows for a common bond to be established and maintained ('social capital'), and thus contributes to value creation by providing access to resources.

Gift exchange serves both *economic* and *social purposes* (Belk 1979; Larsen and Watson 2001; Cheal 1996), and may be mutually supportive (Ferrary 2003;

Smart 1993).[2] While gift exchange is (necessarily) between individuals, these individuals may be from the same organization (e.g., Flynn 2003), or from different organizations, where individuals represent organizations (Child and Faulkner 1998; Ferrary 2003). Gift exchange has been regarded by some as a purely economic exchange between two parties (Larsen and Watson 2001). Gift exchange is not merely an economic transaction, however, it is also a good in itself, a 'process benefit', establishing or affirming, but possibly also damaging, destroying or forestalling a personal relationship (Ferrary 2003; Offer 1997). Gifts not only transfer utility, but are also social interactions embedded in social structures (Cheal 1996). The relation between giver and receiver is primarily personal and can therefore have a value independent of, and in addition to, their instrumental function of regulating transactions (Rose-Ackerman 1998). Darr (2003) thus claims that gift exchange and market transactions are 'inextricably intertwined' in contemporary markets (cf. Granovetter 1985; Dolfsma *et al.* 2005). Smart (1993: 389) avows one should:

> avoid the Scylla of assuming that gift exchange and market exchange are completely different types of relationships and the Charybdis of dissolving the distinction in a unifying theoretical practice of explaining all actions as outcomes of the strategic pursuit of the advantage of the agent.
>
> (cf. Dore 1983)

As there is a limit to the number of relations (ties) one is able to sustain – especially if the ties are strong ties – there is, by necessity, a boundary to one's (immediate) Social Capital Community. One may be able to tap into the social capital that inheres in more indirect connections, but only if one's direct relation allows this (Burt 1992; Coleman 1988; Granovetter 1973; Lin and Dumin 1986). Gift exchange will generally not extend beyond an (emerging) Social Capital Community.

Social capital's ability to facilitate social action, in the absence of any legal enforcement, depends on individuals' willingness and sense of obligation towards the other. Many emphasize generalized reciprocity, such as in the example of voluntary blood donations to unknown others, usually related to concepts such as shared ideology, culture and norms/values (Coleman 1988; Ferrary 2003; Field 2000; Laumann and Pappi 1976; Portes 1998; Putnam 1993; Sandefur and Laumann 1998). Although generalized reciprocity can be defined as part of social capital, it does represent a less potent form of social capital and could be considered as an enabler. Social capital's ability to facilitate action is most effective if and when it is a product of gift exchange resulting from personal obligations between concrete individuals. Individuals generally are more forthcoming towards friends and acquaintances than strangers or persons they are less connected with in general (Coleman 1988). Strong ties generally provide a larger likelihood of reciprocation than weak ties, where reciprocation facilitates actors' access to resources and support (Burt 1992; Hansen 1999). Once established, a Social Capital Community decreases the risk associated with exchange as a result of the reputation (Kreps 1990; Ostrom and Ahn 2003; Coleman 1988; Sherry 1983; Ferrary 2003) and repeated interaction effect (Abreu 1988; Fudenberg and Maskin 1986; Kreps *et al.* 1982), hence actors' preference for dealing with insiders instead of outsiders. Therefore, in contrast to what many authors seem to assume, that social capital does not exist in the absence of a social context, in its most potent form, social capital mainly results from concrete interaction (gift exchange) between concrete individuals.

Social capital thus needs *maintenance* (Adler and Kwon 2002). Gift exchange can be considered as an investment to create a relation that can be drawn on later and can therefore be referred to as social capital (Bourdieu 1986; Nahapiet and Ghosal 1998). 'Gifts can be described as an investment in the relationship between donor and recipient. The greater the value of the gift, the more substantial the investment' (Larsen and Watson 2001: 899). The generosity and voluntaryism observed in gift giving may be an illusion and only an apparent altruism (Blau 1964; Mauss 1954). Indeed, social capital is not simply there for anybody to use, as both Coleman (1988) and Putnam (1993) assume. Investments are necessary since connections are not givens but require continuous maintenance (Bourdieu 1977, 1986). Gift exchange engenders the relationships in which social capital can be said to reside (Bourdieu 1986; Nahapiet and Ghosal 1998). The symbolic denial of economic calculation of gift exchanges then serves the requirement of strategic interaction (Bourdieu 1977). Gift exchange will, therefore, not extend beyond an (emerging) Social Capital Community, while for social capital to be maintained in a community, there needs to be continued gift exchange.

Gifts – Inclusion & Exclusion

Social relationships and group boundaries are formed and sustained through the perpetuating exchange cycle of giving and receiving (Ruth *et al.* 1999). The latter aspect of the gift, its instrumentality in *maintaining* social ties (Belk 1979; Cheal 1988; Mauss 1954; Ruth *et al.* 1999; Sherry 1983; McGrath *et al.* 1996), is highlighted by Belk and Coon (1993) who stress that gift giving creates a bond of goodwill and social indebtedness between people. In their argument, instrumental and altruistic motives are not so neatly separated. This indebtedness, is what highlights gift giving as an exchange, and perpetuates the exchange process – as long as the scales are not balanced. Gift exchange then establishes repetitive, self-enforcing bonds (Offer 1997); the outstanding obligations between the exchange partners make it expedient not to break off relationships, for both 'creditor' and 'debtor', as both have an interest in maintaining their long-term relation (Gouldner 1960). On the other hand, however, it has been argued that a person should not maintain a pattern of gift exchange that is perceived as highly unbalanced. This will not only affect a person's sense of emotional state of mind, but if it were to occur within a firm, for instance, this imbalance would make it less productive (Flynn 2003). Being perceived as a creditor, rather than a debtor, however, does increase one's status or reputation within a community, something which may best be done by exchanging gifts frequently (Flynn 2003). An organization where gifts are exchanged is a caring organization where knowledge creation and diffusion is more likely to occur (Von Krogh 1998).

Belk and Coon (1993) emphasize how gift giving creates a bond of goodwill and social indebtedness between people. Indebtedness perpetuates the exchanges process. A deferred return obligates one individual to another, and therefore creates social debt. At the same time, Belk (1979) has described the tension generated and reduced in imbalanced exchanges as an important dynamic in gift giving. While the giving of large gifts, that the receiver may not reciprocate, enables one person to gain control over another person, exchanges of small or token gifts permit a recipient to demonstrate trustworthiness in the short term ([Blehr 1974] taken from Sherry 1983). Many gift exchanges that are meant to maintain social ties or bonds, occur within a context of ritualized occasions, such as birthdays or during Christmas. These ritualized occasions often serve as maintenance rites (Cheal 1988), keeping the established relationships going (cf. Bourdieu 1977, 1986). A sequence of reciprocal gift exchanges establishes a transactional relationship between individuals (Sherry 1983). Relations are, in other words, reaffirmed by regular gift exchange.

Social capital inheres in the ties between individuals and thus takes both parties to be drawn on. A counter-gift cannot be legally enforced and is, by its very nature, part of the social realm. Individuals can be (purposefully) *included* as well as *excluded* from a Social Capital Community. Understanding the emergence, maintenance and possible disappearance of social capital arising from gift exchange, it becomes clear how, and why, boundaries are drawn between (groups of) social individuals, resulting in processes of inclusion and exclusion (Dolfsma and Dannreuther 2003).

As Levi-Strauss (1996) puts it: 'to give is to receive'. The literature on gifts, as well as empirical findings on gift exchange, show that those who give more are also the ones who receive more (Komter 1996). Actors can try to shape their environment to become members of a group (inclusion) – giving them access to the benefits of social capital present in that particular group. Actors who are unable or unwilling to give, prove to be the poorest recipients (Komter 1996, p. 7) – both a cause and an effect for those individuals to have no social networks (Gouldner 1960). Komter (1996) has, consistent with the abovementioned, observed that 'people seem to choose – probably mostly not consciously – those social partners in their gift relationships who are attractive to them, because they can expect them to give in return at some time'. Homans (1950: 182) points out that 'the higher a man's social rank, the larger will be the number of persons that originate interaction for him' (cf. Darr 2003). Bodemann (1988) indicates that powerful people – being in a position where they can confer benefits to others – will receive more gifts than less powerful individuals, so that they might be more likely to reciprocate the focal agent. The (less-extended) social networks of less powerful or resource-poor individuals lead to less participation in gift exchange and diminishing opportunities to develop feelings of 'faithfulness and gratitude' (Simmel, 1996). Individuals may very well seek supportive relationships with network members who have different – not just more – resources (see, e.g., Lin and Dumin 1986). Although Mauss has stated that gifts should be accepted, there are ways a person may avoid being offered one. Rejecting a gift publicly offered is an offence for both parties. Anticipating that a gift may not be accepted, signalling that a particular kind of gift will not be deemed appropriate, or that a particular giver if and when considering to offer a gift will not be admitted to a community, prevents the gift from being offered in the first place and thus from having to reciprocate later. Such signalling prevents the establishment of a relation or inclusion into a Social Capital Community. Also, an exchange of gifts can start or go awry. As the gift signals the kind of person the giver is (or wants to be), the perception by the giver of the receiver, as well as the perception by the giver of the relationship as it exists or should develop, there is scope for misunderstandings to arise. Certainly because of the necessarily 'silent' nature of the gift. As Sherry (1983, 15) points out: 'those to whom we give differ from those to whom we do not give'.

While trust can emerge and grow due to gift exchange, it can vanish as well: 'Risk-taking and trusting behavior are thus really different sides of the same coin' (Deutsch 1958: 266; cf. Mayer *et al.* 1995). Trust may be betrayed (Elangovan and Shapiro 1998), but if it works, transaction costs can reduce substantially, conferring economic benefits to the parties involved, as well as social ones (Dore 1983). If the wrong gift is offered in the wrong way, a relationship will not begin and an existing relationship can cease to exist, destroying all the social capital that existed between parties in the process. Not only will the parties involved miss out on a potentially lucrative relation, they may also lose 'face' (Smart 1993).

Knowing the right people, and moving in the right circles, is a good start but does not mean that one can use the social capital present (Ingram and Robert 2000). Social capital, as the discussion of gifts suggests, does not float around in the group, but exists between concrete individuals and are tangible expressions of their social relations (Sherry 1983). One person is not generally in a position to profit from the social capital present in the relation between a second and third person. Gifts can be a medium through which social boundaries are expressed, frequently invoked in ritual (e.g. Smart 1993; Schneider 1981 [from Sherry 1983]; Dolfsma and Dannreuther 2003). Reciprocity in gift exchange should not be exclusively considered as affirming or reinforcing social networks (Komter 1996). Douglas and Isherwood (1979) succinctly observed that: reciprocity in itself is a principle of exclusion. Inappropriate gifts, inappropriately given gifts, or inappropriate givers, can therefore lead to exclusion from, or can prevent the inclusion into, a Social Capital Community. Gifts or return-gifts that are too much out of balance, can equally harm the relation. Gifts not, reciprocated or inappropriately reciprocated, will exclude the original givee from a Social Capital Community.

Using Social Capital

Gift exchange not only initiates and facilitates the exchange of resources, it also affects the realm of social relations. Gift exchange, if and when performed using the appropriate rituals, establishes and maintains relationships between individuals. The social capital that inheres in these ties and relationships between actors can be *appropriated* for different purposes. Being connected is a resource in itself since people are able to make use of their connection to obtain other benefits. An important mechanism that underlies this aspect of social capital is reciprocity that was shown to be an important element of gift exchange. Reciprocity is seen to strengthen the rights of the provider to call upon the receiver and the obligation of the latter to provide it at some future point (Blehr 1974; Uehara 1990). Or as Sherry (1983) formulates it: 'to avoid feeling inferior and to safeguard reputation, the recipient must reciprocate. Failure to reciprocate appropriately can result in an asymmetrical relationship'. The need to reciprocate may be seen as an outstanding obligation by the receiver to the giver, that is created between gift exchanging individuals, that, according to Coleman (1990) can be considered as credit slips that can be put to use when the actor requires its use. These 'credit slips', or obligations, then facilitate the mobilization of concomitant benefits and resources and appropriation of existing ties and relationships. In determining whether the resources could be called upon in practice, Coleman (1990) identifies two 'crucial' context specific elements, namely the 'actual extent of obligations held' and 'the level of trustworthiness of the social environment'.

Burt (1992), however, concludes that trust is an essential characteristic of obligations since one never knows a debt is recognized until the trusted person reciprocates. At some point, somehow, failure to reciprocate may well entail excommunication. Burt emphasizes that there is a limit to the extent to which generalized reciprocity (Levi-Strauss 1996, 1969; Ekeh 1974),[3] can be expected to operate within a community. Generalized reciprocity may matter, but, as for instance studies of the development Open Source Software has indicated (Lakhani and von Hippel 2003), generalized reciprocity is likely to be circumscribed and less powerful in eliciting the help of others than direct reciprocity (Bourdieu 1977; Gouldner 1960; Wilke and Lanzetta 1970; Regan 1971; Mauss 1954).[4] The likelihood for reciprocity to occur is, *ceteris paribus* other relevant characteristics of the relationships involved, expected to be higher in case of direct reciprocity as compared to generalized reciprocity. At the same time, the literature on gifts indicates that, from the perspective of the members of a community, there needs to be some balance in the relationship (Sahlins 1972; Walster *et al.* 1976; Adams 1965; Blau 1968; Homans 1974). New members have not contributed to the community to the same extent as established members have and, as a result, their credit and reputation is limited. A person whose position in a community is yet to be established will receive gifts, largely due to the existence of generalized reciprocity in that community, but not to the same extent, and of the same kind, that more established members do. A member of a Social Capital Community cannot draw at will on a relation with other members of that community, demanding a counter-gift. As a counter-gift cannot be (legally) demanded, it may then matter crucially *how* relations in a Social Capital Community are drawn on to elicit a particular counter-gift if and when needed.

3.4 DISCUSSION: NO BLACK BOX, NO BLACK HOLE

Emerson (1981) and Gouldner (1960) conceive exchange relationships as being predicated upon the dependence of two parties on each other's resources. In a situation of dispersed resources, exchange becomes a necessary condition for resource combination (Moran and Ghosal 1996; Nahapiet and Ghosal 1998; Tsai and Ghosal 1998). The bargaining power of participants will vary according to the alternative sources of supply open to them (e.g. Heath 1976). The giving of gifts is a way of conferring material benefit on each other (Sherry 1983). Ostensibly, there is no expectation of equivalent and formal return ([Beals 1970] from Sherry 1983). According to Mauss, people of a community must give, accept or receive a gift, and they must reciprocate. Counter-gifts must not be immediate, or of the same value, as that would turn a gift exchange into a market exchange, and might turn the gift into a bribe. Again ostensibly, the act of giving takes precedence over the gift itself; acknowledgement of the gift invariably involves reference to the value and benefit of the gift (Sherry 1983). The value of a gift is not necessarily defined by the price in the marketplace, but is likely just as much to be a reflection of factors other than the ones one associates with the market place, such as scarcity, monetary price and alternative sources of supply (Belk and Coon 1993).[5]

Gift exchange can lead to lower transaction costs since it allows individuals to trade with one another without relying solely on formal mechanisms such as legal contracts and litigation. In the process of exchanging gifts, both parties get to know each other and the other's perceptions and frame of reference. It is believed by most exchange theorists that actors will engage in gift exchange if both parties believe that exchange provides them with more utility (satisfaction) than any other option currently open to them (Uehara 1990). Offer (1997) and Ferrary (2003) point out that under certain circumstances, reciprocal exchange, without the presence of a contract or financial compensation, is preferred. Firstly, not all goods exchanged are merchandisable in the sense that their circulation cannot be transmitted via the market with a commercial contract and a monetary counter payment (for example certain types of information). Secondly, reciprocal exchange has been preferable when trade involves a personal interaction, and when goods or services are unique, expensive or have many dimensions of quality.

The notion of gift exchange opens up the black box of social capital. Discussing social capital as the result of gift exchange, allows one to understand how social capital is created, maintained and used. This, in turn, makes clear what can and what cannot be usefully attributed to social capital and that, not all good (or bad) can be ascribed to it, almost at will, thereby turning the concept into a black hole. The phenomena of gift exchange shows that the social and the economic sphere should not be conceived of as separate – spheres overlap and are interrelated – and motives for gift exchange are both instrumental and (much) less self-interested (Dolfsma *et al.* 2005). Through gift exchange one may initiate and maintain relationships, as (mutual) obligations are created in its process. As a corollary of the cycle of giving and reciprocating, trust emerges and cooperation between the (exchange) parties involved is more likely to take root (Sahlins 1972; Mauss 1954; Gouldner 1960; Uehara 1990). As such, the benefits ascribed to social capital can now be properly understood.

Gift exchange creates and maintains social capital as a gift requires the receiver to give in return. Relationships between individuals are formed and sustained through the perpetual cycle of giving and receiving (Ruth *et al.* 1999). Frequent gift or favour exchanges lead to positive emotions and reduces uncertainty, generating cohesion and commitment (Lawler *et al.* 2000). Repeated social interactions – only possible if the cycle is not obviously broken – makes it possible for trust to develop (Landry *et al.* 2001; Tsai and Ghosal 1998; Adler 2001; Williamson 1993). The indebtedness of others to the focal actor allows a person to call in favours from those who are indebted to him. However, the exact nature of the counter gift, nor the moment at which it occurs, can be fully determined by the focal agent. No formal, enforceable agreement is involved; if there were to be such an enforceable agreement, one would have to speak of a market transaction with a different dynamic. Building a new Social Capital Community, or extending an existing one, requires protracted investments in the form of gift exchange between individuals. However, gift exchange only occurs when both parties are willing, and able, to give, receive and reciprocate resources in a broad sense of the term. If gifts are not returned, if inappropriate gifts are given in an inappropriate manner, or if too much or not enough is given, the relationship created and sustained by gift exchange can break down and people can be excluded from a Social Capital Community. Thus, in time, social capital is created and sustained by gift exchange, but at the same time, once created, social capital facilitates exchange of both gifts and market commodities particularly in uncertain circumstances (Bourdieu 1986; Nahapiet and Ghosal 1998).

3.5 SOME CONCLUDING REMARKS

Even though the thrust of the argument in this chapter, drawing largely on the anthropological literature on gift exchange, has been that one needs to understand the importance of the frame of reference people in a Social Capital Community entertain, this does not mean that the anthropologists' tool-kit is the only tool-kit for doing empirical research. Certainly, ethnographic research of the kind that Marcel Mauss, Claude Levi-Strauss, Mary Douglass and many others have undertaken to provide 'thick descriptions' (Geertz 1973) is of great use, but other methods of research are as well. Flynn (2003) has shown how the extent to which people subjectively feel they 'owe' others, can explain their (gifting) behaviour in a community. Surveys can thus be used too. A third method that will provide useful insights, perhaps of a theoretical nature in particular, is that of the controlled experiment (Burgess and Nielsen 1974; Greenberg and Frisch 1972; Lawler and Yoon 1998; Pruitt 1968). Each of these methods will illuminate different, but related, aspects of the process of gift exchange and emergence or decay of social capital, thus opening its black box and revealing why it is not a black hole.

APPENDIX TO CHAPTER 3

It is instructive to consider Boulding's (1981) formalization of the exchange of gifts (grants, as he calls them). He considers two individuals (A and B) exchanging two different goods (x and y, respectively). These x's and y's may be commodities, money, but may also represent 'communications, information, threats, promises, affirmations, persuasions, and so on' (Boulding 1981: 19). A sends out something, x, that he perceives as sending x_a, to B; B, similarly, may send something, y, that she perceives as sending y_b to A. When x_a and y_b arrive at B and A respectively, they may be (perceived as) different from what was intended: x_b and y_a. When there is a simultaneous exchange of commodities, a 'complete' market exchange emerges. In such a 'simple' market exchange, it may be unproble-matic to assume that $x_a = x_b$ and $y_b = y_a$; only the solid arrows of Figure A3.1 need be considered. Such alignment of perceptions may not occur. Indeed, as Boulding (1981: 21) argues: 'in many forms, even in commodity exchange, the difference between x_a and x_b and between y_b and y_a may be of great significance'. In many exchanges, then, flows of information and communication are involved: x'_a x'_b and y'_b y'_a – the dashed lines.

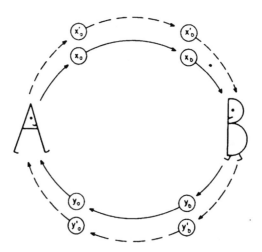

Figure A3.1 'Simple' market exchange
Source: Boulding 1981.

The gift is then that exchange in which one of the commodity flows is zero, for instance $y_b = y_a = 0$. This is presented in Figure A3.2. At some later occasion, A will expect B to reciprocate, but reciprocation may not occur and the value of that which is reciprocated may not 'objectively' be similar or the same. There is, thus, considerable uncertainty involved in gift exchange.

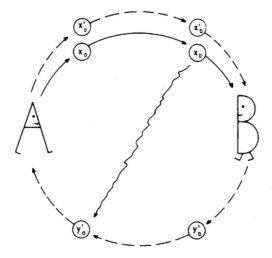

Figure A3.2 Gift exchange
Source: Boulding 1981.

To the extent that gift exchange is instrumental, and thus motivated by self-interest, one may assume that some sense of a terms of trade (T) between A and B will play a role. If v is the quantity of x exchanged, and u the quantity of y, then the terms of trade for A in case of a gift from A to B will be T_a:

$$T_a = (y'_a u'_a)/(x_A v_a) + (x'_B v'_B)$$
(Eq A3-1)

The terms of trade for B can be determined by analogy.[6] One would then expect, *pace* Boulding and others who have emphasized the instrumental nature of gift exchange as mentioned in the main body of the chapter, that both A and B will only engage in gift exchange if: Ta, Tb ≥ 1. Part of the exchange, incorporated in y'_a y'_b is the promise or obligation of a counter-gift. The original gift will be given in the expectation of a counter-gift, and B will communicate to A that one is expected. Gift exchange will go awry if and when either the perception by B of good x given by A to B (x_b), or the understanding by A of the signals from B (y'_b), are misguided. In a knowledge economy, information-communication can in fact be what is expected as a counter-gift; in the present framework, consistent with Bouling's argument, this would be y_b y_a and not y'_a y'_b. Assuming continued interaction, at some later moment in time, another exchange similar to that of Figure A3-2 will occur, in opposite direction.

4 Development of economic knowledge

Paradigms and new ideas[*]

Over time economics has experienced paradigm shifts, and there is every reason to think this will continue. In economics, as in the development of technological knowledge and other disciplinary fields, paradigms do not emerge from nowhere, but build on precursors, possibly from other fields. Our understanding of current thinking can be enhanced by paying greater attention to the role of paradigms, and by using the concepts of myth, plot structure, and cultural endowment as presented by the historian Hayden White. Together, these can help us better understand how ideas from other times and fields may be combined to generate better research (and publications). The history of economics may well be the first, and best, way to enhance our understanding as economists.

4.1 INTRODUCTION

This chapter adds to the understanding of how knowledge develops and what role agents take in the process. It looks at the knowledge held within the community of economists as an example. The development of the discipline of economics might best be understood by using the concept of paradigm. Indeed, Richard Schmalensee has done this when, building on Kuhn's normal science and paradigm shifts, he speculated on the future of economics:

> . . . [M]any, if not most, of the problems on today's research agenda will be solved through 'normal science'. . . . History also suggests, however, that some problems . . . will be solved only by 'paradigm shifts' and that these shifts will change both the tools economists use and the problems they study. Whatever the successes that will be achieved by natural extensions of current lines of research, these revolutions will dominate histories of 21st-century economic thought.
>
> (Schmalensee 1991: 115–116)

The paradigmatic development of knowledge, including that in economics, is inescapable: 'Economic knowledge is path-dependent' (Blaug 2001: 156). Indeed,

[*] With Pat Welch.

the history of economics as a science has seen a number of paradigmatic shifts. One might think of the Marginalist revolution, Keynesianism, Monetarism and New Growth Theory, to name just a few. Paradigm shifts are not to be relegated to the past, however. In our time, there is talk of paradigm shifts: for example, that economics is turning into an information economics (Stiglitz 2002). Subfields are also said to show paradigm shifts. Geographical economics is thought to have gone through two in a very short period of time: one with the publication of Krugman's 1995 book and, more recently, what Bathelt and Glückler (2003) call a 'reflexive' shift.

While the need to study the history of economics has been argued for before (e.g. McCloskey 1976), looking at the development of economics over time in terms of evolving paradigms adds useful insights for economists by opening the way to analyze the contents of thought patterns in terms of routines and rules. Concepts from the historian Hayden White on the impact of cultural perspective can be combined with the concept of a paradigm to deepen the understanding of economic thinking, be it current, previous or upcoming, by studying the history of the economics discipline. Paradigm shifts in economics are not like bolts from the sky. Elaborating mostly on parallels with developments in technology, it is argued that precursors of a shift can always be found. This is significant for contemporary economists, and in this chapter are suggested ways one can be better prepared for possible paradigm shifts. In addition, being aware of paradigms in economics, that have preceded the current paradigm, allows one to better see the contours of the incumbent one. This can be extremely valuable since creative works 'composed' when mindful of the rules of a paradigm, but not slavishly following them, will likely be better than works that neatly and rigidly fit into the paradigm.

4.2 PARADIGMS AND RULES OF THE GAME

The concept of a technological paradigm, or regime, has emerged as an appealing vehicle for studying stability and change in the fields of technological and scientific knowledge (Kuhn 1962 and Dosi 1982).[1] Knowledge does not change haphazardly, so there is a need to understand patterns in its development, and how and why these patterns may change. To this end, the concept of paradigm has received much attention across the academic disciplines, and has been interpreted in various ways (Maasen and Weingart 2000). Some might argue that the claim that new paradigms have emerged is invoked with too much enthusiasm nowadays (Cohen 1999), but nevertheless the paradigmatic nature of knowledge seems inescapable (Blaug 2001).

Whereas the philosopher of science Thomas Kuhn (1962) used the term paradigm as a set of ideas and institutions, here one draws more on works in technology studies where paradigm is defined more narrowly as a set of rules and routines.[2] Perhaps not surprisingly, within economics the concept has been used particularly in fields where the impact of technological development is a primary focus (Dosi 1982).

Rules and routines coordinate the behavior of actors vis-à-vis each other because they create mutual expectations and make the actions of other actors more predictable. Developments from within the technological/knowledge field, as well as the market, may account for a paradigm's emergence as well as its development (cf. Van den Ende and Dolfsma 2005). By conceiving paradigms or regimes as sets of action-guiding rules, social phenomena related to knowledge development is ultimately seen as originating in individual human actions and decisions. The paradigm perspective itself can be seen as constraining the range and development of acceptable solutions that practitioners in the field take into consideration. This focuses attention, allows for specialization, and enables practitioners to direct their efforts toward areas where development is expected to be most fruitfully pursued. These advantages were nicely summarized by Nelson and Winter, who wrote:

> The sense of potential, of constraints, and of not yet exploited opportunities, implicit in a regime focuses . . . attention . . . on certain directions in which progress is possible, and provides strong guidance as to the tactics likely to be fruitful for probing in that direction. In other words, a regime not only defines boundaries, but also trajectories to those boundaries.
>
> (Nelson and Winter 1977: 57)

One of the things that becomes clear from studies of technological paradigms is that new paradigms usually grow out of old ones.[3] However, it is important to acknowledge, as did Schmalensee (1991), that technological change does not necessarily require a paradigm shift or transformation; it may also occur within the bounds of an existing paradigm, constituting an incremental change. An example of incremental change within the bounds of a technological paradigm is the promise-requirement cycle (Van Lente and Rip 1998). Promises or expectations that are shared among players within a technological regime will be translated into requirements that guide the innovative activities of the involved actors.

4.3 PARADIGMS AND THE DEVELOPMENT OF KNOWLEDGE IN ECONOMICS

Concerns over economists, apparent lack of interest in the history of their discipline have been voiced on several occasions (Gordon 1965; Schabas 1992; Reder 1999). It would, however, be fruitful for contemporary economists to raise their awareness of the history of their own field as this could help them better utilize current and dominant paradigms. One may mention three self-interested reasons for contemporary economists to be more mindful of their discipline's history that relate to the development of knowledge along paradigms.

First, new paradigms can take a field by surprise, obviating much knowledge that has been accumulated from the past. However, it must be remembered that these new paradigms are rooted in paradigms developed in the (sometimes distant) past, or that are developing along, or beyond, the profession's fringes (cf. Levinthal 1998). Thus, being aware of some of these other paradigms and understanding their focuses and theoretical structures puts one in a better position to be prepared for a paradigm shift. In addition, because the development of knowledge is not necessarily cumulative and linear, earlier paradigms that have been discarded may again be corroborated (Agassi 1975). For example, the paradigm shift toward a new geographical economics initiated by Krugman (1995) was not entirely new as it could draw on research undertaken in this field for quite some time (Martin 1999).

A second reason is that reflecting on one's knowledge by contrasting it with that of others may allow one to more effectively come up with new, fruitful ideas. As Mill observed:

> It is hardly possible to overrate the value . . . of placing human beings in contact with persons dissimilar to themselves, and with modes of thought and action unlike those with which they are familiar. . . . Such communication has always been, and is peculiarly in the present age, one of the primary sources of progress.
>
> (Mill 1848: 581)

Robert Lucas (Holt 1995) has made this point about research in economics, Feiner and Roberts (1995) and Pressman and Holt (2003) about teaching economics, and somewhat relevant, Burt (2004) about how organizations and firms develop new knowledge.

A third reason is that a study of the peculiarities of other paradigms can make one more aware of the rules of the game of their own paradigm. It is argued, for example, that pieces of music by the likes of Bach, Copeland and the Beatles, that have drawn the bulk of attention, were composed *mindful of*, but not *obedient to*, the rules of composition at the time of their writing (Manns 1994; Porter 1979, Tillekens 1998). A similar argument holds for being able to play chess well. It is said that, thanks to their awareness of boundaries and trajectories, grandmasters are able to recognize patterns in the position of pieces and the branches according to which play may develop, that allows them to break away from conventional thinking in order to win (Simon and Schaeffer 1992; de Groot 1965; Puddephatt 2003). An awareness of these and other examples of movements beyond the boundaries of paradigms in other fields should help someone working in a discipline like economics to depart just enough, and in the right way, from the discipline's rules so as to introduce enough novelty to draw attention from their peers, but not so much novelty as to perplex them (cf. Stigler 1965). This, for example, might help explain the immense impact of Keynes' aggregate equilibrium theory, which combined neoclassical analytic methodology with a trajectory along a path away for Say's Law, that supply creates its own demand to generate an economic paradigm that would revolutionize twentieth Century macroeconomic thinking.

4.4 MYTHS, PLOT STRUCTURES AND CULTURAL ENDOWMENTS

In light of the impact of evolving paradigms there is much to be gained from being more attentive to the often unacknowledged influence of language and culture on our understanding of both contemporary, as well as historical, contributions to the field of economics. This attentiveness can be helped by an awareness of the historian Hayden White's (1978) argument that histories are fictions, not in the sense that they are untrue, but that they are as much invented as found. That is, their forms are closer to what one finds in literature than in science. While White's works have been cited by economists (McCloskey 1985, 1990), the essay in which this argument is made appears to have escaped our attention, despite the fact that it has been widely accepted by other audiences. Here, White develops three concepts: myth, plot structure, and cultural endowment. These concepts offer interesting insights into how one reads and perceives writings that help us discern and understand paradigms in economics.

White describes myths as *stories* through which we shape our perceptions of what we are reading or hearing to give them meaning. The importance of these stories in gaining understanding is suggested by Stark (1958: 105) who observes: 'What we know we know only by and through the categories of our understanding' (cf. Lakoff and Johnson 1980). Accordingly, White's (1978) myth categories include: romantic, comic, tragic, and ironic. Romantic myths are about quests, perhaps seen as sacred, toward a higher state of perfection. Comic myths are not about humor, but rather the attainment of order through evolutionary or revolutionary change. Tragic myths are about decline and fall, and ironic myths are about recurrent or unexpected catastrophe.

Plot structure is the arrangement of elements in the story by the author to give it its shape and provide cues as to which myth is at hand. Regarding the role of plot structure in helping the reader understand what is being presented, White states[4]:

> The reader, in the process of following the . . . account of . . . events, gradually comes to realize that the story he is reading is of one kind rather than another: romance, tragedy, . . . or what have you. And when he has perceived the class . . . to which the story that he is reading belongs, he experiences the effect of having the events in the story explained to him. He has at this point not only successfully *followed* the story, he has grasped the point of it, *understood* it, as well.
>
> (White 1978: 86)

What allows the reader to understand the story is that he or she shares a cultural endowment with the writer that leads to similarities in their perceptions of how significant human affairs take form. Culture provides the context, or template, in which myths and plot structures are interpreted. What distinguishes one culture from another is differences in how their members interpret a myth or plot structure. Thus, the relationship between myths, plot structures and culture is interactive: how you interpret a myth or plot structure defines the culture to which you belong, and if you belong to a particular culture you can be expected to interpret a myth or plot structure in a particular way. For example, how one reads the writings of Adam Smith or Karl Marx will determine whether he or she is more appropriately seen as belonging to a culture endorsing capitalism or a culture endorsing socialism. At the same time, belonging to one or the other of these cultures will influence how he or she reads those writings. It should not be surprising that culture lies at the core of a debate over whether the outcomes of inquiries reflect clearer understandings of truths verifiable to anyone, or truths verifiable only to those who see the world in the same way. Such a debate has been engaged in over how one reads earlier writings on economics, and has been characterized as the truth v. perspective, or chronicler v. constructionist debate (Backhouse 1992).

4.5 MYTHS, PLOT STRUCTURES, AND CULTURAL ENDOWMENT IN ECONOMICS

While 'myth', 'plot structure' and 'cultural endowment' are typically not part of economists' standard operating vocabulary, each can be applied to economics in general. However, as announced before, here the history of economic thought is taken to be examplary for how science develops.

Beginning with myths, White's categories are a fruitful means to 'labor at historical reconstruction' (Blaug 2001: 152). For example, Adam Smith's Invisible Hand and Karl Marx' economic interpretation of history can be read by a capitalism advocate and socialism advocate respectively as a romantic myth since each describes a quest toward a higher state of perfection. For Smith, the quest is toward a fuller realization of the principle of subsidiarity through a reduction in the role of government. For Marx, it is toward a truly human society by way of a progression through epochs of the production process. The general equilibrium model under prefect information, or Say's Law, that supply creates its own demand, can be read as comic since each leads, in an evolutionary way, to an ordered outcome. Joseph Schumpeter's theory of creative destruction when viewed from the perspective of those with a stake in the displaced technology, and David Ricardo's prediction of shrinking capitalists' incomes as production activity expands, can be read as stories of decline and fall, and therefore as tragic. The undoing of the hive in Bernard de Mandeville's *Fable of the Bees* following the bees' conversion from vice to virtue, and Malthus' population theory can be read as ironic.

References to plot structures and cultural endowments, although not named as such, if at all, are also found in the writings of economists. One well-known acknowledgment of plot structures in economics is Schumpeter's 'vision'. He writes:

> Analytic effort starts when we have conceived our vision of the set of phenomena that caught our interest. . . . The first task is to verbalize the vision or to *conceptualize it in such a way that its elements take their places, with names attached to them that facilitate recognition* . . .
>
> (Schumpeter 1954: 42, Emphasis added)

Building on Schumpeter's 'vision,' and suggesting as well the role of myths, Heilbroner observes that:

> . . . [B]ehind scenarios of the most differing sorts lie the precognitive analytic acts . . . that not only fulfill the essential task of reducing raw perceptions to ordered concepts [plot structures], but that also imbue those concepts with qualities of inevitability and rightness [myths].
>
> (Heilbroner 1990: 1110)

In respect of the economics profession's having a particular cultural endowment that impacts understanding, Hayek (1969: 46) writes: 'It is significant that the capacity to respond to signs of which we are not conscious decreases as we move from members of our own culture to those of different cultures'. A similar opinion is voiced by McCloskey (1990: 34), who writes: 'An economist can read the most unreadable and compressed production of a fellow economist if she participates in the same community of speech'.[5] Weintraub takes the role of cultural endowment one step further by explicitly separating it from scientific verifiability. He writes:

> [W]hat constitutes a good theory . . . is not a matter of comparing the theory to some standard of scientific goodness. We have to ask more complex questions of a theory and its interpretations. . . . We seek to understand the way the interpretive community has read the economy text and what makes the community more likely to respond to one interpretation rather than another.
>
> (Weintraub 1991: 7)

Hayden White's concepts of myths, plot structures, and culture further specify these comments by Schumpeter and the others. A heightened awareness of the myths and plot structures employed by earlier writers on economics, as well as of their cultural endowments, can enhance both what we take away from their writings and our understanding of economic paradigms both then and now. Below are two ways in which this heightened awareness can strengthen one's interaction with earlier economic writings: firstly, by allowing a more open and penetrating assessment of what has been written, and secondly by increasing our recognition that the mathematical arguments on which so much of current economics is based are, in fact, plot structures.

Sensitivity to Differing Cultural Endowments When Assessing Earlier Works

Greater sensitivity to differences in the cultural endowments of earlier writers and today's reader should prompt the reader to make an effort to better understand the environments in which the writers found themselves. Thanks to this effort, today's reader might better understand, rather than merely 'follow', the writers' arguments. This sensitivity, and subsequent effort, is important because an understanding of the writers' culture is not automatically conveyed in their writings, and the present-day reader is to some degree a captive of his or her surroundings. As Coats puts it, perhaps overly pessimistically:

> However sensitive his historical imagination, the intellectual historian cannot enter fully into the minds of his subjects, especially if they lived long ago; and however hard he tries, he cannot fully emancipate himself from the ideas and beliefs of his own day.
>
> (Coats 1973: 489)

One example is that the modern economist reading Malthus' population theory should, even if tightly culture bound, readily follow the *analytics* of his argument. However, since he or she cannot enter Malthus' mind, or be fully emancipated from today's ideas and beliefs, the reader's understanding of the motivation and reasoning underlying the theory should be enhanced by a greater awareness that Malthus' society had a largely poor, wealthless and politically under-represented working class, prohibitions against organizing labour and a history of laws hostile to the working class to the point of forbidding its members to read the Bible in English.[6] Malthus' tragic story should be better understood in this context.

Other examples involve economic thought on property rights and the charging of interest on loans. Views on these issues have changed dramatically over time. For instance, there are statements from the *Old Testament* that property shall be returned to the countryman who is its original owner on the jubilee year, and that interest can be charged to foreigners but not fellow countrymen.[7] Or, more recently, consider Thomas Aquinas' influential remark in *Summa Theologica* (1947: 1518), that charging interest is to: '. . . sell what does not exist, and this evidently leads to inequality which is contrary to justice'. Such positions, standing in marked contrast with what today's reader typically views as natural, might seem nonsensical. However, for a largely nomadic society in hostile surroundings, as was often the case for the ancient Jews, or a survival-level society where economic transactions were often non-cooperative zero-sum games, as was the case in Aquinas' time, such rules could well lead to more orderly (or 'comic') outcomes than would more individually-based agreements on property ownership and lending such as those found today. Would one's understanding of this thinking be improved by a greater sensitivity to the similarities and differences between earlier and modern paradigms and the environments in which they were constructed? It would. As both Aquinas and present day economists argue from a comic myth, the example shows how one also needs White's concepts of plot structure and cultural endowment to understand the differences.

Thus, one consequence of a greater appreciation for differences between the writers' and readers' cultures is that it should make us more hesitant to dismiss earlier writings as uninformed or irrelevant because, on first reading, they appear inconsistent with the tenets that underlay modern economics. As Strassman and Polanyi (1995: 143), explain: '. . . [I]n economics, stories which jar with the situated perspective of established practitioners . . . are deemed outside and irrelevant to the important conversations of the field'. Why might stories from the history of economics be jarring and irrelevant to the established practitioner? One answer is because we might be prioritizing and presenting earlier literature with no regard for cultural differences.

Accordingly, the history of economic thought can be approached as an area of inquiry where an awareness of the possibility of paradigm shifts, rather than extensions through normal science, is emphasized more. A greater appreciation for the reality of differences between the cultural endowments, myths and plot structures of earlier writers and today's readers is both a requirement and an outcome of such an exercise. This, in turn, can play a key role in better informing our understanding of *both* earlier and present-day works. This is especially true if, as suggested by Heyne (1996: 2–3), what is taken here as 'preanalytic visions' are in fact 'postanalytic conclusions' following from the perspective of the current literature. A greater openness to cultural differences would, hopefully, lead us to approach the earlier writings with questions like: 'what cultural elements make this viewpoint reasonable, even though it might not at first appear reasonable to residents of today's culture?'; and, subsequently: 'once cultural differences are acknowledged, what can we learn about both then and now from this viewpoint?' This does not mean that no theory should ever be discarded, but it does require that the act be more reasoned as it puts the onus on the ones who do the discarding.

Mathematics as Plot Structure

Heilbroner (1988: 38) writes: 'Economics prides itself on its science-like character, and economists on their ability to speak like scientists, without color, passion, or values, preferably in the language of mathematics'. Given this self-image of economists, one would not expect the word 'poetic' to be the first chosen to describe the economists' method. Yet, the characterization fits. White (1978: 82) describes the poetic method as that which works from, not toward, a unifying form. Certainly a poem's meter and rhyme demonstrate the presence of a unifying form. However, the notion of unifying form goes far beyond the obvious mechanics of poetry. Given this definition, mathematics, with its carefully structured formats and axiomatic approach that allow us to articulate imaginations and come to a fuller understanding of that which surrounds us, can be reasonably described as poetic. Thus, to the extent economists' current method of choice for analyzing and explaining social phenomena is mathematics, the method is poetic.[8]

If the economists' method is poetic in the sense used here, one problem for today's reader approaching earlier economic writings might be the non-mathematical format in which many of their arguments are cast. Specifically, the reader might have what Hexter (1971: 16–17) calls an 'assimilationist' view of the worth of earlier works, which holds that: '. . . "explanation". . . that deviate[s] . . . from the physical-science norm [is] . . . either an inferior or inadequate surrogate for "real", "complete", or "satisfactory" explanation, . . . or it [is] . . . not an explanation at all. . . .'[9] Ultimately, this criticism is of the form of the explanation, not its content.

One example of how this could affect the reading of earlier works in economics occurs where there is a conflict between a currently popular mathematical technique, and a myth or plot structure underlying an earlier presentation. As background to an examination of this conflict consider Nelson's comment that:

> . . . the application of mathematics to problems of human behavior can come only through the explanation of mathematical formulas as metaphors for some real world phenomenon, and this drawing of analogies involves the use of words. In the process, meaning beyond that immediately present in the mathematical analogy will also be suggested.
>
> (Nelson 1992: 114–115)

Nelson's comment suggests that economists' technical analyses might be influenced by their cultural endowments. More pointedly, the economist Boettke (1992: 85), notes in this regard that, '. . ."vision" and "analysis" are not so neatly separated'.

If, as suggested by Nelson and Boettke, the meanings conveyed by mathematical techniques can come from beyond what is immediately apparent in their mechanics, potential conflicts can surface when reading earlier economic writings.[10] Myths, plot structures and cultural endowments do not automatically combine into a single and universally acceptable constellation. For example, mathematical techniques for solving maximizing problems are at the core of a large part of modern economics. However, applying these maximizing techniques to formalize the writings of previous economists may not be easy due to differences in the myths and plot structures dominant in the writers' and readers' cultures, as Marshall found to his dismay when he tried to 'mathematize' Ricardo (Keynes 1933: 151; Pigou 1925: 427). This shows how differing cultural endowments – in Marshall's case separated by a Marginalist Revolution – may affect the core of the argument. The difficulty is partly one of misaligned myths – Ricardo's is tragic, Marshall's is ironic, and that of mathematics, poetic.

Regarding the impact of differences in myths, because of the precision of these mathematical techniques, one meaning likely to be attributed to maximizing behaviour by the modern practitioner is that it leads to orderly (or comic) outcomes. While much of the earlier economics literature is consistent with this modern perception of maximizing behaviour, from the Aristotelian viewpoint, such behavior is questionable because of its association with gain seeking and greed, that can prevent the attainment of higher values (Aristotle 1908 and Langholm 1979). This is consistent with a tragic or ironic myth and leaves the modern economist with a choice: Dismiss the Aristotelian view because it is inconsistent with how stories are plotted today, or ask what would make the viewpoint reasonable, and what can be learned from the viewpoint.

Interestingly, the risk of premature dismissal on mathematics-based grounds is not limited to acceptance of earlier writings; it can also affect acceptance of current writings. This is partly due to the fact that mathematics is not singular, as many economists would seem to hold, but rather plural (Mirowski 1991). For example, modelling out-of-equilibrium dynamics is mathematically possible and well-established within mathematics and biology, but largely incompatible with the equilibrium-directed cultural endowment and myths adhered to by today's economists.[11] Consequently, practitioners of each approach might not readily or fully understand what the other is doing, which makes the concepts highlighted by White useful for evaluating both earlier economic writings and alternative current methodologies.

In summary, one's understanding of earlier writings in economics stands to benefit from a greater awareness that myths and plot structures underlay the interpretation of economic theories, and that the economics profession is a community of inquiry with a defined, but changing, dominant view of reality that informs what tends to be recognized, or accepted, as appropriate myths and plot structures. Given this, Lyotard (1984: 7) writes: 'I do not mean to say that narrative knowledge can prevail over science, but its model is related to ideas of internal equilibrium and conviviality . . . next to which contemporary scientific knowledge cuts a poor figure'. In fact, exactly the opposite may occur when reading literature from the history of economic thought. The scientific (mathe-matical) aspects of earlier theories may pass relatively easily, and understandably, from their writers to today's readers possessing similar analytic skills. What may not pass so easily are the culturally defined myths and plot structures around which the theories were built.

4.6 HOW A FULLER UNDERSTANDING OF THE HISTORY OF ECONOMICS CAN BETTER PREPARE YOU FOR PARADIGM SHIFTS, AND HELP YOU WRITE BETTER ARTICLES IN THE MEANTIME

In an article asking if the past has useful economics, McCloskey (1976: 454) claims that: 'An economist hopping around without a historical leg . . . has a narrow perspective on the present, shallow economic ideas, little appreciation for the strengths and weaknesses of economic data, and small ability to apply economics to large issues'.

Nevertheless, from time to time one encounters the opinion that the modern economist can safely ignore the history of economic thought; either because the earlier thinking has been replaced by better thinking,[12] or because it simply chronicles what was important in the past and is therefore of little interest to the modern economist wrestling with today's problems. These two opinions go by several names: absolutism and relativism; incrementalism and inductivism and economic thought in the tradition of Walras and in the tradition of Adam Smith (Blaug 1968, pp. 2–3; Houghton 1991, pp. 397–399; Fetter 1965, pp. 36–137).

However, do these opinions speak of the worth of the earlier writings, or of how we interact with them? For example, and based on what we have seen from the exploration of White's views, is current thinking really better, or is it just expressed in a way that is more recognizable to today's economist? While some modern theories are unquestionably superior to earlier presentations, the fact that names such as Smith, Marx, Schumpeter, Ricardo, Keynes and Friedman often carry more weight than do the best present-day economists – and not just as signposts in introductions to flag one's supposed erudition – suggests that it is presumptuous to categorically, and out of hand, dismiss earlier works as inferior.

Might we not fully appreciate the importance of what had been written earlier because one is embedded in one's own culture and thus conceive of the history of economic thought as just a chronicle of what used to be important? For example, now that the 'Evil Empire' has been defeated and capitalism has reached global proportions, can we forever close *Das Kapital*? now that the education of children is generally seen as a beneficial human capital investment, can today's reader understand Jevons' position that only after a person has gained adulthood is education perceived of as an investment, and, that before maturity is reached parents (should) provide for their children's education for moral reasons only? (Mosselmans 2002.)

The fact is, a focus on the paradigmatic nature of developments in economic thinking, combined with White's framework, creates an opportunity for the modern economist to confront what Mitchell (1967: 7) describes as, '. . . the limitations of his knowledge, the fallibility of his insights, . . . [and] the degree to which he is a child of his age . . .'. Confronting other paradigms within the fields of economics will increase one's awareness of the peculiarities of one's own sub-field. This will: firstly, make us better prepared for possible paradigm shifts in a field one may happen to find oneself in; secondly imbue one's work with more, and more varied, ideas,[13] and lastly, improve its quality and recognition, as one's work will more likely be composed mindful of, but not strictly obedient to, the rules of one's own paradigm. In short, the history of economics, or that of any field of science, should not be x-rated.[14]

5 Knowledge exchange in networks

Within-firm analysis*

The informal communication networks in organizations are often emphasized as facilitating knowledge transfer. However, formal work-flow networks also contribute significantly to knowledge transfer, and perhaps even more so. This is particularly the case when knowledge is transferred *between* units within a firm. Indeed, formal work-flow and informal communication networks appear to be synergetic; formal work-flow networks may be the basis on which informal communication networks can form. This suggests that knowledge transfer effects, that in previous studies were attributed to the informal communication network, may in fact be a consequence of the prior existence of a formal work-flow network.

5.1 INTRODUCTION

Knowledge is frequently considered to be the most valuable asset of an organization (Grant 1996) and a key source for competitive advantage (Teece *et al.* 1997). Yet, at the same time, it is one of the most difficult resources to manage: for instance, knowledge is usually spread throughout the organization and may not be available where it might best be put to use (Cross *et al.* 2001; Moorman and Miner 1998; Szulanski 2003). Thus, transfer of knowledge within the organization has gained considerable attention in the literature (Hansen 1999; Powell *et al.* 1996; Argote *et al.* 2003). Scholars have emphasized that effective transfer of knowledge between employees within an organization actually increases the organization's innovativeness (Davenport and Prusak 1998; Tushman 1977; Moorman and Miner 1998; Perry-Smith and Shalley 2003; Tsai 2001; Moran 2005; Hansen, Mors and Lovas 2005). However, such transfer is not automatic (Szulanski 1996). Some potential difficulties in knowledge transfer lie in its incompatibility with incentive structures, it's threat to existing strategic positions and incompatible frames of reference (Amabile *et al.* 1996; Davenport and Prusak 1998; Carlile 2004). Another important barrier is the lack of information regarding the knowledge that exists in other divisions, the individuals who possess this knowledge, and, once located, how it can be transferred (Hansen 1999;

* With Rick Aalbers, Otto Koppius.

Szulanski 2003; Winter and Szulanski 2001; Hansen, Mors and Lovas 2005). These latter questions have been addressed frequently from a network perspective.

In the literature, different types of intra-organizational networks or relations that are involved in knowledge exchange are discussed, including formal work-flow, informal communication (trust), political support and advice networks (Krackhardt and Hanson 1993). Studies tend to investigate one particular type of tie or network (Hansen, Mors and Lovas (2005) are an exception), and in many cases the role that informal ties play in effective knowledge transfer is emphasized (e.g. Granovetter 1973; Freeman 1991; Hansen 1999; Powell *et al.* 1996; Reagans and McEvily 2003). This focus is equally true for studies that focus on knowledge exchange between firms (e.g. Dahl and Pedersen 2004). Formal work-flow networks have received much less research attention in this regard and when they have, they are equated with the organizational chart and found to be of marginal influence for knowledge transfer (Krackhardt and Hanson 1993; Cross and Prusak 2002). However, if we are prepared to conceive of work-flow networks as broader than just the organizational chart, this dismissal may be premature. Decisions to assign employees to divisions, work units, teams or projects all determine a person's place in the formal network. Such decisions will affect knowledge transfer, but have not always been considered as such in studies taking a narrow view of formal structures. They put individuals in a certain position in the work-flow network, and it seems plausible to expect at least some sort of impact on knowledge transfer processes arising from formal networks (Allen and Cohen 1969; Stevenson 1990; Stevenson and Gilly 1991). Despite assertions that different *types* of ties or networks can be conducive for different purposes, or in different circumstances, a comparison between the different networks, for instance to determine which one contributes to knowledge transfer best, has rarely been undertaken to date (see Hansen, Mors and Lovas (2005) for a recent exception).

5.2 KNOWLEDGE TRANSFER IN MULTI-UNIT FIRMS

In line with previous research (Carlile 2004; Cummings 2004; Hansen 1999, 2002; Szulanski 2003; Tsai 2001), we focus attention on multi-unit firms, since this is where the knowledge transfer problem is most pertinent.

Multi-unit (or multi-divisional) firms tend to be organized according to either the products they develop and markets they aim for, or on the basis of disciplinary knowledge. In many cases the two coincide. This structure offers units a relatively high level of autonomy. Although a unit structure offers benefits such as focus and specialization, at the same time it may limit the inter-unit knowledge utilization and transfer because units may be primarily concerned about their own performance. Given Schumpeter's (1934) point of combining, and re-combining, existing knowledge as a source of innovation (cf. Cohen and Levinthal 1990), this inherent limitation of the multi-unit structure is problematic and hence, many firms are seeking ways to overcome it. Unfortunately, combining and recombining knowledge is by no means obvious, especially due to the social dimensions of communication patterns (Szulanski 1996, 2003). To be able to use existing knowledge, firms need to have sufficient insight in the knowledge actually available, and the actual processes of, and structures for, knowledge transfer (Kogut and Zander 1992). The structure of the communication patterns within organizations that facilitate the knowledge transfer to take place is believed to be of considerable importance to direct the transfer of knowledge in an effective way (Tsai 2001; Hansen 2002).

As an example, finding the person that has the knowledge that one is looking for may be difficult within a large, multi-unit organization (Szulanski 2003; Hansen 1999; Hansen and Haas 2001). The relative autonomy of divisions within a multi-unit organization structure creates a lack of awareness of each other's activities on an individual and a unit level, possibly limiting knowledge-transfer. Also, within a unit that specializes in a certain knowledge field, knowledge tends to be of the tacit kind. The advantage of the tacit nature of knowledge is that imitation by competitors is relatively difficult (Nonaka and Takeuchi 1995), but at the same time the tacit nature of knowledge requires a high degree of personal contact in order to be effectively dispersed throughout the company (Teece 1998; Hansen 1999). As a result, interpersonal networks within an organization play a significant role in intra-organizational knowledge transfer (cf. Allen 1977; Tushman and Scanlan 1981).

5.3 FORMAL WORK-FLOW AND INFORMAL COMMUNICATION NETWORKS

Networks within an organization affect the organization's activities and performance in a number of different ways. The contribution to knowledge transfer within the organization has been studied by focusing on informal communication networks. Monge and Contractor (2001: 440) define networks as 'the patterns of contact between communication partners that are created by transmitting and exchanging messages through time and space'. A broadly accepted distinction, when discussing intra-organizational networks, is between the formal work-flow and the informal communication network (e.g. Allen and Cohen 1969; Allen 1977; Madhaven and Grover 1998). The work-flow network is the communication that is derived from the formal relations as formulated and standardized by corporate management (Kilduff and Brass 2001). Communication that flows through the work-flow network is based on the planned structure established for the organization (Simon 1976: 147). This planned structure is only partly reflected in the organization chart because it also includes formal procedures, schemes and rules deemed important mostly for the execution of daily operations (Adler and Borys 1996). Formal structures are relatively transparent. They allocate responsibility, may prevent conflict, and can reduce ambiguity (Adler and Borys 1996), thereby reducing uncertainty regarding the location of expertise and obtaining the resources for intra-firm knowledge transfer as an example. The formal structure also dictates to some extent who interacts with whom. These repeated interactions can build a shared understanding between two parties, and this knowledge base can in turn facilitate transfer of further knowledge (Cohen and Levinthal 1990). Formal structures also allow for specialization as individuals in particular positions store experience and best practices; the formulation and realization of a common goal is thereby promoted (Adler and Borys 1996). Therefore, the formal work-flow network may be said to contribute positively to knowledge transfer within an organization.

Blau and Scott (1962) observed that it is impossible to understand processes within the formal organization without investigating the influence of the informal relations within it. Adler and Borys (1996) argue that, depending on the task, formal structures may enable or hamper employees' autonomy and creativity, and may thus increase or decrease their commitment (cf. Rogers 1983). Certainly, for the kind of non-routine activities related to knowledge transfer and innovation, highly formalized structures might be problematic (Adler and Borys 1996: 63). Although altering formal structures may be more easily accomplished than changing informal ones that are more explicit, intentionally changing formal relations may not yield intended benefits (Krackhardt and Hanson 1993). This is mainly due to neglecting the influence of informal networks that cut through the formal structures and thereby operate as a 'communication safety net' (Cross *et al.* 2002).

When communication via the formal work-flow network takes too long, or when the relations required to get certain things done have not been formally established, the informal communication network ('the grapevine') may come into play. The informal communication network refers to the 'interpersonal relationships in the organization that affect decisions within it, but either are omitted from the formal scheme or are not consistent with that scheme' (Simon 1976: 148). Informal communication networks are the contacts actors have with others within the organization that are not formally mandated. This may, for instance, include friendships with co-workers, but also contacts unrelated to the day-to-day work-flow. The informal communication network provides insight into the general way 'things are getting done' within the organization, often bypassing, and sometimes undermining, the formal communication structure (Schulz 2003) because information may be transferred relatively fast in the informal network (Cross *et al.* 2002). Thus, informal channels may provide insight into the *de facto* authority within the organization (Krackhardt and Hanson 1993). Besides this, the informal communication network provides the opportunity for information and knowledge to flow in both vertical and horizontal directions, that contributes positively to the overall flexibility of the organization (Cross *et al.* 2002). As such, drawbacks of an inflexible formal network might be mitigated (Kilduff and Brass 2001; Molina 2001; Krackhardt and Stern 1988). Based on the above argument, the informal communication network contributes positively to knowledge transfer within an organization.

H1   Both the formal workflow and the informal networks contribute positively to knowledge transfer within an organization.

Although formal and informal networks may be expected to contribute to knowledge transfer, this review indicates that most scholars expect the informal network to be the main driver of knowledge transfer (Cross *et al.* 2002; Stevenson and Gilly 1991; Jablin and Putnam 2001; Madhaven and Grover 1998). Compared to the formal work-flow network, this may offer a higher degree of flexibility as the relative ease of knowledge-transfer makes it possible to adapt quickly to changing market circumstances and to tap into unconventional/new knowledge sources, even when an informal network might be less transparent compared to a formal network (Cross *et al.* 2002: 26). Albrecht and Ropp (1984) suggest that employees tend to discuss new ideas with colleagues in their informal network first. Hansen (2002) argues that informal networks allow units to tap into knowledge available outside one's own organizational unit more easily – informal networks allow for flexibility if they do not turn into old boys networks. In addition to the flexibility argument, informal communication networks may be the primary basis for the creation of trust. Trust in turn is necessary for knowledge transfer to take place in practice (Kramer *et al.* 2001; Szulanski *et al.* 2004). Thus, although formal work-flow ties may prove to be helpful to knowledge transfer, its benefits are likely to be marginal compared to those of an informal communication tie. Hence, drawing on existing literature comparing both networks, the informal communication network contributes more to knowledge transfer than the formal work-flow network.

We thus hypothesize that both the formal work-flow, as well as the informal communication networks, contribute to knowledge transfer, constituting different roads to the same end. Informal relations are often seen as allowing for more flexible responses by the organization as a whole to deal with perceived needs (Krackhardt and Stern 1988). Informal communication networks may offer avenues for the exchange of knowledge where no established avenue is readily available. As formal structures follow, and in fact partly constitute, unit boundaries, inter-unit knowledge transfer presents precisely such a situation of uncertainty regarding the relevance of the sought knowledge and/or the best way of transferring it (Schulz 2001, 2003). Hence, in such situations, informal relations are more likely to have a beneficial effect on knowledge transfer compared to knowledge transfer within units. Within a unit, there are more likely to be established patterns of work-flows that provide a basis for knowledge transfer irrespective of the presence of informal ties, therefore, compared to inter-unit knowledge transfer, formal networks are likely to be more effective for intra-unit knowledge transfer. Two additional hypotheses that further explore the nature of the differences between the formal and informal network should also be considered:

H2 The formal work-flow network contributes to intra-unit knowledge transfer more than to inter-unit knowledge transfer.

H3 The informal communication network contributes to inter-unit knowledge transfer more than to intra-unit knowledge transfer.

5.4 RESULTS

Using UCINET (Borgatti *et al.* 2002) the formal network and the informal network can be graphically displayed (where peripheral nodes of individuals

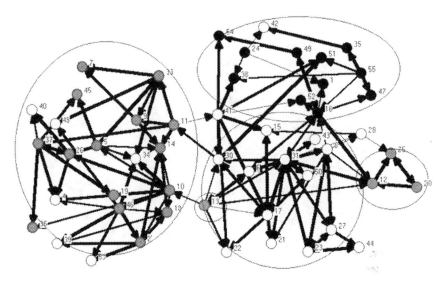

Figure 5.1 The formal workflow network (N_{total} = 110, N_{figure} = 52)

who did not have further contacts have been removed for clarity), as in Figures 5.1 and 5.2. The colours of the nodes represent different organizational units, the circles roughly (although not perfectly) correspond to these units. What is immediately striking is that both the formal and informal network closely follow divisional boundaries.

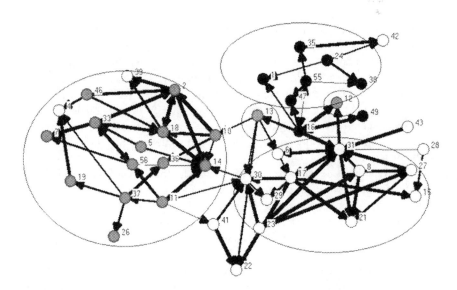

Figure 5.2 The informal network (N_{total} = 87, N_{figure} = 41)

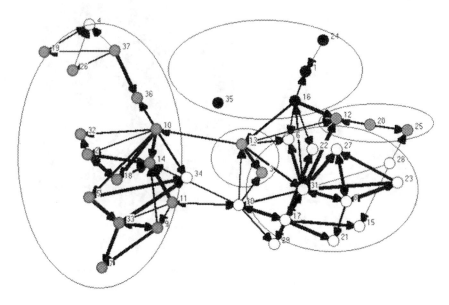

Figure 5.3 The 'innovation' network (N_{total} = 82, N_{figure} = 37)

As discussed above, formal work-flow and informal communication networks explain the knowledge transferred within this organization. The network where new ideas, innovations and improvements regarding products and processes are discussed might be called the 'innovation network'; it is presented in Figure 5.3.

As is to be expected (see for example Homans 1951), the formal work-flow and informal communication networks overlap to a certain extent (QAP correlation 0.529, p < 0.001). At the same time, the two networks are sufficiently different – in line with findings by, a.o., Fernandez (1991) – to be able to determine their separate effects on knowledge transfer. In addition, as discussed above, even if, and to the extent that the formal and the informal network overlap, they provide separate or alternative avenues for knowledge transfer. Two individuals can, and do, relate to each other in a number of different ways, depending on the purpose and the circumstance of the communication, the content of the communication will be different accordingly.

To test hypothesis 1, the correlation between the formal work-flow and inno- vation the informal communication and the innovation network will be measured using the QAP procedure with 2,500 permutations (Hubert and Schulz 1976; Krackhardt 1987). From this calculation, the correlation coefficient (r-squared) and the standardized regression coefficient (beta) can be derived. The r-squared gives an indication of the explanatory value of the informal and formal net- work on the innovation network. The interpretation of the derived beta will be used to interpret the individual influence of the independent variables, formal work-flow network and informal communication network on knowledge transfer. The independent variable with the highest beta-value has the largest influence on the innovation network as dependent variable.

The QAP correlation between the formal work-flow network and the innovation network is 0.739 ($p < 0.001$). The QAP correlation between the informal communication and the innovation network is 0.649 ($p < 0.001$). This shows that both the formal and the informal networks contribute separately to knowledge transfer. A QAP regression analysis was conducted with the innovation network as the dependent variable in which both independent variables were included. The combined model of formal and informal networks explains fifty nine per cent ($p < 0.001$) of the variance in the innovation network. The coefficients for both networks are positive and significant (formal network $\beta = 0.460$, $p < 0.001$; informal network $\beta = 0.360$, $p < 0.001$). This emphasizes that *both* the formal and the informal network have a strong positive influence on knowledge transfer, where previous research has often acknowledged only the role of the informal network.

The standardized beta for the formal work-flow network is larger than the standardized beta of the informal communication network. As the size of the standardized beta-score serves as an indicator of the influence of the respective independent variable on the dependent variable innovation network, it seems valid to conclude that the formal work-flow network affects knowledge transfer somewhat more than the informal communication network. Not only should hypothesis 1 be accepted, but one might conclude that the formal network contributes more to knowledge transfer than the informal one.

To investigate hypotheses 2 and 3, each of the three networks was split in two mutually exclusive sub-networks: one consisting of intra-unit ties and one consisting of inter-unit ties (unit membership for each respondent was obtained from company records). Separate QAP regressions were run with the innovation network as the dependent network for the intra- and inter-unit case. Hypothesis 2 predicts that the QAP regression coefficient for the formal workflow network will be larger in the intra-unit regression than the inter-unit regression. Hypothesis 3 predicts a larger QAP regression coefficient for the informal communication network in the inter-unit regression than the intra-unit regression.[1]

Both the intra- and inter-unit regression models are significant and have a fairly large R^2 (intra-unit $R^2 = 0.671$, inter-unit $R^2 = 0.431$). The differences between standardized betas are in the opposite direction from what is predicted. The formal work-flow network is slightly *more* influential for inter-unit ($\beta = 0.487$, $p < 0.001$) than for intra-unit ($\beta = 0.401$, $p < 0.001$) knowledge transfer, thus rejecting Hypothesis 2. Perhaps even more surprising, is that the informal communication network is considerably more influential for intra-unit ($\beta = 0.460$, $p < 0.001$) than for inter-unit ($\beta = 0.221$, $p < 0.001$) knowledge transfer, thereby rejecting Hypothesis 3.

These results also provide an additional test of Hypothesis 1, albeit at the intra- or inter-unit level. Hypothesis 1 is supported since both formal work-flow, and informal communication networks, contribute to both intra-unit and inter-unit knowledge transfer. In addition, for knowledge transfer between units, formal work-flow relations are more important than informal communication relations. Within units, informal communication relations do seem somewhat more important than formal work-flow relations.

5.5 DISCUSSION: THE DIFFERENT ROLES FOR FORMAL AND INFORMAL NETWORKS

The results of the analysis support the contention that the formal network plays an important role in knowledge transfer – one that has not always been acknowledged. How does the role of the formal network differ from that of the informal network? Results for Hypotheses 2 and 3 suggest that they do, but since the effects were in the opposite of what was expected, based on the existing theory regarding formal and informal network, it is clear that a refinement of the theory is needed. While more evidence or more specific measures at the tie level would have been helpful in this regard, the data available allows for some additional analysis that can help to shed some more light on this issue.

First of all, the role of the centrality of the transferring actors in both networks is of importance. Given the organization's explicit goal of promoting inter-unit knowledge transfer, and based on qualitative data, monopoly power over communication is not an issue in this research setting – thus, the measure of degree centrality is opted for (Freeman 1979). Degree centrality scores were calculated per employee engaged in the formal respectively informal network using Ucinet 6.0. (Borgatti *et al.* 2002).[2] The relative number of outgoing relations, or the extent to which an individual communicates across unit boundaries, is analyzed as the percentage share of such communication in relation to total communication. The relationship between centrality within *either* the formal network *or* the informal network on the *one* hand, and the degree of inter-unit knowledge-transfer regarding innovation on the *other* hand, was analyzed using non parametrical Mann-Whitney tests to correct for the absence of a normal distribution in the dependent variable. The results show that a high degree of centrality within the formal network strongly increases the involvement in inter-unit communication (Mann-Whitney $U = 265.0$, $p < 0.001$, effect size[3] $r = 0.717$). In addition, a strong relationship (Mann-Whitney $U = 245.0$, $p < 0.001$, effect size $r = 0.560$) between the level of centrality in the informal network and the percentage of inter-unit knowledge transfer is present. The extent to which an individual is central in a network appears to be a useful predictor of the level of involvement in inter-unit knowledge transfer, as underscored by the large effect sizes (Cohen 1992). This finding is in line with, but gives further specification for, the often-found importance of centrality for knowledge transfer (Tsai 2001). The difference between the effect sizes of the formal and informal network suggests that a central position in the formal network might be more important for inter-unit knowledge transfer than a central position in the informal network.

Table 5.1 Frequency distribution of ties

Formal workflow tie	Informal communication tie	Innovation tie	Frequency
–	–	√	9
√	–	–	33
√	–	√	26
–	√	–	6
–	√	√	5
√	√	–	34
√	√	√	82

Secondly, a 'conversion rate' for ties may be suggested: given a tie between two actors in the formal network only, the informal network only, or a combined formal/informal tie, what is the likelihood of each tie resulting in a tie in the knowledge transfer network? The frequency data given in Table A5.1 in the Appendix suggests a possible answer to this question. Figure 5.4 displays the same data graphically[4] grouped by the three possible antecedent categories (formal only, informal only, combined formal + informal) of knowledge-transfer ties. One of the things that is immediately obvious from the chart is that informal ties without an accompanying formal tie are very uncommon compared to the other two types (eleven vs. sixty nine and 116). However, when they do occur, they result in a knowledge-transferring tie in forty six per cent of the cases (five

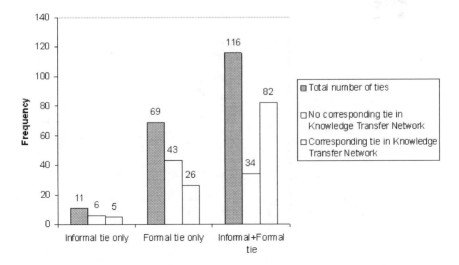

Figure 5.4 Knowledge transfer – full network

out of eleven). Another striking fact is that not only are formal ties without informal ties fairly common, but a considerable portion of those result in knowledge
transfer: thirty eight per cent. Examination of the most common category (a
combined informal and formal tie) shows that there is a strong synergy effect
between the formal and informal network when it comes to knowledge transfer:
seventy one per cent of ties result in a corresponding knowledge-transferring
tie. When taken together, these observations, although purely descriptive and
not permitting a significance test, are in line with the hypothesis regarding the
positive effects of formal ties and informal ties. However, they paint a more mixed
picture when it comes to the presumed importance of the informal network. On
one hand, an informal tie adds considerable value to a formal tie for knowledge
transfer (conversion rate thirty eight per cent → seventy one per cent), but on
the other hand, so does adding a formal tie to an informal tie (conversion rate
forty six per cent → seventy one per cent). If one were to compare solely on the
basis of whether or not an informal tie adds to knowledge transfer, one would
conclude that it does. Interaction effects between the formal and informal network seem primarily to be at work, however. This apparent synergy effect could
not have been found, had informal ties only been looked at. Focusing solely on
informal ties when explaining knowledge transfer in an organization would
not only disregard these synergy effects but also that well over a quarter of all
knowledge-transferring ties are entirely formal.

Figures 5.5 and 5.6 show the corresponding charts for the intra- and inter-
unit networks respectively. The results are qualitatively similar to those found
for the entire network, although it is interesting to note that the synergy effect
between the formal and informal network is stronger in the intra-unit case

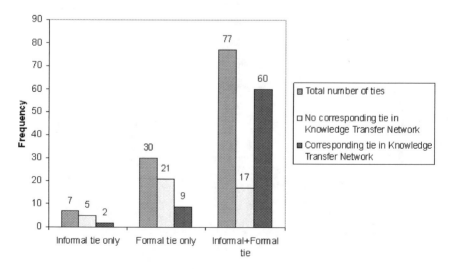

Figure 5.5 Knowledge transfer – inter-unit

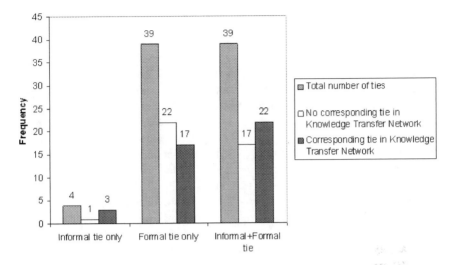

Figure 5.6 Knowledge transfer – intra-unit

compared to the inter-unit case. In fact, nearly forty per cent of all inter-unit knowledge transferring ties result only from a formal tie, this seems to run counter to the presumed importance of informal ties, particularly for the inter-unit case (Cummings 2004; Hansen 1999).

The oft-reported important role of informal ties for knowledge transfer – a role found here as well – contrasts with the finding that formal ties are at least as important. These findings may be reconciled by taking a longitudinal perspective. While it is certainly possible that informal ties develop between two actors that do not work directly together, it is more likely that such informal ties develop on top of existing formal (work-flow) ties. Frequent interaction allows the more social aspects of a relationship to develop, that can then lead to an informal tie (cf. Homans 1951). As Powell and Dimaggio. (1996: 121, italics added) state: 'Collaboration *becomes* emergent – stemming from ongoing relationships – informal and nonpremeditated'.

Formal and informal ties also offer different bases for new innovative knowledge to be transferred. Formal ties involve work-interaction regarding domain knowledge and, as the interaction continues for a longer period of time, the shared knowledge-base between these actors deepens. This in turn offers opportunities for sharing more complex, tacit knowledge (Cohen and Levinthal 1990; Gabarro 1990; Hansen 1999). Informal ties, involving a trust component ensuring an open climate required for transferring complex, innovative knowledge (Szulanski *et al.* 2004; Hansen 1999, 2002), may subsequently grow. Both the formal and informal networks thus offer distinct and possibly complementary enablers for knowledge transfer.

5.6 CONCLUSION

Knowledge transfer is necessary to increase the innovative potential of an organization, whether within units of a firm or between them. Reviewing the literature on knowledge exchange within an organization, from a network perspective, informal communication networks have been identified as contributing to knowledge transfer in particular (Cross *et al.* 2002; Stevenson and Gilly 1991; Jablin and Putnam 2001; Madhaven and Grover 1998). A direct comparison between networks is rare, however. This study is unique in comparing different networks in terms of their contribution to knowledge transfer and innovation at the firm level as opposed to a single network (Hansen and Lovas 2004; Hansen *et al.* 2005). It appears that the hypotheses that may be derived from the network literature are not fully supported by the findings presented. Informal communication networks for knowledge transfer within the organization may thus have been overemphasized and the role of the formal work-flow network underemphasized. The analysis shows that *both* the formal work-flow network and the informal communication network contribute significantly to the transfer of new, innovative knowledge (Allen and Cohen 1969). Evidence suggests that the formal work-flow network may even be somewhat more important in this regard, particularly in the case of inter-unit knowledge transfer. This is the first, and most significant, insight made in this chapter makes.

The second insight is the further specification of the ways the two networks differ regarding knowledge transfer. The majority of ties between actors have both a formal workflow component as well as an informal communication component. However, relations between actors that are formal only are fairly common, whereas informal ties between actors without a formal component are rare. Furthermore, a combined formal work-flow and informal communication tie between actors is much more likely to lead to the transfer of new, innovative knowledge than either tie separately. This suggests a synergetic effect between formal work-flow and informal communication ties. This, in turn, suggests that knowledge transfer effects, that in previous studies were attributed to informal networks only, may in fact need to be attributed in part to prior formal work-flow relations that had existed. The synergy effects for knowledge transfer between formal work-flow and informal communication ties are strong especially for intra-unit knowledge transfer. Formal ties, without the support of informal ties, are comparatively more conducive to inter-unit knowledge transfer than to intra-unit knowledge transfer.

Formal relations are more purposefully malleable in nature. Considering the contribution of the formal network to knowledge transfer, and given that formal relations seem to provide the basis for which informal relations develop, these findings offer opportunities for management to influence knowledge transfer. Obviously, by mapping organizational networks, as indicated, an organization can anticipate possible disruptions of both the formal and informal networks. The consequences of an employee's departure from the organization for communication and knowledge transfer networks can be assessed and dealt with better. Shaping formal networks in ways that are thought to contribute to a company's goals is feasible and not necessarily in conflict with existing informal networks. Rather, informal relations may draw on formal ones, creating a potentially synergetic path for knowledge transfer.

Limitations

Needless to say, there are some limitations to this study that should be acknowledged. The sample size was relatively small and the centrality measure, especially, may be skewed to some degree. Although the formal network is important for knowledge transfer, the actual mechanisms through which this takes place need to be explored more for instance by looking at the different brokerage roles that individuals in a network can adopt (Gould and Fernandez 1989; Fernandez and Gould 1994). Finally, there are also some factors that may limit the generalizability of the results. The organization studied is part of a large multinational and, much like other large firms, has a fairly formal organizational culture (Pugh *et al.* 1969a). This may have contributed to findings about the prevalence of formal ties, but in actual fact has not substantially affected the findings regarding the effect of formal ties on knowledge transfer. This is partly because people in the country where the subsidiary of the multinational is located are known for their aversion to hierarchical relations. Orders based on authority claims without providing supporting arguments are certainly not accepted per se, yet the role of formal networks is evident despite these a-hierarchical tendencies. Thus the findings of the importance of formal networks for knowledge transfer and its synergetic effects with the informal network are not likely to be an artifact of the research setting.

The distinct, as well as combined, contributions of formal and informal networks and ties to knowledge transfer need to be studied more closely. Inclusion of both these networks in future research can improve our understanding of what drives a firm's innovation.

APPENDIX TO CHAPTER 5: METHODOLOGY

Organizational setting

The setting for this study is a multinational electronics and engineering company with headquarters in a European country. The subsidiary studied, operating since the late nineteenth century, is in a different European country and employs over 4,000 employees. The organization employs over 400,000 people worldwide making it one of the world's largest conglomerates. In the business press this organization is sometimes referred to as Europe's most successful conglomerate. Revenue generated by this subsidiary is equivalent to some 6.5 per cent of the total revenue for the company. At corporate level, over 6.8 per cent of revenue is spent on Research and Design, emphasizing the importance of innovation and making this a high-tech company according to OECD criteria. The company is organized according to a unit structure with a high level of autonomy and responsibility for the separate divisions that are organized according to product-market segmentation. Recently, the company shifted from offering specific products towards offering integrated and innovative solutions to its customers, based on its technical competencies that cross unit boundaries. As a consequence of the strategic shift, the company has reorganized its activities according to a number of strategic multi-disciplinary themes.

We decided to focus on one specific theme. Focusing on knowledge transfer related to a single theme, as opposed to knowledge transfer in general, has two main advantages: firstly, because the focus of the questions is clear and close to the respondents' day-to-day activities, the reliability of the answers will be increased. Secondly, identifying a clear theme allows us to more precisely specify the boundaries of the network to be investigated (Laumann *et al.* 1983). The focus is on the theme of 'transportation'; according to top management, this theme has a high priority but is currently being insufficiently explored. As a result, this study focuses on a subset of the overall organization, namely the four functional divisions related to transportation as well as two main staff functions related to new business development (the innovation department and the market information department). The unit structure constitutes a natural membership boundary (see Hansen 1999) therefore it is employees, sorted by unit membership, that form the object of analysis in this study of inter-unit transfer of knowledge. Access to the company was negotiated through the senior innovation manager of the subsidiary who operates directly under the supervision of the board of directors. The selection of these divisions was based on the input gathered during several interviews with the new business managers in the separate divisions and the senior innovation manager, who also secured the commitment of the unit directors.

Data collection procedure

To test the formulated hypotheses, data on the social relations within the company was gathered. The focus is on the formal work-flow and informal communication networks within the organization as independent variables to explain the endogenous variable. The dependent variable for this study is the innovation network.

In order to be able to study the formal work-flow and the informal communication structures in a firm, they need to be defined in comparative terms. At the same time, crucially, it must be guaranteed that different entities are measured in the survey. The methodology of network analysis has progressed tremendously, and so questions (name generators) to be included in a survey have been honed in many previous studies of both an empirical and methodological-theoretical nature. Thus, even when in some cases relations in, for instance, the formal work-flow network may involve the same individuals as in the informal communication network, it is clear that the ties serve different purposes for the individuals involved as well as for the organization.

We follow Farace *et al.* (1977) in defining social networks as repetitive patterns of interaction among members of an organization. Data is collected using two separate methods: semi-structured interviews with managers and other employees and a network survey. The interviews served a two-fold purpose: firstly, to become familiar with the organizational setting and thus gain input for the proper design of the network survey and secondly, they served as the first round in a snowball sampling procedure. Snowball sampling is especially useful when the population is not clear from the beginning (Wasserman and Faust 1994), as is the case here because of the focus on inter-unit cooperation and the resulting blurring of unit boundaries. Snowball sampling is based upon several rounds of surveying or interviewing where the first round helps to determine who will be approached as a respondent in the second round and so on. The first round of snowball sampling can be totally at random but it can also be based on specific criteria (Rogers and Kincaid 1981). To reduce the risk of 'isolates', i.e. isolated persons within the organization who possess relevant knowledge to a particular subject, but who are being left out by the study due to the lack of accuracy of random sampling (Rogers and Kincaid 1981), this study opted for a first round consisting of specifically targeted respondents. The selection of the first round of respondents was based on the expertise of the innovation management department (one of the two staff departments involved in the study). This department was asked to create an overview of employees who are most active in the field of transportation and who are members of the earlier selected divisions. This resulted in as list of nine employees in four functional divisions. The selection was validated by seeking the judgment of the manager of the market information department (the other staff department involved in the study). These nine people completed the survey during a personal interview. They named forty two other employees who formed the second round of targeted respondents and who were sent the survey by email. Respondents in this second round, who did not reply initially, were approached to complete the survey during a personal interview, resulting in an overall response rate of ninety six per cent. This percentage includes the sixty three per cent who completed the whole questionnaire including the matrix and the 33% who indicated that they did not have any relationship with the transportation theme. 4% did not respond to the first mailing and the later mailings and interview requests. Responses from the second round indicated that the vast majority of people related to the transportation theme had been identified and surveyed. Thus, one can be sure to have included all relevant actors in the network, and therefore reduced the boundary specification problem common to an egocentric approach (Laumann *et al.* 1983 and Marsden 1990, 2002).

The survey was constructed as a digital version that could be distributed by e-mail and every survey form was accompanied by a personalized cover email introducing the project to the respondent. An email survey was chosen to reduce the time needed to complete the questionnaire, thus improving response rates. This was signed by the innovation manager to further improve response rates. To further reduce the time needed to fill in the survey, the survey form was constructed in a matrix style, such that names only had to be inserted once in the horizontal column of the survey form by the respondents after which they could automatically be used for all three network questions. The number of contacts that could be listed was not fixed throughout the survey because the number of employees named partially determines the position of the individual employee in the network (Friedman and Podolny 1993). However, a guideline of naming, at most, six employees was issued to make sure that only the most important contacts per employee were mentioned. To reduce ambiguity in the interpretation of questions by the respondents, the network questions were formulated in the native language.

Variables

The independent variable formal work flow network is put into operation in a broader sense than the more commonly chosen organizational chart measure. Firstly, it is well-recognized that the organization chart is a poor indicator of dynamics in an organization on the day-to-day basis that is the focus of this study (Krackhardt and Hanson 1993). Secondly, an organization chart is often focused more on hierarchical, vertical relations, while formally mandated horizontal relations (for instance temporarily created teams) are emphasized less. Again this renders it an incomplete measure for the purposes of predicting knowledge transfer. According to Mehra *et al.*, the workflow network was defined as: 'the formally prescribed set of interdependencies between employees established by the division of labor in the organization' (Mehra *et al.* 2001: 130, italics added). Thus, relations that are mandated by the organization, but that are not part of the organizational chart, are captured as well. This includes temporary, yet formal, organizational elements such as teams (cf Blindenbach-Driesen and van den Ende 2006). The work flow network was measured by asking respondents to indicate the persons with whom they exchange information, knowledge, documents and schemes to successfully carry out their *daily activities* within the organization (Mehra *et al.* 2001: 130). The focus of communication in this network is on existing projects, goods and services already developed, or relations with customers that had already been established.

The independent variable informal communication network was put into operation as the communication network and measured by asking with whom one discusses what is going on within the organization (Ibarra 1993: 479–480; Brass 1984: 526). Thus, one may gain insight into the personal preferences and insights of employees regarding informal communication within the organization.

The dependent, or endogenous, variable is the network in which individuals indicated with whom they discuss *new* ideas, innovations and *improvements* to products and services (Cross and Prusak 2002: 107; Krebs 1999). In this case, for methodological reasons, the specific focus has been on the transportation theme, as explained earlier. Clearly, this concerns communication that was *not* perceived as related to the ongoing business of the organization. This network is the 'innovation network', since the focus is specifically on the transfer of innovative knowledge. The terms innovation network and knowledge transfer network are used interchangeably.

A potential concern with this particular operationalization of the dependent variable is that it might, by definition, be considered a subset of either the formal work flow network (since it involves work-related knowledge), or the informal communication network (since it involves communication). However Table A5.1 below shows that the three variables do indeed represent three distinct networks. The table presents frequency counts for all possible combinations of ties between two actors in the network (except the case of two totally uncon- nected actors in all three networks). Had, for instance, the innovation network been a subset of the informal communication network, then one would not observe the twenty six ties between actors who were only connected in the formal work flow network and the innovation network. Similarly, the innovation network is not a subset of the formal work flow network.

6 Knowledge exchange between firms

Economic geography of high-tech firms[*]

In contrast to findings in other countries, and surprisingly in view of the literature, high-tech economic activity in the Netherlands is not spread geographically
according to either relevant labour market characteristics, or to localized agglomeration economies. Instead, statistical analysis shows that the Netherlands is an urban
field and that the knowledge infrastructure is the only variable that can offer an
explanation of the high-tech presence throughout the country. By being close to
knowledge institutes, high-tech firms may reap both the intended, and the unintended, knowledge spill-overs. By analysing similar relationships for younger firms,
quite a strong case about causation can be made.

6.1 INTRODUCTION

Due to their continuous Research and Design (R&D) efforts, high-tech firms are
allegedly highly competitive, and fast growing, in terms of employment and
output (Geroski *et al.* 1993). Their R&D efforts, and rate of growth, constitute a
comparative advantage for the countries in which they are located and thus boost
national economic growth. Some regions accommodate more high-tech firms than
others. Despite regional efforts to attract high-tech firms, the success stories are
few in number. Regional characteristics are apparently important and cannot
easily be modified. An important strand of research in the field of economic
geography analyses regionalized economic activity. The regional accumulation of
knowledge, and locally occurring knowledge spillovers, are major topics of such
research (cf. Krugman 1995; Martin 1999). Three knowledge-related elements,
originating in the industrial district argument first developed by Alfred Marshall,
are emphasized in the literature: the eminence of the regional labour market, agglomeration externalities, and characteristics of the regional knowledge infrastructure.

In this chapter, the extent to which these three elements explain the spread
of firms in high-tech industries throughout the Netherlands is assessed. Some
studies show that, in a technical sense, clusters of high-tech firms do not exist
in this country (Swann 1999; Wever and Stam 1999; Hoen 2001). The *tendency*

---

[*] With Gerben van der Panne.

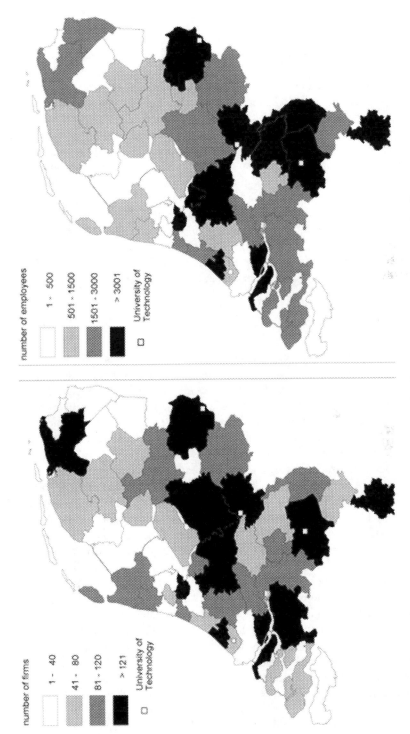

Figure 6.1 Location pattern of high-tech firms (A), and total high-tech employment (B), by Corop region(‡)

Source: Calculations based on data available from Marktselect plc, 2002.

(‡) Depicting the data in relative numbers yields roughly the same patterns.

to cluster is studied: although there are no clusters, high-tech firms tend to concentrate in particular regions (see Figure 6.1).

The Dutch case differs from other cases described in the literature. To anticipate the results to some extent, the Dutch case shows that, where physical distance is deemed less important in location choices, *cognitive* distance becomes of greater significance (cf. Nooteboom 2000). This element, thought to be of increasing importance, is included in the study by examining the effects of the knowledge infrastructure on the geography of high-tech economic activity. Material reasons for the spread of economic activity through the Netherlands, at least for high-tech activity, become less important, indicating that the Netherlands is indeed an 'urban field'; regional differences in material factor endowments do not seem to have any systematic impact on the location pattern of high-tech activity.

In section 6.2, the location factors deemed important in the literature are discussed. Section 6.3 presents the model with which the high-tech location pattern will be explained. The results are discussed in section 6.4. Section 6.5 elaborates on the original model, testing the causality of relations between location factors and the location pattern at Section 6.6 concludes.

6.2 LOCATION FACTORS

Economic activity tends to have an uneven geographic spread. It is not surprising, therefore, that firms in high-tech industries are not evenly distributed across the Netherlands (see Figure 6.1). The literature generally recognizes three factors on the basis of which firms decide on their location. These are in line with Alfred Marshall's (1920) industrial district argument. They are well understood today and need little elaboration. Marshall has argued that the local labour market may have particular characteristics that are attractive to firms. The type of products, and the production process used, may require employees with particular skills and knowledge. Assuming that the labour market is not perfect, and may be fragmented regionally, as well as according to skills and knowledge, firms may not scatter evenly as would be the case in the perfect market of neoclassical economics. A second factor discussed by Marshall is that of agglomeration externalities. Suppliers to, or buyers (customers) of, a firm may be concentrated in a region. In the case of high transport costs, in particular, agglomeration externalities may be strong. In what increasing numbers of observers call a (emerging) 'knowledge' economy, factors hinted at by Marshall, such as knowledge spillovers and things being 'in the air' in a regional context, become more important.

In a knowledge economy, the first factor may take a different role. Various characteristics of potential employees in the region may become important. The need that they should respond adequately to the economic and technological dynamism has increased the demand for employees with a formal education. Professionalization and the need for objective criteria regarding the selection of future employees illustrate the eminence of the regional labour market as a genuine location factor (Malecki 1991; Weiss 1995). High-tech industries, in particular, need employees who are trained in engineering, for instance at the academic level. De Grip and Willems (1996) show that Dutch high-tech firms actually employ more professionals relative to medium- and low-tech firms.

Agglomeration externalities may also differ in a knowledge economy. In addition to Marshall's industrial districts argument, agglomeration can offer a favourable environment for the innovating firm in which to create and sustain its knowledge base. As distance hinders the exchange of tacit knowledge (Jaffe 1989), the regionally bound stock of tacit knowledge increasingly becomes a source of competitive advantage for the region (Maskell and Malmberg 1999). Moreover, proximity fosters collaboration (Fritsch and Schwirten 1999), that creates relations of trust among economic actors within the agglomeration (Harrison 1992). Hence, agglomerations not only offer the advantages of Marshall's 'traded linkages', but possibly also the more elusive 'untraded interdependencies' (Storper 1997). As Hägerstrand (1967) has shown for Europe, innovations tend to be introduced in major cities and then spread across the urban hierarchy. More recently, it has been shown empirically that innovative activities tend to be concentrated in agglomerated milieus in the USA (Audretsch and Feldman 1996), the UK (Baptista & Swann 1998) and France (Carrincazeaux *et al.* 2001). As such, agglomerations are alleged breeding places for innovations (Brouwer *et al.* 1999). Proximity may thus economize on communication and interpretation costs involved in the creation of new knowledge.

For firms in high-tech industries, particularly, the role of knowledge-creating and diffusing institutes, such as universities and non-academic research centres, both private and public, could play an important role in understanding regional economic differences (cf. Florax 1992). In line with other research, (non-) academic research institutes are constituents of the regional knowledge infrastructure and are a separate location factor for high-tech firms. Joint research projects, the spillover of research undertaken at these institutes, and the informal exchanges of (tacit) know-how are their main contributions to the regional knowledge base. As these effects are regional, firms in high-tech industries might benefit from knowledge spillovers if and when they locate nearby knowledge institutes. Jaffe (1989), for instance, provides evidence that knowledge can spillover from university research to industrial R&D efforts (see also Audretsch and Feldman 1996; Mansfield and Lee 1996; Anselin and Varga 1997). In Germany, the same holds for universities that engage in applied sciences (Engel and Fier 2000) as well as for non-academic research institutes (Fritsch and Schwirten 1999; Sternberg 1999). For present purposes, and from a theoretical point of view, it seems reasonable to separate knowledge infrastructure from the more general agglomeration effect. A focus on high-tech industries points in this direction. The course that modern economies, in general, take towards a knowledge economy is a more general argument in favour of including the knowledge infrastructure as an explanatory variable in the analysis.

Although this study is able to explain the location of high-tech activity throughout the Netherlands, it should be clear that the set of location factors included is not exhaustive: the location pattern of high-tech activity may also be affected by regional living amenities appreciated by qualified personnel, by the regional physical infrastructure and industrial zoning policies (cf. Ouwersloot and Rietveld 2000; Atzema 2001). These location factors reach beyond the scope of this study, however.

6.3 THE MODEL

In this section, we use the OECD definition of high-tech industries. When, on average, firms in an industry spend at least 4.5 per cent of total sales on R&D, that industry is considered high-tech (OECD 1986). The creation and use of new knowledge is then important. Industries covered by this definition include pharmaceuticals, office equipment, computers, electronic devices, communication devices, scientific instruments and aerospace. For the Netherlands, this adds up to 4,424 high-tech firms, or 0.4 per cent of the total population of firms. The definition used by OECD is not the only one, and has several drawbacks (cf. Kleinknecht 2000). For instance, it focuses on the level of the industry. Firms in industries that OECD does not recognize as high-tech could spend more than 4.5 per cent of revenue on R&D – intra-branch differences with respect to R&D intensity may be considerable. Statistical information used to establish the extent to which an industry is innovative, such as that used by OECD, tends to under-estimate innovation in service industries. The OECD classification is based on R&D inputs only, whereas output measures are more direct proxies of the level of innovation. However, the branches designated as high-tech by this OECD definition are also classified as such by most alternative definitions. Moreover, the OECD definition is most common in scientific research; using it here makes our study comparable to other studies.

The model tests whether the three sets of regional factors discussed in section two (labour market characteristics, agglomeration externalities and knowledge infrastructure) can explain the spread of high-tech activity in the Netherlands, explaining the pattern in Figure 6.1. Malecki (1991) emphasizes the need for employees with a strong technical background. Two indicators for the regional labour market are included: those who have a university degree (Master's) or a degree from a polytechnic for vocational training (Bachelor's) in a field of the natural sciences on the one hand, or who have such a degree in a different field of study. Data provided by Statistics Netherlands are used for these indicators.[1] Our hypothesis, deriving from the literature, is that the higher the proportion of BAs and MAs – technical or non-technical – in a region's labour force, the more likely it is that high-tech firms will locate there. Although these labour market characteristics are correlated to some degree, tests show that this is not significant and does not preclude both variables from being included in the model.[2]

In the literature, linkage-density parameters among proximate firms are used to catch the influence of agglomeration externalities (Richardson 1973). Inter-firm linkage-density, however, is an inappropriate indicator for agglomeration. Agglomeration externalities enhance the local knowledge base, which is resembled by 'traded' linkage-density parameters, only to a very limited extent (Malmberg and Solvell 1997). Indeed, for the Netherlands, it is acknowledged that inter-firm linkage density does not run parallel with physical proximity (Wever and Stam 1999; Atzema 2001; Heijs and Schmitz 2001). Rather than measuring linkage densities, whether agglomerated regions accommodate more high-tech firms compared to less agglomerated regions, is tested. Manshanden's (1996) agglomeration index is used as an indicator of agglomeration externalities. It distinguishes five ordinal degrees of agglomeration externalities according to physical distances between a Corop region's central town and those in all other Corop regions, weighted by the region's population density. Similar to the linkage-density approach, this index does not capture all relevant dimensions of agglomeration externalities, e.g. the degree of specialization, competition and diversity of the local production milieu (Ouwersloot and Rietveld 2000; Van Oort 2002). Nevertheless, the indicator is used for reasons of data availability and comparability; other scholars in the field have also used it (Kleinknecht and Poot 1992; Manshanden 1996; Brouwer *et al.* 1999).

Our third hypothesis is that the regional knowledge infrastructure, measured by the number of knowledge institutions in Corop regions, is conducive to high-tech economic activity within a region. In particular, testing was used to ascertain whether the presence of a university, a university of technology or non-academic (private) research institute (for agricultural, medical, scientific and societal research) in a region made a difference in terms of high-tech activity. The Netherlands has eleven universities without any clear focus on technology and a further four universities of technology in Delft, Enschede, Eindhoven and Wageningen. Non-academic research institutes add up to 1,820 in total. The regional impact achieved by such institutions obviously depends on their size. To account for size differences, the presence of non-academic research institutes is weighted by the total number of employees.

A comparison of the results from the model developed here, with an earlier study using data from Statistics Netherlands which lacked data on total employees (Van der Panne and Dolfsma 2001) indicates that the availability of more detailed information on this count is highly valuable. Marktselect, a private firm, offers such detailed data for non-academic research institutes and high-tech firms by complementing data provided by Chambers of Commerce with information concerning the exact number of establishments (Statistics Netherlands on the other hand, rounds off in units of five). For each non-academic research institute and high-tech firm, not only is size in terms of the total number of employees known, but so is the year of foundation.

Estimation results naturally hinge on the level of aggregation applied, especially regarding agglomeration externalities (Van Oort 2002). Both dependent, and explanatory, variables are defined at the regional level of Corop, distinguishing forty three regions that are relatively homogeneous, although aggregated, in economic terms. Alternatively, the focus might be on a more local level, such as city or postal code. It does not seem, however, that such increased disaggregated geographical demarcations are more economically homogeneous.[3] In addition, as the Corop level is the prevailing level of analysis in Dutch research on economic geography, its use makes this analysis more comparable to other studies.

The data used allows for use of ordinary-least-squares-technique, that offers results that are most readily interpretable.[4] Two models are estimated, one in which the number of high-tech firms in a region is the dependent variable (Figure 6.1a), and the other in which high-tech employment in a region is explained (Figure 6.1b). Both models are relevant: whereas the first is more likely to indicate reasons for a high-tech firm to select a location, the second takes size differences into account and may therefore indicate growth potential. The explanatory variables relate directly to the factors deemed important in the theory. As the relationship between the variables cannot be presumed to be linear at this stage, logarithms are taken. Hence, the following models are estimated at the Corop level:

$$\ln Y_{1,2} = \alpha + \beta_1 \ln \text{(share of bachelors and professionals in the regional labour market)} +$$
$$\beta_2 \ln \text{(share of technicians in the regional labour market)} +$$
$$\beta_3 \ln \text{(agglomeration externalities)} +$$
$$\beta_4 \ln \text{(university)} +$$
$$\beta_5 \ln \text{(university of technology)} +$$
$$\beta_6 \ln \text{(non-academic research institutes)} + \varepsilon \qquad \text{(Eq. 6.1)}$$

Where: Y_1 = number of high-tech firms in Corop region (Fig. 6.1a), and
Y_2 = total high-tech employment in Corop region (Fig. 6.1b)

Table 6.1 presents the results of our analysis. The models using logarithms of variables perform better than those that don't (not presented) which indicates that

Table 6.1 Two models explaining the location of high-tech activity

		1. Number of high-tech firms (fig 6.1A)		2. Total high-tech employment (fig 6.1B)	
		Beta	t-value	Beta	t-value
Labour market	Technicians	−0.08	−0.35	−0.32	−0.71
	Bachelors and professionals	0.23	1.23	0.50	1.29
Agglomeration externalities	**Agglomeration Index‡**	0.37	0.72	1.44	1.37
Knowledge infrastructure	University	−0.29	−1.43	−0.62	−1.45
	University of technology	0.32	1.18	0.48	0.84
	Research institutes	0.39	8.68*	0.60	6.50*
Adjusted R-squared		0.76		0.59	

* significant at 1% level.
‡ Values given are averages of 4 dummies representing 5 ordinal categories of agglomeration.

the relationships between the variables is indeed non-linear. The results of each of these models are discussed in Section 6.4, which also compares the two in order that some of the dynamics of high-tech economic activity throughout the Netherlands might be understood.

6.4 RESULTS

Care should be taken in interpreting Fig. 6.1. A number of elements are striking. The economically-active Rotterdam region shows little high-tech activity: its main sectors are transport and the chemical industry. The south-east again proves to be the region where technology-intensive firms locate (Wintjes 2001). It remains to be seen if the Twente-region, a central-eastern Corop region bordering Germany, with a university of technology in the city of Enschede, can convert itself from being a low-tech region, traditionally strong in textiles etc., and become a high-tech region. The region is home to a few larger high-tech firms these are subsidiaries of other firms that do most of the research (Ministry of Economic Affairs 1997). A comparison of maps A and B shows which regions have relatively smaller high-tech firms, the central Veluwe and northern Groningen being cases in point. Regions with a relatively high number of high-tech firms show up where Corop regions in Figure 6.1B have a darker shade of grey than in Figure 6.1A.

Table 6.1 shows that the regional labour market is not responsible for the location of high-tech firms. Foreign studies indicate that labour markets are an important factor in deciding the attractiveness of various regions (c.f., Malecki 1991; Weiss 1995). The Netherlands stand out in this respect. Observations on the Amsterdam region, with relatively many high-tech firms and substantial high-tech employment as shown by Figure 6.1, corroborate our results about the labour market: a third of Amsterdam's labour force does not live in the region but commutes (Van der Vegt et al. 2000). Indeed, there was in the Amsterdam region, between 1988 and 1993, an increase in the number of 'higher technicians, mathematicians and natural scientists' (Van der Vegt et al. 1995). Indicating considerable willingness to commute, this is consistent with our finding that regional labour market characteristics are not explanatory.

As is the case for the labour market, agglomeration externalities do not play a role in explaining the location of high-tech firms: the coefficients are not significant. This agrees with Atzema (2001) with regard to the Dutch ICT sector. In accordance with Atzema, this may be due to the structure of the Dutch urban system: in a poly-nuclear urban system, agglomeration externalities arise almost throughout the Netherlands (Atzema 2001). Brouwer et al. (1999), however, find that the degree of urbanization correlates positively with the announcements of new products in specialist trade journals. This seems to be largely caused by their use of a different indicator of innovation.[5] The findings on labour market and agglomeration combined, confirm earlier conclusions derived from studies with a slightly different focus, that of the Netherlands as an 'urban field' (Wever and Stam 1999; Atzema 2001; Heijs and Schmitz 2001).

Contrary to the above, a region's knowledge infrastructure does make a significant difference. The positive effect of the presence of knowledge institutes is consistent with Winter's (1984) argument that high-tech economic activity is science-based. Delving more deeply into the reasons why the knowledge infrastructure attracts high-tech firms to locate in one region rather than another it appears that universities and universities of technology make little difference. This contrasts with international research (Engel and Fier 2000), but corroborates results obtained by Ouwersloot and Rietveld (2000) for the Dutch case. Non-academic research institutes have the strongest effect on the location of high-tech firms in the Netherlands. This finding runs parallel with Fritsch and Schwirten (1999), but contradicts partly with Engel and Fier (2000), who observe that regions with non-academic research institutes do not accommodate many high-tech start-ups.

The two models presented in Table 6.1 explain seventy six and fifty nine per cent respectively of total variance in high-tech activity. The remaining unexplained variance may be accounted for by additional location factors earlier-mentioned, such as living amenities, physical infrastructure and industrial zoning policies (e.g., Ouwersloot and Rietveld 2000).

6.5 DISCUSSION: CAUSATION

Statistical significance is not synonymous with scientific significance (cf. McCloskey and Ziliak 1996). In order to stand on firmer ground in our claim that the pattern for the spread of high-tech activity throughout the Netherlands can be explained by the presence or absence of either of three variables, some additional tests may be necessary. The data allow for discrimination between ages of firms and to disentangle the process of cumulative causation that underlies geographical clustering. Is an economic activity located in a particular region because of its specific characteristics, or does the region apparently have attractive characteristics (partly) as a result of the firms that are located there? Assuming that the decision to start a firm at a specific location is a rational one, weighing all important costs and benefits, it makes sense to study the clustering of younger firms. The model presented earlier has been regressed for firms of three and ten years; both for the number of high-tech firms as for high-tech employment. Findings on the number of high-tech firms are presented only, as these dynamics can be assumed to be more pronounced: three and ten-year-old firms (772 and 2,222 firms, respectively). After three years, firms in the Netherlands are no longer entitled to any tax breaks intended to encourage entrepreneurship.[6] Three years is thus an important threshold. Ten years is another threshold as during that period a knowledge base, or absorptive capacity of some kind, can be assumed to have been established. Subsidiaries of foreign firms in the Netherlands, for instance, irrespective of sector, move to another location in the Netherlands within a few years in order to take advantage of the knowledge infrastructure in the new location (Wintjes 2001).

Table 6.2 Explaining the location of young high-tech firms†

		3. Number of high-tech firms (3 year old)		4. Number of high-tech firms (10 year old)	
		Beta	t-value	Beta	t-value
Labour market	Technicians	−0.13	−0.42	−0.10	−0.32
	Bachelors and professionals	0.26	0.24	0.31	1.47
Agglomeration externalities	Agglomeration Index‡				
	category 1	−	−	−	−
	category 2	−0.07	−0.42	−0.12	−0.84
	category 3	0.71	2.99*	0.52	2.59*
	category 4	0.10	0.40	−0.17	−0.68
	category 5	0.23	1.22	0.22	0.93
Knowledge infrastructure	University	−0.30	−1.04	−0.21	−0.95
	University of technology	0.36	1.02	0.41	1.11
	Research institutes	0.37	4.32*	0.33	4.18*
Adjusted R-squared		0.65		0.65	

* significant at 1% level.
† Ordinary Least Squares Estimation with White heteroskeasticity-consistent standard errors and covariance.
‡ The Agglomeration Index would be an average of the 4 dummies representing 5 ordinal categories of agglomeration shown.

Consistent with the findings for the total population of high-tech firms (see Table 6.1), an attractive labour market does not attract high-tech start-ups. This consistency applies for agglomeration externalities as well, except for agglomeration at the medium level. Agglomerated areas at the medium level do accommodate more high-tech start-ups relative to the least agglomerated regions. The findings for the regional knowledge infrastructure also follow our earlier findings closely: a comparison of the findings presented in Table 6.2 with those of Table 6.1 indicates that a strong case can be made about the causality of the presence of a relevant knowledge infrastructure on the location choice of a high-tech firm.

6.6 CONCLUDING REMARKS

Of the three factors recognized in the literature – labour market, agglomeration externalities and knowledge infrastructure – the first two are insignificant in explaining the spread of high-tech economic activity throughout the Netherlands. As far as these location factors are concerned, the Netherlands is indeed an 'urban field'.

Our findings are noteworthy for another finding: the significance of the knowledge infrastructure – more important than any other variable. Non-academic research institutes have a positive influence on the activity of high-tech firms in a region, whereas universities and universities of technology do not.

There are indications of causation; as the general findings are confronted with the same test for groups of firms of more recent origin the same pattern emerges. Younger firms in high-tech industries also tend to locate close to non-academic knowledge institutes and, in contrast to older firms, preferably in agglomerations at the medium level. As proximity appears relevant only for specific knowledge relations, the role of proximity in those relations can be considered odd.

7 The knowledge base of an economy

What contributes to its entropy?*

Can the knowledge base of an economy be measured? In this study, the perspective of regional economics and the triple-helix model on the interrelationships among technology, organization, and location are combined to offer the mutual information in three dimensions as an indicator of the knowledge base of an economy. When this probabilistic entropy is negative, the configuration reduces the uncertainty that prevails at the systems level. Data concerning more than a million Dutch companies are used for testing the indicator. The data contains postal codes (geography), sector codes (proxy for technology), and firm sizes in terms of number of employees (proxy for organization). The configurations are mapped at three geographical levels: national, provincial, and regional. The levels are cross-tabled with the knowledge-intensive sectors and services. The results suggest that medium-tech sectors contribute to the knowledge base of an economy more than high-tech ones. Knowledge-intensive services have an uncoupling effect, but less so at the high-tech end of these services.

7.1 INTRODUCTION

Ever since evolutionary economists introduced the concept of a 'knowledge-based economy' (Foray and Lundvall 1996; Abramowitz and David 1996), the question of how to measure this new type of economic coordination has been asked (Carter 1996; OECD 1996). Recently, Godin (forthcoming) argued that the concept itself has remained a rhetorical device because the development of specific indicators has failed. However, the concept of a 'knowledge-based economy' has been attractive to policy-makers at the level of the European Union, perhaps as an alternative to the 'national systems of innovation' approach. For example, the European Summit of March 2000 in Lisbon was specifically held in order 'to strengthen employment, economic reform, and social cohesion in the transition to a knowledge-based economy' (European Commission 2000; cf. European Commission 2005).

Can something as elusive as the knowledge base of a system be measured? (Foray 2004; Leydesdorff 2001; Skolnikoff 1993). Is a structural transformation

---

* With Loet Leydesdorff, Gerben van der Panne.

of the economy at the global level indicated, with potentially different effects, in various world regions and nations? When originally proposing their programme of studies at the OECD, David and Foray (1995: 14) argued that the focus on *national* systems of innovation had placed too much emphasis on the organization of institutions and economic growth, and not enough on the distribution of knowledge itself. However, Lundvall's (1988) argument for considering the nation as a first candidate for defining innovation systems was carefully formulated in terms of an heuristics: 'The interdependency between production and innovation goes both ways. [...] This interdependency between production and innovation makes it legitimate to take the national system of production as a starting point when defining a system of innovation' (Lundvall 1988: 362). The choice of the nation as a frame of reference enables the analyst to use national statistics about industrial production and market shares, to make systematic comparisons among nations (Lundvall 1992; Nelson 1993), and to translate the findings into advice for national governments. The relevant statistics have been made comparable among nations by the OECD and Eurostat (OECD/Eurostat 1997).

The hypothesis of a transition to a 'knowledge-based economy' implies a systems transformation at the structural level across nations. Following this lead, the focus of the efforts at the OECD and Eurostat has been to develop indicators of the relative knowledge-intensity of industrial sectors (OECD 2001, 2003) and regions (Laafia 1999, 2002a, 2002b). Alternative frameworks for 'systems of innovation' like technologies (Carlsson and Stankiewicz 1991) or regions (Braczyk *et al.* 1998), were also considered (Carlsson 2004). However, the analysis of the knowledge base of innovation systems (e.g., Cowan *et al.* 2000) was not made sufficiently relevant for the measurement efforts (David and Foray 2002). Knowledge was not considered as a coordination mechanism of society, but mainly as a public or private good.

Knowledge as a coordination mechanism was initially defined in terms of the qualifications of the labour force. Machlup (1962) argued that in a 'knowledge economy' knowledge-workers would play an increasingly important role in industrial production processes. Employment data has been central to the study of this older concept. For example, employment statistics can be cross-tabled with distinctions among sectors in terms of high- and medium-tech (Cooke 2002). However, the concept of a 'knowledge-based economy' refers to a change in the structure of an economy beyond the labour market (Foray and Lundvall 1996; Cooke and Leydesdorff 2006). How does the development of science and technology transform economic exchange processes? (Schumpeter 1939).

The social organization of knowledge production and control was first considered as a systemic development by Whitley (1984). Dasgupta and David (1994) proposed to consider science as the subject of a new economics. Because of the reputational control mechanisms involved, the dynamics of knowledge production and diffusion are different in important respects from economic market or institutional control mechanisms (Mirowski and Sent 2001; Whitley

2001). When a third coordination mechanism is added as a sub-dynamic to the interactions and potential co-evolution between economic exchange relations and institutional control (Freeman and Perez 1988), non-linear effects can be expected (Leydesdorff 1994). The possible synergies may lead to the envisaged transition to a knowledge-based economy, but this can be expected to happen to a variable extent: developments in some geographically defined economies will be more knowledge-based than others.

The geographical setting – the (knowledge-based) technologies as deployed in different sectors – and the organizational structures of the industries, constitute three relatively independent sources of variance. One would expect significant differences in the quality of innovation systems among regions and industrial sectors in terms of technological capacities (Fritsch 2004). The three sources of variance may reinforce one another in a configuration so that the uncertainty is reduced at the systems level. A knowledge-based order of the economy can therefore be shaped.

Our research question is whether one is able to operationalize this configurational order and then also to measure it. For the operationalization, elements from the two research programmes that have supported this collaboration are needed: economic geography and scientometrics. Using Storper's (1997: 26ff.) notion of a 'holy trinity' among technology, organization, and territory from regional economics, one may elaborate on Leydesdorff's (1995) use of information theory in scientometrics.

7.2 A COMBINATION OF TWO THEORETICAL PERSPECTIVES

Storper defined a territorial economy as *stocks of relational assets*. The relations determine the dynamics of the system:

> Territorial economies are not only created, in a globalizing world economy, by proximity in input-output relations, but more so by proximity in the untraded or relational dimensions of organizations and technologies. Their principal assets – because scarce and slow to create and imitate – are no longer material, but relational.
>
> (Storper 1997, p. 28)

The 'holy trinity' is to be understood not only in terms of elements in a network, but as the result of the dynamics of these networks shaping new worlds. These worlds emerge as densities of relations that can be developed into a competitive advantage when and where they materialize by being coupled to the ground in regions. For example, one would expect the clustering of high-tech services in certain (e.g., metropolitan) areas. The location of such a niche can be considered as a consequence of the self-organization of the interactions (Bathelt 2003;

Cooke and Leydesdorff 2006). Furthermore, Storper argued that this extension of the 'heterodox paradigm' in economics implies a reflexive turn.

In a similar vein, authors using the model of a triple helix of university-industry-government relations have argued for considering the possibility of an overlay of relations among universities, industries and governments to emerge from these interactions (Etzkowitz and Leydesdorff 2000). Under certain conditions, the feedback from the reflexive overlay can reshape the network relations from which it emerged. Because of this reflexive turn, the parties involved may become increasingly aware of their own and each others' expectations, limitations and positions. These expectations and interactions can be further informed by relevant knowledge. Thus, the knowledge-based subdynamic may increasingly contribute to the operation of the system.

The triple helix model of university-industry-government relations has hitherto been developed mainly as a *(neo)institutional* model for studying the knowledge infrastructure in networks of relations (Etzkowitz *et al.* 2000; Powell and DiMaggio 1991). From a *(neo)evolutionary* perspective, a triple-helix can be formulated dynamically as the interactions among three (or more) subdynamics of a system (Leydesdorff 1997; Leydesdorff and Etzkowitz 1998). To what extent do the networks allow for a synergy among (1) economic wealth generation, (2) technological novelty production, and (3) institutionally organized retention? How can the economic exchange, the innovation dynamics upsetting the market equilibria, and the locally organized interfaces among these subdynamics be integrated at a systems level?

The knowledge-based overlay, and the institutional layer, operate upon one another in terms of frictions that provide opportunities for innovation both vertically within each of the helices, and horizontally among them. The quality of the knowledge base in the economy depends on the locally-specific functioning of the interactions in the knowledge infrastructure, and on the interface between this infrastructure with the self-organizing dynamics at the systems level. A knowledge base would operate by diminishing the uncertainty that prevails at the network level, that is, as a structural property of the system.

The correspondence between these two perspectives can be extended to the operationalization. Storper (1997: 49), for example, used the following depiction of 'the economy as a set of intertwined, partially overlapping domains of action' in terms of recursively overlapping Venn-diagrams:

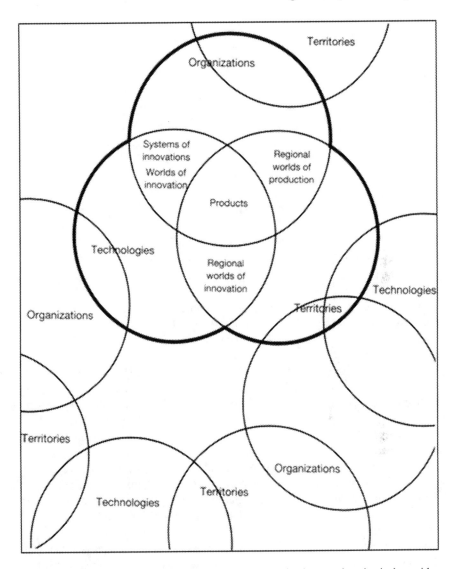

Figure 7.1 Storper's 'holy trinity of technologies, organizations, and territories' provides an overlap in the resulting 'products'

Using the triple helix model, Leydesdorff (1997: 112) noted that the three circles boldfaced in Figure 7.1 do not have to overlap in a common zone like the area indicated with 'Products'. He proposed the following configuration as an alternative:

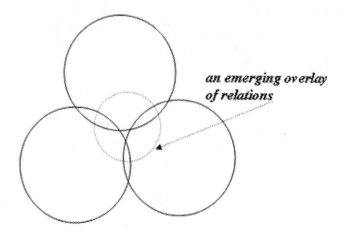

Figure 7.2 The neo-evolutionary variant of the triple helix model

In a networked arrangement, an overlay of interrelations among the bilateral relations at interfaces can, to a certain extent, replace the function of central integration. In this case, a virtual hyper-cycle potentially integrates the complex system by providing an additional structure.

The gap in the overlap between the three circles in Figure 7.2 can be understood as a negative entropy, that is, a reduction of the uncertainty in the system. Unlike the mutual information in two dimensions (Shannon 1948; Theil 1972), information among three dimensions can thus become negative (McGill 1954; Abramson 1963). This reduction of the uncertainty is in this case a consequence of the networked configuration. However, the 'configurational information' is not present in any of the subsets (Jakulin and Bratko 2004).[1] In other words, the overlay can be considered as an additional source or sink of information. A configurational reduction of the uncertainty locally, counteracts the prevailing tendency at the systems level towards increasing entropy and equilibrium (Khalil 2004).[2]

Using scientometric indicators like co-authorship relations, it could be shown that the configurational information among the three helices varies considerably among nations and world regions (Leydesdorff 2003). In this study, the scientometric approach to measuring the knowledge base is extended to economic regions at the national and sub-national levels by applying the operationalization to data concerning the distribution of Dutch firms in three dimensions. This data has been used extensively in previous studies by the other authors of this study (Van der Panne and Dolfsma 2001, 2003; Van der Panne 2004).

7.3 METHODS AND DATA

7.3.1 Data

The data consists of 1,131,668 records containing information based on the registration of enterprises by the Chambers of Commerce of the Netherlands. This data is collected by Marktselect plc on a quarterly basis. Our data specifically corresponds to the CD-Rom for the second quarter of 2001 (see Chapter six). Because registration with the Chamber of Commerce is obligatory for corporations, the dataset covers the entire population. Dedicated programmes were developed for further processing and computation where necessary.

In addition to information at the company level, the data contains three variables that can be used as proxies for the dimensions of technology, organization and geography at the systems level. Technology will be indicated by the sector classification (Pavitt 1984; Vonortas 2000), organization by the company size in terms of the number of employees (Pugh *et al.* 1969a, 1969b; Blau and Schoenherr 1971), and the geographical position by the postal codes in the addresses. Sector classifications are based on the European NACE system. This classification was further elaborated by the Dutch Chambers of Commerce into a five-digit system (BIK-codes).[3] In addition to major activities, most companies also provide information about second and third classification terms. However, the focus below is on the two-digit level unless otherwise indicated.

The distribution by company size is provided in Table 7.1. The data contains a first class of 223,231 companies without employees. The category in included because it contains, among others, spin-off companies which are already on the market, but whose owners are employed by mother companies or universities. Given our research question, these establishments are relevant economic activities.

Table 7.1 Distribution of company data by size

Size	Number of employees	Number of companies
1	None	223,231
2	1	453,842
3	2 to 4	279,835
4	5 to 9	88,862
5	10 to 19	42,047
6	20–49	27,246
7	50–99	8,913
8	100–199	4,303
9	200–499	2,313
10	500–749	503
11	750–999	225
12	> 1000	348
		N = 1,131,668

Postal codes are a fine-grained indicator of geographical location. The two-digit level, providing details on ninety districts was used. Using this information, the data can be aggregated into provinces (NUTS-2) and so-called COROP regions. The COROP regions correspond with the NUTS-3 level used for the statistics of the OECD and Eurostat.[4] The Netherlands are thus organized in twelve provinces and forty regions, respectively.

7.3.2 Knowledge-intensity and high-tech

The OECD (1986) first defined knowledge-intensity in manufacturing sectors on the basis of R&D intensity. R&D intensity was defined for a given sector as the ratio of R&D expenditure to value added. Later this method was expanded to take account of the technology embodied in purchases of intermediate and capital goods (Hatzichronoglou 1997). This new measure could also be applied to service sectors which tend to be technology users rather than technology producers. The discussion continues about how best to delineate knowledge-intensive services (Laafia 1999, 2002a, 2002b; OECD 2001, 2003: 140). The classification introduced in the *2001 STI Scoreboard* will be used here (OECD 2001: 137ff.). The relevant NACE categories for high- and medium-tech are as follows:

Table 7.2 Classification of high-tech and knowledge-intensive sectors according to Eurostat

High-tech Manufacturing	*Knowledge-intensive Sectors (KIS)*
30 Manufacturing of office machinery and computers	**61** Water transport
32 Manufacturing of radio, television and communication equipment and apparatus	**62** Air transport
	64 Post and telecommunications
	65 Financial intermediation, except insurance and pension funding
33 Manufacturing of medical precision and optical instruments, watches and clocks	**66** Insurance and pension funding, except compulsory social security
	67 Activities auxiliary to financial intermediation
Medium-high-tech Manufacturing	**70** Real estate activities
24 Manufacture of chemicals and chemical products	**71** Renting of machinery and equipment without operator and of personal and household goods
29 Manufacture of machinery and equipment n.e.c.	**72** Computer and related activities
	73 Research and development
31 Manufacture of electrical machinery and apparatus n.e.c.	**74** Other business activities
	80 Education
34 Manufacture of motor vehicles, trailers and semitrailers	**85** Health and social work
	92 Recreational, cultural and sporting activities
35 Manufacturing of other transport equipment	Of these sectors, **64**, **72** and **73** are considered *high-tech services.*

Source: Laafia 2002a: 7.

These classifications are based on normalizations across the member states of the European Union and the OECD, respectively. However, the percentages of R&D, and therefore the knowledge-intensity at the sectoral level, may differ in the Netherlands from the average for the OECD or the EU. In a recent report, Statistics Netherlands (CBS 2003) provided figures for R&D intensity as percentages of value added in 2001. Unfortunately, this data is aggregated at a level higher than the categories provided by Eurostat and the OECD. For this reason, and, because the Dutch economy is heavily internationalized so that knowledge can easily spill over from neighboring countries, Eurostat categories provided in Table 7.2 are used to distinguish levels of knowledge-intensity among sectors.

7.3.3 Regional differences

The reader may need some descriptive statistics to understand the context, since the geographical make-up of the Netherlands is different from its image. The share of employment in high-tech and medium-tech manufacturing in the Netherlands rates only above Luxembourg, Greece, and Portugal in the EU-15 (OECD 2003: 140f.). The economically leading provinces of the country, like North- and South-Holland and Utrecht, rank among the lowest on this indicator in the EU-15.[5] The south-east part of the country is integrated in terms of high- and medium-tech manufacturing with neighbouring parts of Belgium and Germany. More than 50% of private R&D in the Netherlands is located in the regions of South-east North-Brabant and North-Limburg (Wintjes and Cobbenhagen 2000).

The core of the Dutch economy has traditionally been concentrated on services. These sectors are not necessarily knowledge-intensive, but the situation is somewhat brighter with respect to knowledge-intensive services than in terms of knowledge-based manufacturing. Utrecht and the relatively recently reclaimed province of Flevoland score high on this employment indicator,[6] while both North- and South-Holland are in the middle range. South-Holland is classified as a leading EU region in knowledge-intensive services (in absolute numbers), but the high-tech end of these services has remained underdeveloped. In summary, the country is not homogenous on any of these indicators. On the basis of these employment statistics, the geographical distribution seems almost opposite for high-tech manufacturing and knowledge-intensive services, with provinces specialized in one of the two.

7.3.4 Methodology

Unlike a covariation between two variables, a dynamic interaction among three dimensions can generate a complex pattern (Schumpeter 1939: 174f.; Li and Yorke 1975). The two configurations possible among three subdynamics were depicted above as integrating or differentiating (in Figures 7.1 and 7.2, respectively). In the case of overlapping Venn diagrams, the dynamics can be considered as relatively integrated, e.g., in the resulting products (Storper 1997: see Figure 7.1), while in the absence of overlap the system remains more differentiated. In this latter case, it operates in terms of different systems interfacing with each other at the network level. In other words, the overlap among the three domains has become negative, and by using the mutual information this can be indicated as negative entropy.[7] Negative entropy reduces the uncertainty that prevails.

Information that is shared among three dimensions can thus be used to measure the extent of integration and differentiation in the interaction between three subsystems. In general, two interacting systems determine each other in their mutual information and condition each other in the remaining uncertainty. They reduce the uncertainty on either side with the mutual information or the transmission. Using Shannon's formulas, this mutual information is defined as the difference between the sum of the uncertainty in two systems without the interaction $(H_x + H_y)$, minus the uncertainty contained in the two systems when they are combined (H_{xy}). This can be formalized as follows:

$$T_{xy} = H_x + H_y - H_{xy} \qquad \text{(Eq. 7.1)}$$

H_x is the uncertainty in the distribution of the variable x (that is, $H_x = -\Sigma_x\, p_x^2 \log p_x$), and analogously, H_{xy} is the uncertainty in the two-dimensional probability distribution (matrix) of x and y (that is, $H_{xy} = -\Sigma_x\, \Sigma_y\, p_{xy}^2 \log p_{xy}$). The mutual information will be indicated with the T of Transmission. If basis two is used for the logarithm, all values are expressed in bits of information.

Abramson (1963: 129) derived from the Shannon formulas that the mutual information in three dimensions is:

$$T_{xyz} = H_x + H_y + H_z - H_{xy} - H_{xz} - H_{yz} + H_{xyz} \qquad \text{(Eq. 7.2)}$$

While the bilateral relations between the variables reduce the uncertainty, the trilateral integration (represented above as the overlap among the Venn diagrams) adds to the uncertainty. The layers thus alternate in terms of the sign. The sign of T_{xyz} depends on the magnitude of H_{xyz} relative to the mutual information in the bilateral relations.

For example, the trilateral coordination can be associated with a new coordination mechanism that is added to the system. In Figure 7.1, Storper (1997) indicated the positive overlap with 'Products.' In the network mode (Figure 7.2), however, a system without strong integration in a centre reduces uncertainty by providing a differentiated configuration. The puzzles of integration at the interfaces are then solved in a non-hierarchical, that is, reflexive or knowledge-based mode.

7.4 RESULTS

Applying this measure to the data first provides the descriptive statistics of Table 7.3. As noted, the data allows us to disaggregate in terms of geographical regions (NUTS-2 and NUTS-3), and high-tech sectors can be distinguished from

Table 7.3 Expected information contents (in bits) of the distributions in the three dimensions and their combinations

	$H_{Geography}$	$H_{Technology}$	$H_{Organization}$	H_{GT}	H_{GO}	H_{TO}	H_{GTO}	N
NL	6.205	4.055	2.198	10.189	8.385	6.013	12.094	1,131,668
% H_{max}	95.6	69.2	61.3	82.5	83.2	63.7	75.9	
Drenthe	2.465	4.134	2.225	6.569	4.684	6.039	8.413	26,210
Flevoland	1.781	4.107	2.077	5.820	3.852	6.020	7.697	20,955
Friesland	3.144	4.202	2.295	7.292	5.431	6.223	9.249	36,409
Gelderland	3.935	4.091	2.227	7.986	6.158	6.077	9.925	131,050
Groningen	2.215	4.192	2.220	6.342	4.427	6.059	8.157	30,324
Limburg	2.838	4.166	2.232	6.956	5.064	6.146	8.898	67,636
N-Brabant	3.673	4.048	2.193	7.682	5.851	6.018	9.600	175,916
N-Holland	3.154	3.899	2.116	6.988	5.240	5.730	8.772	223,690
Overijssel	2.747	4.086	2.259	6.793	5.002	6.081	8.749	64,482
Utrecht	2.685	3.956	2.193	6.611	4.873	5.928	8.554	89,009
S-Holland	3.651	3.994	2.203	7.582	5.847	5.974	9.528	241,648
Zeeland	1.802	4.178	2.106	5.941	3.868	6.049	7.735	24,339

medium-tech sectors and knowledge-intensive services. The various dimensions can also be combined in order to compute the mutual information in a next step (Table 7.4).

7.4.1 Descriptive statistics

Table 7.3 shows the probabilistic entropy values in the three dimensions (G = geography, T = technology/sector, and O = organization) for the Netherlands as a whole and the decomposition at the NUTS-2 level of the provinces. The provinces are very different in terms of the number of firms and their geographical distribution over the postal codes. While Flevoland contains only 20,955 units, South-Holland provides the location for 241,648 firms.[8] This size effect is reflected in the distribution of postal codes: the uncertainty in the geographical distribution – measured as $H_{Geography}$ – correlates significantly with the number of firms N ($r = 0.76$; $p = 0.005$). The variance in the probabilistic entropies among the provinces is high (> 0.5) in this geographical dimension, but the variance in the probabilistic entropy among sectors, and the size categories, is relatively small (< 0.1). Thus, the provinces are relatively similar in terms of their sector and size distributions[9] and can meaningfully be compared.

The second row of Table 7.3 informs us that the probabilistic entropy in the postal codes of firms is larger than ninety five per cent of the maximum entropy of this distribution at the level of the nation. Since the postal codes are more fine-grained in metropolitan than in rural areas, this indicates that the firmdensity is not a major source of variance in relation to the population density. However, the number of postal-code categories varies among the provinces, and postal codes are nominal variables which cannot be compared across provinces or regions.

The corresponding percentages for the technology (sector) and the organization (or size) distributions are 69.2 and 61.3 per cent, respectively. The combined uncertainty of technology and organization (H_{TO}) does not add substantially to the redundancy. In other words, organization and technology have a relatively independent influence on the distribution different from that of postal codes. In the provincial decomposition, however, the highly developed and densly populated provinces (North and South-Holland, and Utrecht) show a more specialized pattern of sectoral composition (H_T) than Friesland, Groningen, and Limburg. These latter provinces are further distanced from the centre of the country. Flevoland shows the highest redundancy in the size distribution (H_O), perhaps because certain traditional formats of middle-sized companies may still be under-represented in this new province.

The combination of technological and organizational specialization exhibits a specific position of North-Holland (H_{TO} = 5.730 or 60.7 per cent of the maximum entropy) versus Friesland (H_{TO} = 6.223 or 65.9 per cent of the maximum entropy) at the other end of the distribution. Since the mean of the distribution in this case is 63.8 per cent with a standard deviation of 1.3, North-Holland is an exception in terms of an interaction effect between the technological specialization and its relatively low variation in the size distribution.

7.4.2 The mutual information

Table 7.4 provides the values for the transmissions (T) among the various dimensions. These values can be calculated simply from the values of the probabilistic entropies provided in Table 7.3 using Equations 7.1 and 7.2 provided above. The first line for the Netherlands as a whole shows that there is more mutual information between the geographical distribution of firms and their technological specialization ($T_{GT} = 0.072$ bits) than between the geographical distribution and their size ($T_{GO} = 0.019$). However, the mutual information between technology and organization ($T_{TO} = 0.240$) is larger than T_{GO} by an order of magnitude. The provinces exhibit a comparable pattern.

While the values for T_{GT} and T_{GO} can be considered as indicators of the geographical clustering of economic activities (in terms of technologies and organizational formats, respectively), the T_{TO} provides an indicator for the correlation between the maturity of the industry (Anderson and Tushman 1991) and the specific size of the firms involved (Suárez and Utterback 1995; Utterback and Suárez 1993; cf. Nelson 1994). The relatively low value of this indicator for Flevoland indicates that the techno-economic structure of this province is less mature than in other provinces. The high values of this indicator for Groningen and Drenthe indicates that the techno-economic structure in these provinces is perhaps relatively over-mature. This indicator can thus be considered as representing a strategic vector (Abernathy and Clark 1985; Watts and Porter 2003).

All values for the mutual informations in three dimensions (T_{TGO}) are negative. When decomposed at the NUTS-3 level of regions, these values are also negative, with the exception of two regions that contain only a single postal code at the two digits level. In these two cases the uncertainty is by definition zero.[10] At first glance, the figures suggest an inverse relationship between the mutual

Table 7.4 The mutual information in two and three dimensions disaggregated at the NUTS-2 level (provinces)

	T_{GT}	T_{GO}	T_{TO}	T_{GTO}
NL	0.072	0.019	0.240	−0.034
Drenthe	0.030	0.005	0.320	−0.056
Flevoland	0.068	0.006	0.164	−0.030
Friesland	0.054	0.008	0.274	−0.056
Gelderland	0.040	0.004	0.242	−0.043
Groningen	0.065	0.007	0.353	−0.045
Limburg	0.047	0.006	0.251	−0.033
N-Brabant	0.039	0.016	0.223	−0.036
N-Holland	0.065	0.030	0.285	−0.017
Overijssel	0.040	0.004	0.263	−0.035
Utrecht	0.031	0.005	0.221	−0.024
S-Holland	0.062	0.006	0.223	−0.027
Zeeland	0.038	0.039	0.234	−0.039

information in three dimensions, and the intuitively expected knowledge intensity of regions and provinces, with North-Holland, Utrecht, and South-Holland
at the one end and Drenthe and Friesland at the other. However, these values
cannot be compared among geographical units without a further normalization.
As noted, the postal codes are nominal variables. Later the focus will turn to the
relative effects of decompositions in terms of high- and medium-tech sectors on
the geographical units of analysis, but let us first turn to the normalization in the
geographical dimension because this dimension provides us with recognizable
units (like provinces and regions) that may allow us to validate the indicator.

7.5 THE REGIONAL CONTRIBUTIONS TO THE
KNOWLEDGE BASE OF THE DUTCH ECONOMY

One of the advantages of statistical decomposition analysis is the possibility to
specify the within-group variances and the between-group variances in great detail
(Theil 1972; Leydesdorff 1995). However, a full decomposition at the lower level
is possible only if the categories for the measurement are similar among the groups.
Had a different indicator for the regional dimension – for example, percentage
'rural' versus percentage 'metropolitan' – one would have been able to compare
and therefore to decompose along this axis, but the unique postal codes cannot be
compared among regions in a way similar to the size or the sectoral distribution
of the firms (Leydesdorff and Fritsch 2006).

The decomposition algorithm (Theil 1972) enables us to study the nextorder
level of the Netherlands as a composed system (NUTS-1) in terms of its lower-
level units like the NUTS-2 provinces and the NUTS-3 regions. Note that in this
case, the regions and provinces are not compared in terms of their knowledge
intensity among themselves, but in terms of their weighted contributions to the
knowledge base of the Dutch economy as a whole. The distributions are weighted
in the various dimensions for the number of firms in the groups i by totalling
first the uncertainties within the different groups ($\Sigma_i(n_i/N) * H_i$; $N = \Sigma_i n_i$). The
in-between group uncertainty H_0 is then defined as the difference between this
sum and the uncertainty prevailing at the level of the composed system:

$$H = H_0 + \Sigma_i(n_i/N)H_i \qquad \text{(Eq. 7.3)}$$

Or for the transmissions:[11]

$$T = T_0 + \Sigma_i(n_i/N)T_i \qquad \text{(Eq. 7.4)}$$

For example, if one uses the right-most column of Table 7.3 indicating the
number of firms in each of the provinces for the normalization, given the total
number of firms registered ($N = 1,131,668$), one obtains the following table for
the decomposition of the mutual information in three dimensions at the level of
the provinces:

Table 7.5 The mutual information in three dimensions statistically decomposed at the NUTS-2 level (provinces) in millibits of information

	$\Delta T_{GTO}\ (= n_i * T_i/N)$ in millibits of information	n_i
Drenthe	−1.29	26,210
Flevoland	−0.55	20,955
Friesland	−1.79	36,409
Gelderland	**−4.96**	131,050
Groningen	−1.20	30,324
Limburg	−1.96	67,636
N-Brabant	**−5.56**	175,916
N-Holland	**−3.28**	223,690
Overijssel	−1.98	64,482
Utrecht	−1.86	89,009
S-Holland	**−5.84**	241,648
Zeeland	−0.83	24,339
Sum ($\Sigma_i\ P_i\ T_i$)	−31.10	1,131,668
T_0	**−2.46**	
NL	−33.55	N = 1,131,668

The table shows that the knowledge base of the country is concentrated in South-Holland ($\Delta T = -5.84$ mbits), North-Brabant (−5.56), and Gelderland (−4.96). North-Holland follows with a contribution of −3.28 mbits of information. The other provinces contribute to the knowledge base less than the in-between provinces interaction effect at the national level ($T_0 = -2.46$ mbit). Figures 7.3 and 7.4 visualize how the knowledge base of the country is geographically organized at the NUTS-2 and NUTS-3 level, respectively.

The further disaggregation in Table 7.6 informs us about the contribution of regions at the NUTS-3 level (Figure 7.4). The contribution of South-Holland is concentrated in the Rotterdam area, the one in North-Brabant in the Eindhoven region, and North-Holland exclusively in the agglomeration of Amsterdam. Utrecht, the Veluwe (Gelderland) and the northern part of Overijssel also have above average contributions using this indicator. However, an important factor in the reduction of the uncertainty is provided at a level higher than the NUTS-3 regions ($T_0 = -9.09$ mbit).[12] We shall therefore focus in the next section on the NUTS-2 level.

These tables and pictures correspond with common knowledge about the industrial structure of the Netherlands (e.g., Van der Panne and Dolfsma 2001, 2003). The contribution of northern Overijssel to the knowledge base of the Dutch economy is surprising because this region has not previously been recognized as an economically active region. However, it is possible it profits from a spill-over effect of knowledge-based activities in the neighbouring regions.

As noted, the normalization involves the number of firms in the geographical unit of analysis as a factor in the weighting. Therefore, these results inform us both about the industrial structure of the country and the knowledge base of the economy,[13] and may differ depending on the aggregation level analyzed. Among

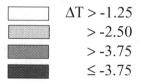

$\Delta T > -1.25$
$\quad\ > -2.50$
$\quad\ > -3.75$
$\quad\ \leq -3.75$

Figure 7.3 Contribution to the knowledge base of the Dutch economy at the provincial (NUTS-2) level

ΔT > -0.50
> -1.00
≤ -1.00

Figure 7.4 Contribution to the knowledge base of the Dutch economy at the regional
(NUTS-3) level

Table 7.6 The mutual information in three dimensions statistically decomposed at the NUTS-3 level (COROP regions) in millibits of information
Regions with a $\Delta T > 1.00$ mbit are boldfaced; $\Delta T = 1.00$ mbits in italics.

	NUTS-3 Regions (Corop)	ΔT_{GTO} $(= n_i * T_i/N)$ in millibits of information	n_i
1	Oost-Groningen	−0.20	7,571
2	Delfzijl en omgeving	0.00	2,506
3	Overig Groningen	−0.81	20,273
4	Noord-Friesland	−0.99	17,498
5	Zuidwest-Friesland	−0.37	7,141
6	Zuidoost-Friesland	−0.41	11,744
7	Noord-Drenthe	−0.44	9,702
8	Zuidoost-Drenthe	−0.39	9,121
9	Zuidwest-Drenthe	−0.13	7,327
10	**Noord-Overijssel**	**−1.04**	20,236
11	Zuidwest-Overijssel	−0.16	7,333
12	Twente	−0.57	36,971
13	**Veluwe**	**−1.38**	43,489
14	Achterhoek	−0.76	24,995
15	Arnhem/Nijmegen	−0.85	43,388
16	Zuidwest-Gelderland	−0.69	19,192
17	**Utrecht**	**−1.86**	88,997
18	Kop van Noord-Holland	−0.30	25,978
19	Alkmaar en omgeving	−0.39	17,145
20	IJmond	−0.07	11,017
21	Agglomeratie Haarlem	−0.16	17,376
22	Zaanstreek	−0.07	9,865
23	**Groot-Amsterdam**	**−1.15**	117,518
24	Het Gooi en Vechtstreek	−0.42	24,818
25	Agglomeratie Leiden en Bollenstreek	−0.42	26,738
26	*Agglomeratie 's-Gravenhage*	*−1.00*	50,603
27	Delft en Westland	−0.28	19,489
28	Oost-Zuid-Holland	−0.67	25,262
29	**Groot-Rijnmond**	**−1.61**	92,255
30	Zuidoost-Zuid-Holland	−0.91	27,301
31	Zeeuwsch-Vlaanderen	0.00	6,840
32	Overig Zeeland	−0.39	17,499
33	West-Noord-Brabant	−0.78	43,954
34	Midden-Noord-Brabant	−0.61	32,332
35	*Noordoost-Noord-Brabant*	*−1.00*	47,214
36	**Zuidoost-Noord-Brabant**	**−1.13**	52,416
37	Noord-Limburg	−0.53	16,753
38	Midden-Limburg	−0.17	15,272
39	Zuid-Limburg	−0.79	35,611
40	Flevoland	−0.55	20,928
	Sum $(\Sigma_i \, P_i \, T_i)$	−24.46	1,131,668
	T_0	**−9.09**	
	NL	−33.55	N = 1,131,668

the regions, for example, Utrecht (region 17) contributes most to the reduction of the uncertainty at the national level, while as a province, the same value for Utrecht ($\Delta T = -1.86$ mbits), remains below the average contribution. In general, the mutual information in three dimensions provides a composite measure of the three factors involved in Storper's holy trinity (geography, technology, and organization). These three factors can be decomposed along each axis. The next section looks at the sectoral axis, and in particular to the effects of indicating knowledge intensity along this axis.

7.6 THE SECTORIAL DECOMPOSITION

While the geographical comparison is compounded with traditional industrial structure, like firm density, all effects of the decomposition in terms of the sectorial classification of high- and medium-tech sectors and knowledge-intensive services will be expressed as a relative effect. That is, as a percentage increase or decrease of the negative value of the mutual information in three dimensions when a specific selection is compared with the complete population. In the remainder of this study, the categories provided by the OECD and Eurostat (see Table 7.2 above) are used as selection criteria for subsets, and compare the results with those of the full set provided in the previous section as a baseline. A greater negative score for the probabilistic entropy, compared to the overall score, indicates a reduction of the uncertainty, and is therefore considered as a more favourable condition for a knowledge-based economy.

Table 7.7 shows the results of comparing the subset of enterprises indicated as high-tech manufacturing (sectors 30, 32, and 33) and high-tech services (64, 72, and 73) with the full set. The column headed 'All sectors' corresponds

Table 7.7 The mutual information in three dimensions when comparing high-tech sectors in industrial production and services

T_{xyz}	All sectors	High Tech	% change	N
NL	−0.034	−0.060	80.2	45,128
Drenthe	−0.056	−0.093	67.6	786
Flevoland	−0.030	−0.036	20.6	1,307
Friesland	−0.056	−0.136	144.9	983
Gelderland	−0.043	−0.094	120.1	4,885
Groningen	−0.045	−0.066	48.1	1,204
Limburg	−0.033	−0.068	105.9	2,191
N-Brabant	−0.036	−0.058	61.2	6,375
N-Holland	−0.017	−0.034	103.4	9,346
Overijssel	−0.035	−0.079	127.6	2,262
Utrecht	−0.024	−0.039	65.9	4,843
S-Holland	−0.027	−0.044	61.7	10,392
Zeeland	−0.039	−0.067	73.3	554

to the right-most column in Table 7.3. The third column provides the mutual information in three dimensions for the high-tech sectors in both manufacturing and services. In the fourth column, the percentage change is indicated in relative terms. This indicates the influence of these high-tech sectors and services on the knowledge base of the economy. The results confirm our hypothesis that the mutual information, or entropy that emerges from the interaction between the three dimensions, is more negative for high-tech sectors and high-tech services than for the economy as a whole. The dynamics created by these sectors deepen and tighten the knowledge base more than is the case for firms at the average level.

Table 7.8 provides the same figures and normalizations, but on the basis of selections according to the classifications provided in Table 7.2 for high- and medium-tech manufacturing combined (middle section of Table 7.2), and knowledge-intensive services (right-side columns of Table 7.2), respectively. These results indicate a major effect on the indicator for the sectors of high- and medium-tech manufacturing. The effect is by far the largest in North-Holland with a 943 per cent increase relative to the benchmark of all sectors combined. Utrecht follows with 859 per cent. A number of provinces (Limburg, South-Holland, Flevoland) have above average effects of 647, 635 and 594 per cent, respectively. Zeeland has the lowest value on this indicator (365 per cent), but the number of establishments in these categories is also lowest for this province. North-Brabant, however, has the largest number of establishments in these categories, while it does not seem to profit from an additional effect on the configuration.

The number of establishments in knowledge-intensive services is more than half (51.3 per cent) of the total number of companies in the country. These companies are concentrated in North- and South-Holland, with North-Brabant in third position. With the exception of North-Holland, the effect of knowledge-intensive services on this indicator of the knowledge base is always negative, that is, it leads to a decrease of configurational information. This is indicated with an opposite sign for the change. In the case of North-Holland, the change is marginally positive (+1.0 per cent), but this is not due to the Amsterdam region.[14] North-Brabant is second in this rank order with a decrease of −16.6 per cent.

These findings accord with a theoretical expectation about the different contributions to the economy of services in general and KIS in particular (Bilderbeek *et al.* 1998; Miles *et al.* 1995; OECD 2000). Windrum and Tomlinson (1999) argued that to assess the role of KIS, the degree of integration is more important than the percentage of representation in the economy. Unlike output indicators, the measure adopted here focuses on the degree of integration in the configuration. However, our results indicate that KIS unfavorably affects the synergy between technology, organization and territory in the techno-economic system of the Netherlands, its provinces, and regions. This indicates a relative uncoupling effect from the geographically defined knowledge bases of the economy. The effects of KIS are spilling over geographic boundaries more easily than knowledge-based manufacturing.

Table 7.8 High-tech and medium-tech manufacturing versus knowledge-intensive services and the effects on the mutual information in three dimensions

	All sectors	High & medium tech Manufacturing	% change	N	Knowledge-Intensive Services	% change	N
NL	-0.034	-0.219	553	15,838	-0.024	-27.3	581,196
Drenthe	-0.056	-0.349	526	406	-0.034	-39.1	11,312
Flevoland	-0.030	-0.206	594	401	-0.018	-37.9	10,730
Friesland	-0.056	-0.182	227	951	-0.037	-32.6	14,947
Gelderland	-0.043	-0.272	536	2,096	-0.025	-40.8	65,112
Groningen	-0.045	-0.258	479	537	-0.029	-34.0	14,127
Limburg	-0.033	-0.245	647	1,031	-0.018	-45.1	30,040
N-Brabant	-0.036	-0.190	430	2,820	-0.030	-16.6	86,262
N-Holland	-0.017	-0.173	943	2,299	-0.017	1.0	126,516
Overijssel	-0.035	-0.207	496	1,167	-0.020	-42.8	30,104
Utrecht	-0.024	-0.227	859	1,020	-0.013	-45.0	52,818
S-Holland	-0.027	-0.201	635	2,768	-0.015	-45.5	128,725
Zeeland	-0.039	-0.180	365	342	-0.028	-27.8	10,503

This result contrasts with the expectations expressed in much of the relevant literature on the role of knowledge-intensive services in stimulating the knowledge base of an economy. For example, the conclusion of the European Summit in Lisbon (2000) was, among other things, that 'the shift to a digital, knowledge-based economy, prompted by new goods and services, will be a powerful engine for growth, competitiveness and jobs. In addition, it will be capable of improving citizens' quality of life and the environment'.[15] Our results suggest that the knowledge-based economy, and the digital economy, are not the same: the manufacturing of goods, or the delivering of services, can be expected to have other geographical effects and constraints.

Knowledge-intensive services seem to be largely uncoupled from the knowledge flow within a regional or local economy. They contribute negatively to the knowledge-based configuration because of their inherent capacity to deliver these services outside the region. Thus, a locality can be chosen on the basis of considerations other than those relevant for the generation of a knowledge-based economy in the region. For example, the proximity of a well-connected airport (or train station) may be a major factor in the choice of a location.

Table 7.9 shows the relative deepening of the mutual information in three dimensions when the subset of sectors indicated as 'high-tech services' is compared with KIS in general. 'High-tech services' are only 'post and telecommunications' (NACE code 64), 'computer and related activities' (72), and 'research and development' (73). More than knowledge-intensive services in general, high-tech services can be expected to produce and transfer technology-related knowledge (Bilderbeek *et al.* 1998). These effects of strengthening the knowledge base seem highest in regions that do not have a strong knowledge base in medium- and high-tech manufacturing, such as Friesland and Overijssel. The effects

Table 7.9 The subset of high-tech services improves the knowledge base in the service sector

T_{xyz}	Knowl-intensive services	High-Tech services	% change	N
NL	−0.024	−0.034	37.3	41,002
Drenthe	−0.034	−0.049	45.2	678
Flevoland	−0.018	−0.018	−4.6	1,216
Friesland	−0.037	−0.087	131.5	850
Gelderland	−0.025	−0.046	82.3	4,380
Groningen	−0.029	−0.044	49.5	1,070
Limburg	−0.018	−0.039	118.7	1,895
N-Brabant	−0.030	−0.035	16.1	5,641
N-Holland	−0.017	−0.020	17.0	8,676
Overijssel	−0.020	−0.046	133.1	1,999
Utrecht	−0.013	−0.020	49.8	4,464
S-Holland	−0.015	−0.025	69.8	9,650
Zeeland	−0.028	−0.045	59.7	483

of this selection for North-Brabant and North-Holland, for example, are among the lowest. However, this negative relation between high- and medium-tech manufacturing on the one hand, and high-tech services on the other, is not significant ($r = -0.352$; p = 0.262). At the NUTS-3 level, the corresponding relation is also not significant. Thus, the effects of high- and medium-tech manufacturing, and high-tech services on the knowledge base of the economy, are not related to each other.

7.7 CONCLUSIONS AND DISCUSSION

Before drawing conclusions and considering policy implications, it should be emphasized that the initial focus in this chapter has been on methodological considerations. In the first instance, an indicator of interaction effects at the network level providing a quantitative measure for the reduction of the uncertainty that cannot be attributed to the individual players in a network, is developed. The reduction of this uncertainty is configurational, indicating that a next-order system is operating as an overlay. In the second instance, the data and insights from economic geography allowed us to use proxies for the three main dimensions of Storper's 'holy trinity' of technology, organization and territory. This approach is quite novel, and may be counter-intuitive for some as neither the outcome or the analysis relates directly to the actions of concrete agents in the system. An essentially scientometric indicator of triple-helix relations is thus validated in an economic context, as it supplies a measure of the knowledge base of an economy and its decompositions along different dimensions.

Nevertheless, results of the analysis at the system level indicate that indeed a national innovation system in the Netherlands can be said to exist. Uncertainty is reduced as three theoretically relevant dimensions interact at the systems level. Decomposition along two of the three dimensions allows formulation of the following hypotheses:

1. The knowledge base of a (regional) economy is carried by high-, but more importantly, medium-tech manufacturing; high-tech services favourably contribute to the knowledge-based structuring, but to a smaller extent.
2. Medium-tech manufacturing provides the backbone of the techno-economic structure of the country; this explains why high-tech manufacturing contributes less to the knowledge infrastructure than might be expected, for example, on the basis of patent portfolios (Leydesdorff 2004).
3. The knowledge-intensive services that are not high-tech have a relatively unfavourable effect on the territorial knowledge base of an economy. One could say that these services tend to uncouple the knowledge base from its geographical dimension.
4. The Netherlands is highly developed as a knowledge-intensive service economy, but the high-tech end of these services has remained more than an order of magnitude smaller in terms of the number of firms.

These conclusions are corroborated by analysing data for another country: Germany (Leydesdorff and Fritsch 2006). In terms of policy implications, these conclusions suggest that regions that are less developed may wish to strengthen their knowledge infrastructure by trying to attract medium-tech manufacturing and high-tech services. The efforts of firms in medium-tech sectors can be considered as focused on maintaining absorptive capacity (Cohen and Levinthal 1989) so that knowledge and technologies developed elsewhere can more easily be understood and adapted to particular circumstances. High-tech manufacturing may be more focused on the (internal) production and global markets than on the local diffusion parameters. High-tech services, however, mediate technological knowledge more than knowledge-intensive services that are medium-tech. The latter services seem to have an unfavourable effect on territorially defined knowledge-based economies.

It should be noted that the indicator measures a synergy at the structural level of an economy and is not a measure of knowledge creation or economic output (Carter 1996). The synergy among the industrial structures, geographical distributions, and technological capacities can be considered crucial for the strength of an innovation system (Fritsch 2004). In other words, this indicator measures only the conditions in the system for innovative activities, and thus specifies an expectation (compare chapter 8 below). Regions with a high potential for innovative activity can be expected to organize more innovative resources than regions with lower values of the indicator.

Perhaps the most important insight is the procedure presented for measuring the synergy as the expected knowledge base of an economy. The various dimensions correspond to the classifications that are already available from the OECD and Eurostat databases, and the geographical address information of the units is also used. In principle, the dimensionality of the mutual information can further be extended. Unlike the focus on comparative statics in employment statistics and the *STI Scoreboards* of the OECD (OECD 2001, 2003; Godin 2006), this indicator was developed for measuring the knowledge base of an economy as an emergent property (Jakulin and Bratko 2004; cf. Ulanowicz 1986: 142ff.). Furthermore, the indicator could be specified as an operationalization with reference to two bodies of theorizing in evolutionary economics, namely regional studies (e.g. Storper 1997, Chapter 6) and the study of knowledge-based systems of innovation (e.g. David and Foray 2002; Leydesdorff and Etzkowitz 1998).

8　A dynamic welfare perspective for the knowledge economy

'Since it is rooted in a contradiction, there can be no such thing as an ideally beneficial patent system, and it is bound to produce negative results in particular instances'

– Joan Robinson

'[O]wnership . . . gives the owner not only the right of use over the community's immaterial equipment, but also the right of abuse and of neglect and inhibition'

– Thorstein Veblen

It is argued that an economy where knowledge plays an important role should be evaluated in terms different from Paretian welfare economics. Ingredients and a structure for a Dynamic (Schumpeterian) Welfare Economics are proposed. The framework is applied to evaluate recent developments in a set of institutions that are central to the knowledge economy: intellectual property rights such as patents and copyrights.

8.1 INTRODUCTION

Does a focus on the role of knowledge in the economy, and the theoretical coming to grips within economics that has only just started to occur, have an impact on the way in which economists and others should evaluate situations and developments that they encounter? My answer to this question is a resounding 'yes!'. Reasons for this have become clear in the previous discussion. I would now like to develop some thoughts on what such a welfare economics might look like and what it might incorporate. As existing welfare economics, drawing on Pareto, is foremost a static perspective, and since this line of thinking is strongly influenced, directly and indirectly, by the work of Schumpeter, a Dynamic (Schumpeterian) Welfare Economics would emphasize the development of knowledge and its use in the economy. In this respect, in chapter seventeen of his Capitalism, Socialism and Democracy, Schumpeter (1943: 190, italics in original) has introduced some fundaments for a dynamic welfare economics. One passage is especially worth noting:

'we shall call that system relatively more efficient which we see reason to expect would *in the long run* produce the larger stream of consumers' goods per equal unit of time'.

Relatedly, the argument in favour of competition in the market, and dynamic efficiency, is emphatically not based on Paretian considerations of perfect competition (Baumol 2002; Blaug 2001a or b; Mokyr 2002; Nelson 1981, 2004). I suggest some elements for a different welfare economic perspective. A much debated policy issue that is very relevant for the knowledge-based economy is subsequently looked at to evaluate some measures that governments are currently implementing. How would a dynamic welfare economics evaluate changes in the system of intellectual property right law? One thus needs to discuss Paretian welfare economics first, albeit briefly, develop thoughts on a Dynamic (Schumpeterian) alternative and explain a bit on Intellectual Property Rights (IPRs). The alternative framework may be applied to look at the effects of these developments in IPRs for the parties involved, including consumers, producers of information goods and third world countries.

8.2 PARETIAN WELFARE ECONOMICS

Historian of economic thought, Mark Blaug, has lamented on several occasions the 'replacement of the process conception of competition by an end-state conception [which] drained the idea of competition of all behavioural content' (Blaug 2001a or b: 39), where not the existence of an equilibrium, but rather the stability of that equilibrium state, is analyzed (cf. Vickers 1995). Blaug traces the origins of this approach to Cournot, Walras, and blames Samuelson, Hicks and Robbins for establishing it as the mainstream.

Every first-year student of economics is presented with the picture of perfect competition between large groups of suppliers and consumers of homogenous products. The Pareto optimum welfare conditions to attain a first-best situation are well known and need not be reproduced here. The thinking about welfare economics in the 1930s up to the 1950s has moved from discussing cardinal utility functions, to the Hicks-Kaldor compensation criteria, to the Lipsey & Lancaster second-best theorem and to Arrow & Debreu's impossibility theorem. I will not discuss this development in the economics literature at length.

Central assumptions in Paretian welfare economics are, among others, three postulates: 'consumer sovereignty, individualism in social choice, and unanimity' (Blaug 1980: 148). Every individual (agent) is the best judge of his own welfare, social welfare is defined only in terms of the welfare of individuals and the welfare of individuals may not be compared. These, together with assumptions about parties' objective functions and motivation (Profit and Utility maximization), allow one, for the analysis, for instance, of a world where two goods (A and B) are offered to determine the optimum situation at the point of Tangency, in Figure 8.1, where marginal costs of production equals marginal utility. At the same time, the relative price ratio between the two goods equals marginal utility, constituting a Pareto-optimal situation. Changes in either the Supply or the Demand curve in Figure 8.2, for whatever reason, will be evaluated in terms of welfare triangles. In the figure, a movement of the Supply curve is

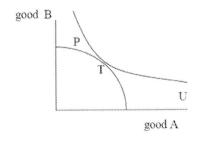

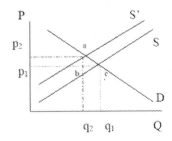

Figure 8.1 Paretian welfare

Figure 8.2 Welfare triangles

shown (from S to S'), leading to a 'deadweight welfare loss' of the size of triangle ABC.

To date, Paretian welfare theory still dominates, while a characterization made in a 1960 survey of welfare economics still holds as well:

> No growth or innovation takes place, no uncertainty exists and individual tastes remain unaltered. In addition, the working population is fixed and is, in some sense, fully employed. Within this framework it is further assumed that individual behaviour is consistent, and (. . .) that the individual is the best judge of his own wants.
>
> (Mishan 1960: 198)

For my purposes, the first part of the quote is especially noteworthy. As Paul Romer (1994) argues, however, the conditions that are here placed under the c.p. clause are far from rare. The kind of analysis that needs to posit these assumptions may thus not be as relevant as one might assume: 'to keep things simple, set aside the niggling disputes about consumer surplus as a welfare measure' is what he suggests (Romer 1994, p. 15; cf. Blaug 2001a or b: 47).

8.3 A DYNAMIC (SCHUMPETERIAN) WELFARE PERSPECTIVE

A more appropriate (additional) welfare theory would be acknowledging the dynamics in today's knowledge economies. The comparative static foundations of a Paretian approach are less appropriate in such circumstances. Indeed, as Tyler Cowen (2000) has argued, there have been more attempts at suggesting different theories to the established welfare economics of Vilfredo Pareto. Cowen (2000: xiii) distinguishes 'three dominant yet incompatible strands': ordinalist Paretian welfare theory; applied cost-benefit analysis used in practical policy and cardinalism of which Amartya Sen is a representative. The latter 'returns to the purely theoretical realm but rejects Paretianism'; it 'is less systematic and unified than the other two strands'.

The public interest in the creation of new knowledge has been long established, mainly due, in more recent decades, to Richard Nelson (1959, 1990). In a dynamic economy, a static approach to welfare, emphasizing the end-state kind of competition is not very appropriate, however. Thus, 'welfare loss triangles are admitted and downplayed' as Nelson (1981: 106) has expressed it, following Schumpeter (1943). A welfare perspective emphasizing the dynamics in an economy will need to combine insights from a diverse set of related fields as such a perspective has not been developed to date (cf. Mokyr 2002: 21–27).

Schumpeter (1942, especially Chapter 17) indicates that the effects of choices made by private or public parties should (also) be evaluated in terms of their long-term effects – which alternative leads to the most attractive outcome in the future? Schumpeter seems to indicate that both measurable effects in the market, as well as more immeasurable effects inside and outside of the market, should be taken into consideration, although he is not very clear about how to develop these ideas into more operational terms. In line with Schumpeter's work, and prompted by a number of other scholars, I would suggest that 'communication' between agents plays an important role in shaping the processes through which an economy evolves from one stage to the next. To be more exact, it would seem that there is a positive association between the ease with which communication may occur and economic development (see, e.g., Dudley 1999; Mokyr 2002).

In this contribution, a main starting point will be to use a Cobb-Douglass type function for the production of knowledge. The use of this function to model the production of knowledge is far from unique (Audretsch 1998; Dudley 1999), despite the use of production functions being questioned in general (Shaikh 1990) and in part due to the failure of the efforts at growth accounting (Denison 1967). It starts from the idea that communication between parties can be more or less difficult, and that these difficulties can be translated into costs. The extent to which communication is difficult (costly) relates directly to the technology used, as well as to the established (cultural) mores about communication (cf. Mokyr 2002; Nelson 1990), as well as to more formal institutions. The costs can be direct or more mediated, and the effects are both on levels of welfare as on the ways organizations take shape (Milgrom and Roberts 1988). Certainly when 'more than sixty per cent of the labor force in the United States is engaged in activities in the "information sector" of the economy' (Baumol 2002: 2) it is important to analyze the creation of new information and knowledge and its effects on the economy and its rate of growth.

In line with what Dudley (1999) suggests, three kinds of costs are related to communication – the level of the costs involved determines the kind of communication that one may expect.[1] One may distinguish Storage, Decoding and Transmission costs of communication.[2] In a way, communication is an input that would lead to the 'output' in newly used and created knowledge. As it can often only be determined ex post if the knowledge involved signifies an incremental or a radical development, the discussion here applies to both these situations.[3]

When all of these costs are high, no communication occurs.[4] When transmission costs are low, but the others remain high, communication will be centralized, much as Figure 8.3a presents. As Storage costs decrease, as in Figure 8.3b, a decentralized communication structure emerges. Finally, when decoding costs are low, a distributed type of communication will be observed (Figure 8.3c). The

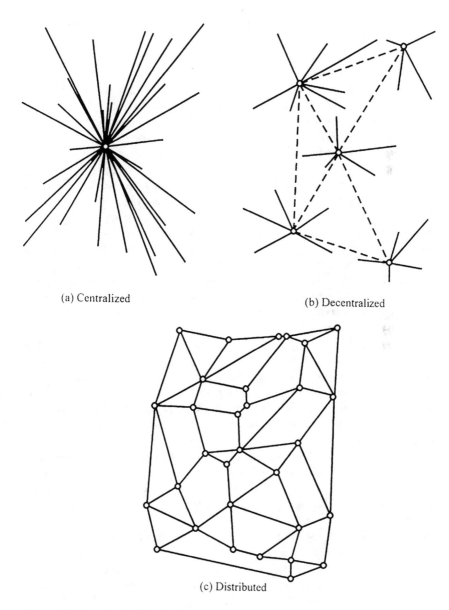

(a) Centralized

(b) Decentralized

(c) Distributed

Figure 8.3 Communication structures

Table 8.1 Communication and communication costs

Costs of	Communication None	Centralized (a)	Decentralized (b)	Distributed (c)
Transmission	High	Low	Low	Low
Storage	High	High	Low	Low
Decoding	High	High ·	High	Low

suggested sequence for decreases in these communication costs seems to match with what may be observed when one considers developments in the use of techniques involved in communication. Table 8.1 summarizes this discussion. Communication that is distributed (Figure 8.3c) is to be preferred from the position of the public interest, as knowledge and information is exchanged most readily and conditions for economic and societal development are most conducive.

The basic insight that centralization of communication raises costs, and is not beneficial for society, was also argued for by Nelson (1981: 101): 'the argument that centralization imposes high information and calculation costs carries considerable weight in a dynamic context'. Indeed, for him it is a central argument for favouring capitalism over socialism, as it was for Hayek too. This view contrasts with 'the standard theoretical analysis [which] implies that only zero spillovers [of knowledge] are compatible with optimality in innovative activity' (Baumol 2002: 121). Rather, extensive dissemination of new knowledge benefits society, and it is of course this truth that is one fundament for the system of IPRs may be the most important. In exchange for a temporary exclusive right to use newly developed knowledge, a party is to make this knowledge publicly available in order for others to build on it. Many firms even consider it directly beneficial for themselves to disseminate their newly developed knowledge (Baumol 2002: 73), for instance because network effects can kick in more readily (Shapiro and Varian 1999). It is for this reason that firms cluster geographically (Saxenian 1994), especially firms in high-tech sectors – this should be considered a causal link (Chapter six above).

In line with Dudley (1999), one could include the three different communication costs in a Cobb-Douglass production function in order to assess the effects of changes in communication costs for economic welfare (Eq. 8.1). The main purpose of this production function is to evaluate changes in communication costs in terms of their effect on social welfare, and less so to study the affect of the absolute size of these costs. For my discussion here issues of returns to scale are irrelevant. A Cobb-Douglas production function makes most sense when the analysis is at an aggregate level, while there is also support for the use of this function at a disaggregate level (e.g., Gurbaxani *et al.* 2000). Given the nature of the exogenous variables involved, there is no point in assuming constant elasticities of substitution and hence adopt a CES production function. The

Cobb-Douglass production function is the most readily interpretable production function and is used most often in the literature (cf. Audretsch 1998). The suggested Cobb-Douglass production function primarily provides a heuristic tool here. Nonetheless, it seems plausible to assume that total output, q, increases as a given population exchanges its information more readily. At any moment (t), a community of size (n)[5] will experience a social welfare (q) generated by communication that can be represented as:

$$q_t = A \left(\frac{n_t}{s_t} \right)^{\alpha} \left(\frac{1}{tr_t} \right)^{\beta} \left(\frac{n_t - 1}{d_t} \right)^{\gamma} \qquad \text{(Eq. 8.1)}$$

Where: $0 < \alpha, \beta, \text{ en } \gamma < 1$; $n \gg 1$; and s_t, tr_t, and $d_t > 0$[6]

In this equation A is the well-known efficiency parameter. The concrete shape of the production function makes economic sense. A rise in any of the communication costs will hamper economic activity and thus economic welfare – for this reason communication costs are shown as the denominator in the equation.

It seems obvious to assume that an increase in any of the three communication costs will negatively affect social welfare. Hence indicating why these costs should be the denominator. Decoding communicated messages is proportional to the size of a population, but needs only to be done by the receiver of a message. On this Dudley further remarks that:

> the efficiency of markets depends on people's ability to negotiate and enforce contracts, output is decreasing in the cost, d, of decoding a unit of information. Owing to network effects, this transaction cost is offset by increases in the number of other people, n_{t-1}, with whom each individual can communicate.
>
> (Dudley 1999: 602)

Due to the impact of knowledge on productivity and output, q increases with the amount of information stored. The relationship between q and storage cost (s) is inverse under competitive market conditions in particular. There is, furthermore, a direct link between the size of a population and the storage costs that need to be incurred. Transmission costs, tr, are not directly related to the size of a population; depending on circumstances (costs), a population of a given size can transmit knowledge extensively. However, if there are scale economies to joint production, for example because (co-) workers or partners need to be coordinated, increases in transmission costs will decrease q.

Usually, in reality, any development that affects one type of communication cost is likely also to affect other communication costs. A dynamic welfare perspective, for which some suggestions are brought forward in these pages, might suggest policy measures that violate the Pareto criterion. This would then be for different reasons than possible violations of the Pareto criterion as proffered by Pigou. Pigou also suggests that an income re-distribution from rich to the poor would be justifiable because that would allow 'more intense wants to be satisfied' (Pigou 1924: 78). Indeed, for the dynamic welfare perspective suggested here, utilitarian considerations play a less prominent role than in the Paretian view. How the suggested dynamic and the Schumpeterian welfare perspective suggested here fits in Cowen's classification introduced at the start of this section is not clear. I would not present this approach as necessarily incompatible with the other three kinds, including a Paretian one.

8.4 INTELLECTUAL PROPERTY RIGHTS

Intellectual objects are non-exclusive: consumption or use by non-payers cannot be excluded. In addition, intellectual objects are partly non-rivalrous also as they are not consumed by their use. This makes intellectual objects (quasi-)public goods, giving governments a reason to influence relevant processes in society. As the costs of imitating or communicating intellectual objects tend to be low, there may be a tendency for these to be under-produced (Nelson 1959; Romer 2002). IPRs would provide a way to compensate creative individuals that saves on transactions costs by stipulating that the commercial use of knowledge is exclusive to the right-holder. Discussion of the need for IPRs has waxed and waned (Towse and Holzhauer 2002). Notwithstanding such discussions, the scope and duration of IPRs has increased steadily over time.

Rationales for IPRs fall into four, partly related, categories (Hettinger 1989). The extent to which rationales are stressed in law differs between countries, reflected in the authority that administers them. In the UK and the US, the incentive for creative individuals or organizations that IPRs offer is emphasized: development and diffusion of new knowledge is promoted by the prospect of a period of time in which one is able to commercially exploit the innovation.[7] Relatedly, IPRs are said to be necessary for firms to entice them to invest in facilities for the production of goods based on the intellectual object protected under IPRs. Without it, firms would face more than the usual business risk and refrain from the production of such goods. In the UK and the US, these are the rationales emphasized, and this is reflected in the fact that the Commerce Department administers such rights. The two other rationales are not related to such utilitarian considerations and are specifically emphasized in the legal systems of continental Europe (and those based on, or influenced by, them). The first is one of desert. If someone has produced an intellectual object, they deserves some kind, and measure of, reward. The final rationale is a personal/moral one. In creating an intellectual object, someone expresses one's personality.[8]

Over time, the first and second rationales have become increasingly dominant in discussions. Philosopher John Locke's argument in his *Second Treatise of Civil Government* (1690) for a 'natural' property right in what one makes has a strong intuitive appeal. In reality, however, it is a government that creates and polices IPRs; they are a socially created privilege. Intellectual objects differ from physical ones. In their creation, for instance, one draws on work done (by others) in the past; creation is not *de novo*. When use of existing work is restricted, society may be hurt. As intellectual objects are public goods, granting a (temporary) monopoly on their commercial exploitation may not leave 'enough and as good'.[9] Independent inventors are hurt as they may be prohibited from using something they have developed themselves but another party was granted a patent for earlier. It is further argued that intellectual objects are, more often than physical ones, the result of cooperation – a cooperation that may or may not be promoted by IPRs.

This Chapter does not call into question the need for a system of IPRs per se, yet it does elaborate on criticisms of it for possible hampering of future economic development even for developed economies. The IPR system also presents immanent problems, especially for developing countries. The immanent problems referred to relate to the consequences of the system of IPRs for the distribution of national incomes within and among countries. In order to reap the benefits believed to result from joining consecutive rounds of negotiations to liberalize international trade, developing countries have had to accept World Trade Organization (WTO) standards for IPRs. The remainder of the chapter proceeds as follows. Firstly developments particularly in copyrights and patents are presented and discussed from the perspectives and angles developed so far and secondly, the patent system, is discussed, particularly with a view to the effects of patents for developing countries.

8.5   IPRS, KNOWLEDGE DEVELOPMENT AND WELFARE

IPRs are central institutions in a knowledge economy. The relevant legal and technological changes are easily identified, even though not all of their effects are clear. Evaluating developments in IPRs from a perspective of their effects on the dynamics of an economy is entirely appropriate given the objectives for this part of the system of law. Indeed, the purpose of establishing IPRs is twofold: firstly to stimulate the creation of new (useful) knowledge, and, secondly, to stimulate its dissemination. As Levin *et al.* (1987) observed, however, the positive effects of the presence and extension of IPRs is often assumed to be self-evident. IPRs are believed to be beneficial for both the firm that has obtained them, as well as for society as a whole. There is, of course, some discussion in academic circles about the effects of IPRs and how to evaluate these (cf. Towse and Holzhauer 2002), but these are mostly in comparative-static Paretian terms. The duration and scope of patents is one such a topic. Even from this perspective, a disregard of IPRs need not hurt the innovating firm. Other means to protect ones innovations might be preferred (Levin *et al.* 1987), or network effects may come into effect in urging the innovating firm to enforce its IPR position less (Takeyama 1994).

In what follows, I will discuss a number of changes in particularly with regard to patent law and copyright law in terms of their effects on communication costs. The changes I discuss are not exhaustive, although they do include the most significant ones. Each of the changes in IPRs discussed will have effects on all of the three communication costs. The breadth of the system of IPRs has grown over time, both by adding new IPRs, such as the law protecting legal rights in databases, or by extending existing laws, such as allowing for the protection under patent law of software or business models. In addition, the (statutory) limitations on the commercial exploitation of the knowledge developed, have decreased in number. This is no mixed picture: IPRs have grown stronger over time, especially in the past decade where a number of noteworthy developments can be mentioned. Often, the development in the United States is followed by changes in Europe. In this article, the differences between the two legal systems (US and Europe) are not so much discussed, as the similarities between the two. The purpose of the discussion here is thus to evaluate the potential effects of changes to a system of IPRs and not so much an analysis of the systems as they exist in a way that is relevant for economists.[10] In doing so, attention will be drawn to elements that are un- or undernoticed from a more standard welfare approach. From this perspective, too, the undesirable effects of IPRs in general, and patents in particular, have been noted. It is argued, for instance, to possibly distort the direction of technological change (Adams and Encaoua 1994), possibly slow down technological progress (Takalo and Kanniainen 2000), or possibly reduce incentives to compete in R&D or in downstream product markets (Encaoua and Hollander 2002). To reiterate, the discussion here about the dynamic welfare effects of changes in IPRs need not be perceived of as a substitute for a more mainstream economic, Paretian approach.

Following the US, Europe is now considering that software can be protected under patent law in addition to copyright law, under which it would be protected previously. The protection patent law offers is shorter than copyright law, but is more powerful.[11] Copyright law protects the particular expression of an idea, while patent law protects the idea itself irrespective of the way in which it is expressed. As ideas can usually be expressed in more than one way, copyrights offer a weaker kind of protection than patents do. Copyrights do not need to be registered in most countries, albeit that registration may facilitate enforcement in some cases, and is in force immediately after publication of the material. A patent needs to be filed and approved, involving a variety of expenses.[12]

The scope of patent law is currently being hotly debated, both in the US and Europe, in relation to the question of whether business models and software should be patentable in Europe as it is in the US. Does Amazon.com's patent for 'one-click shopping' not violate the requirement that a patent should involve a physical component and must involve an inventive step? It is true that software is often not clearly distinguishable from hardware, and the demand that a patent application needs to constitute an inventive step might be difficult to uphold. Reneging on these requirements too easily might, however, give rise to rent-seeking behaviour on the part of the producing firms. However, in this case, only software is involved, and the software ('cookies') had already been developed prior to the application by others. The particular business model is a useful invention, to be sure, but does it not unduly raise communication costs? Certainly it does for other firms who would like to use this method and now have to license it. In addition, the model also allows firms to increase the extent to which they may differentiate their products and discriminate on price. The net result of the latter is likely to be that consumers suffer (Dolfsma 2004). The decision to extend the scope of patents to include living tissue is also contested. Besides the moral aspects of the debate, there is the issue that the distinction between discovering and inventing, never entirely clear, is blurred to the extent that it no longer exists. The latter (invention) used to be a precondition for a patent to be granted. The ability to patent living tissue might, but need not, have speeded up the discovery of the exact shape of the human genome, for instance, but it will severely restrict the use to which that knowledge can be put for the coming years.

The duration of patents has increased too, most recently (1998) from eighteen to twenty years in the US. The lengthening of the patent for pharmaceutical products is probably less problematic in this light, given the requirements these face before they are allowed on the market, although it does fit the general picture. Fisher (2001) provides a more extended discussion of the development in patent law and its effects on innovative activity.

Copyrights are equally extended in scope and duration; legal scholar Lawrence Lessig (1999, 2001) is among the more prominent people to lament this develop-ment.[13] Most recently, the duration of copyrights in the US was lengthened from the life of the author plus fifty years to the life of the author plus seventy years, effective retrospectively. Several years ago, both the US and Europe started protecting databases as part of copyright laws. In the past, a collection of 'brute facts' would not constitute a creative act and would thus not warrant protection, now a database is protected (Maurer *et al.* 2001). The American Digital Milennium Copyright Act (DMCA), which came into force 1998, as well as the European Directive on Copyright (2000) prohibit agents from making available technical measures that might be used to circumvent measures taken to protect copyrighted work (Koelman 2000). As these means can often also be used for other, legitimate purposes, this element of the new copyright law is much debated. It is also unclear what 'making available' means: does a scientist in the field of, cryptology, for example, presenting his work to fellow scientists make available a means to circumvent the technical protection (encryption) of copyrighted work? Encryption is also used to prevent consumers from making copies of work to be used in different regions of the world than their own. The world is divided into regions that each has different hardware specification, that prevents software from one region being recognized in another.[14] The cost to soci-ety seems evident as consumers are restricted in the consumption of something they have legally obtained (Dunt *et al.* 2002). Encryption is also being used to prevent consumers from playing a CD on a personal computer, making a copy for personal use or to share with family and close friends, or as a back-up. This increases storage costs especially.

The tendency to strengthen the protection offered by copyright law is also clear in the way in which it is enforced. A law can never spell out exactly how it should be applied, and perhaps, as a matter of principle, it should not. Therefore, when applying the law, judges have room for their own interpretation. This is certainly the case in a Roman Law system but also applies in a Common Law system, where the leeway for a judge looking at a specific case is more limited by rulings given in other, similar cases. Considerations about the effect of enforcing copyrights for competition in a market are rarely aired – the different fields of law are quite separated even when one sees them conflict in reality, such as IPR clashing with anti-trust law (Encaoua and Hollander 2002; Dolfsma 2002). An example is the ruling on Napster, where what is called in legal terms 'normal exploitation' of a work is extended to the full exploitation, covering the publication of a work in ways that were not foreseen at the time of the creation. Walt Disney could not have foreseen that his creation Mickey Mouse (formerly known as Steamboat Willey) would be published digitally and distributed over the Internet. Now this existing work is also protected under copyright law from distribution over the Internet. In actual fact, there is another catch to this court case against Napster. The court decided that existing players should first be allowed to develop a means by which to make music available in digital form legally, without limiting the time they could take.[15] Copyright law is now no longer just a de facto entry barrier preventing possible entrants from moving into this market, it is a de jure one. How this constitutes an incentive for innovation is difficult to conceive. The tension between copyright law and anti-trust law thus mounts.

The developments listed above restrict the use of a legally acquired work by a consumer. Either directly or indirectly the limitation built into copyright law of 'fair use' is restricted by a combination of legal and technical means.[16] At present, legal and technical developments are thus under way to make a 'strong' system of digital rights management (DRM) possible for copyright law. In addition to a strict enforcement of a strengthened copyright law, techniques such as encryption are required. The circumvention of the latter needs then to be prohibited by law as well. Even when these requirements are met, the question is raised whether such a development would increase communication cost to the extent that the public interest would be hurt, either directly or indirectly.

Relating the discussion about the development of IPRs to the different kinds of communications costs introduced earlier is quite straightforward. Indeed, communication costs increase in relative terms as a result of the full-scale application of IPRs to the knowledge economy, a result further supported by the developments in the system of IPR itself. Decoding costs rise as a result of the technical measures to prevent copyrighted works from being copied, used in certain electronic equipment, or outside certain geographical boundaries. One therefore needs to acquire more information carriers than one would otherwise. Using available knowledge will become more expensive when the scope and duration of IPRs expand – this basically relates to direct transmission costs (licenses), but also to costs that need to be borne to find out if one tries to discover one would be violating another party's legal rights (Lessig 2001). As the development of knowledge is necessarily cumulative, such costs may be high, and having to incur such costs will not be a stimulus for innovation. Storage costs rise as a consequence and the fact that transmission costs rise seems clear, certainly when discussing developments in the area of copyrights. For copyright law two central notions come into play: publishing and copying. Transmitting knowledge, either using an existing channel or using a new way of publishing material, becomes more expensive due to the developments discussed as the right holders' position has become stronger over the years. A right holder can refuse to publish a work through a new means of communication. More kinds of works are protected, while the number of limitations to a legal position has been restricted, thus increasing transmission costs. This holds for transmission of knowledge protected under patent law as well, as circumstances under which a party would need to take a license proliferate. Unless the authorities impose a compulsory license when the public interest would demand it, the right holder can prevent the use by others of a particular piece of knowledge, implying a steep increase in transmission costs.

8.6 IPRS AND DEVELOPING COUNTRIES: PATENTS

Under current circumstances knowledge and innovation play an increasingly significant role in the economy (Foray and Lundvall 1996; Cowan, David and Foray 2000; Cooke 2002; Dolfsma and Soete 2006). In the year 2000, some $142 billion in royalties were paid internationally by users of specific pieces of knowledge that were protected under Intellectual Property Right law (IPR) to those parties that owned these rights.[17] IPRs have become increasingly prominent in debates and are almost unanimously deemed to favour economic development by policymakers, and certainly by policymakers in developed countries. While it has been acknowledged that some parties may benefit more from a system of IPRs than others, in relative terms a Pareto improvement is the expected outcome (Langford 1997). This has not always been the case. In addition, the academic (economic) community is almost unanimous about the system of IPR overshooting its goals.[18] This has been the motivation to include IPRs in the WTO negotiations that, in 1994, resulted in the TRIPS agreement (Trade-Related Aspects of Intellectual Property Rights). The number of patents granted has grown tremendously, in particular during the 1990s, despite the fact that many a scholar still supports Machlup's conclusion that:

> it would be irresponsible, on the basis of our present knowledge of its consequences, to recommend instituting one. But since we have had a patent system for a long time, it would be irresponsible, on the basis of our present knowledge, to recommend abolishing it.
>
> (Machlup 1958: 28)

From other corners, where specific effects of IPRs are considered, a different and less circumspect sound may be heard. Examples of this are attempts to make available HIV/AIDS drugs at a reduced price compared to what the pharmaceutical companies, that hold the patents on these drugs, demand.[19]

Some Remarks on the Practice of Patenting

While one may quarrel about the theory that supports a system of IPRs in general, and patents in particular, there is also the practice of filing, evaluating and granting. This practice differs between countries, with effects for the firms involved (OECD 1997). While most countries maintain a 'first-to-file' policy, the US maintains a 'first-to-invent' policy. This difference has major consequences for strategic behaviour of firms seeking patents under the different regimes. Another difference is between the scope of the claim staked in a patent. In Japan, for instance, the claim must be much more narrowly defined than in the US. A broad claim in a patent is a stronger claim in a pre-emptive action than a narrow claim is. There are also features about patent systems in general that have been lamented. Some point to the granting of patents that obviously do not meet the criteria for patents: patents have been given for technology that had already been developed, for technology that had no industrial application or physical component, &c. Others, in contrast, point to the losses in terms of forgone license payments due to poor IPR law and/or poor protection.

The expansion in both scope and length has been criticized for representing 'a new stage in commodification', 'corrupting society' 'destructing productivity' (Perelman 2003). In recent years, plant variety rights have been strengthened, business models and software have come to be protected under patent law. The number of patent applications has risen by an annual six per cent since 1990 to total 350,000 a year; 190,000 are awarded, half of which are to non-US firms.[20] In 2003, a backlog of 500,000 applications was reported. The US Patent Office is now receiving its income from parties that have been awarded a patent – no incentive to diligently search for 'prior art' and determine whether an application meets the criteria. The burden of proof seems to be on the side of the USPTO to prove that a patent application is *not* to be granted. Indeed, half of all patents that were apparently important enough to be litigated were found to be invalid. Only twenty three per cent of new drugs developed provide therapeutic benefit over existing drugs (Hubbard and Love 2004) – a notable figure for an industry that relies heavily on patents (Levin *et al.* 1987; Arundel 2001). A mere one per cent is spent on 'neglected diseases.'

Baumol (2002) has estimated that twenty per cent of the benefits associated with an invention are appropriated by the parties directly *or* indirectly involved with the invention. Only partly will the appropriation of benefits be due to IPRs. Patents offer no certainty of appropriating market rents. Many will not have economic value; increasing numbers have very little technical value. Of all US patents granted, fifty five to seventy five per cent lapse for failure to pay maintenance fees; if litigation against a patent's validity is a sign of commercial value of that patent, the fact that only 1.5 per cent of patents are litigated, and only 0.1 per cent litigated to trial, does not bode well (Lemley and Shapiro 2005).

'Even' mainstream economic literature has argued at length and in great detail the drawbacks and pitfalls of current IPR law, and developments therein. Let me discuss the most important findings.

Empirical and theoretical findings bearing on the question of IPRs' effect on technological development, and thus prospect for economic development, are reviewed. Static and dynamic effects are distinguished. Areas where static effects may be expected include transfer of knowledge, balance of payment effects, effects for large as opposed to small firms, and effect on the 'extent of the market'. Areas for dynamic effects include technological development and technological preemption.[21] The list may not be exhaustive, and effects are interlocking: they may be mutually reinforcing or they may conflict. I will mostly focus on 'dynamic' effects.

Static Effects of IPRs

It is becoming increasingly difficult for developing countries to ignore IPR policies. Only when a country has a sufficiently attractive internal market and/or has a sufficiently strong research tradition itself will it be able to negotiate on an equal footing. China, India and Brazil are examples of countries that are able to credibly use the threat of drawing on the compulsory license clause in TRIPS to make right holders lower the price of the products they offer. Particularly if the product and its uses can draw a lot of attention in the media – as in the case of HIV/AIDS medication – such an approach may be successful.

If a country offers protection of IPRs that is perceived as too weak, Foreign Direct Investments (FDI) might suffer and exports of products that embody new technology might be lower to for fear of such products being re-imported. Although not in the spirit of the WTO, parallel imports of IPRs, or products embodying protected rights are forbidden, thus setting boundaries to the 'extent of the market'. In legal terms, IPRs exhaust nationally not internationally. This has the effect of driving up market prices, obviously, as market structure and competitive relations are affected (Klaes 1997). Alternatives to any product may exist that draw on technology that is not patented, or that a second firm owns the patent for. Demand elasticity and pricing regulations are other elements that might affect prices. Administrative price ceilings – allowed under TRIPS – are a common strategy of developing countries. These may not prompt foreign patent-owning firms to supply countries that have such measures in the first place. As ceilings tend to be based on a cost-plus formula, there is an incentive for supplying firms to inflate transfer prices. A ceiling in any particular (developed) country might also be indexed to prices in other (developing) markets. There is thus an incentive to negotiate high prices in index-countries such as India.

Dynamic Effects of IPRs

Patents may raise incentives for R&D in neglected areas of technology. Yet, it may not lead to such investments, and might thus be said to have perverse effects. Overly stringent protection might lead to more resources being devoted to IP management (Langford 1997): technology transfer cost may well increase. Overly stringent protection offered by patents (and other IPRs) may also lead to wasteful research spending such as patent races and the construction of patent portfolios. Levin *et al.* (1987) and Arundel (2001) have found that patents are not seen by firms as the most important way to appropriate the benefits of their innovative efforts: secrecy, lead time and complementary capabilities are. Certainly this holds for smaller firms. In a classical study, Mansfield (1986) suggests that in most industries firms seek patents mostly for strategic reasons.

Having a patent can lead a firm to delay products based on it, as competing firms may not be able to offer alternatives (Takalo and Kanniainen 2000). Although the monopoly awarded by a patent or any kind of IPR is never perfect, it may well induce a firm to consciously forgo the development of a new technology that would be socially more desirable – it may for instance develop a technologically inferior technology that yields it higher profits (Adams and Encaoua 1994). Another dynamic effect may be that research effort may shift from areas where IPRs are less extensive and not as strictly enforced to areas where they are (Langford 1997). Firms are deterred from trying to invent 'in the neighbourhood' of patents granted previously, including undertaking follow-up inventive work (Mazzoleni and Nelson 1998; Scotchmer and Green 1990). This holds particularly where the technology involved is 'complex' and its development cumulative: much research as well as development is highly cumulative in nature.[22] In a patent race, an incumbent might want to maintain its position by preempting entry rather than developing technology (Harris and Vickers 1985). If an incumbent does obtain a patent it may not be a valuable one in an economic or a technical sense (Gilbert and Newbery 1982).

For complex technologies whose development is highly cumulative, where economies of scale are substantial, and given additional means to appropriate the benefits of innovation, the extent to which agents in developing countries can imitate is limited, whether they would like to imitate or not. In such cases, a tightening of IPR will actually hurt the developed countries as product lines will shift to or remain in these countries (Helpman 1993). Cost advantages of production in developing, assuming such advantages would benefit consumers, would favour the developed countries. A tighter IPR regime in case of a slow imitation pace hurts developed countries in general, even though it may benefit producers of the goods involved. When imitation rates are high, a tighter IPR regime will benefit developed countries but certainly not developing countries – it is under these circumstances that the general interest of the two groups of countries conflict.[23]

Pooling of patents may be efficient, but it certainly also constitutes an entry barrier and is disadvantageous for smaller firms (Lanjouw and Schankermann 2004).[24] Litigation costs can be so inhibiting that individual and small firm patent holders strike a deal with a large firm that filed a suit even when, on legal grounds, they would have a strong case; listed firms have lower filing rates (ibid.). Small firms have been found not to pursue innovative paths where the threat of a law suit by a larger firm is high (Lerner 1995). Rent seeking may thus have an effect not just on the application of new technology, but on the kind of new technology that firms seek to develop.

Certainly, then, there is a tension, in general, between anti-trust law and IP law. Surely, too, there is a possible tension between IPR and development, especially in the early phases of economic development.

Developed countries stand to gain most from liberalizing the trade in IPRs with protection levels and scopes determined as they are in these countries, specifically in industries where imitation can be rapid and thus the benefits of diffusion are substantial. Mazzoleni and Nelson (1998) argue that the US has pushed TRIPS most adamantly, attributing its zeal to self-interest as well as an 'honest believe'.

That zeal has not always been there. The US and other countries that now have developed economies have been haphazard in implementing and enforcing IPRs when they were not yet so relatively developed themselves. Had Japan done so with regard to patents, it might not have had its strong electronics industry (Mazzoleni and Nelson 1998). Had the US done so with regard to copyrights, it might not have had its strength in the entertainment industry that it now has.[25]

So, what should be done to prevent the system of IPRs from being hijacked by larger firms particularly for strategic purposes? Raising standards for obtaining patents, aligning incentives of patent officers with those of the general interest, and making sure that incentives to initial inventors are more clearly and evenly weighed against incentives for follow-on innovators (Barton 2000) is not enough. Narrowing the scope of patents is one option, shortening the duration of (some) patents is another. Differentiating between patents covering different areas has been suggested by Bill Gates. In addition, anti-trust policy should be as zealously pursued at the global level as IPRs are at the moment by such organizations as World Intellectual Property Organization (WIPO) and WTO. Such an organization could focus in particular on the effects for technological development in or technology transfer to developing countries.

There are other suggestions. First, to phase in a system where innovation is stimulated by (optionally) rewarding innovators. This system is superior to the IPR system under a range of circumstances (Shavell and van Ypersele 2001; Wright 1983). Veblen's spirit of workmanship can be trusted to some extent to produce new and useful technology even without direct monetary reward – the application of the idea of open source development proves this case. Direct monetary reward can decrease people's efforts to reach a specific goal as much as it can stimulate them (Le Grand 2003).[26]

8.7 IPRS, AND SOCIAL WELFARE

Considering this discussion of the development of IPRs in light of the proposed dynamic welfare perspective developed in an earlier session, one could claim along with Stiglitz (1999: 9) that 'it is possible that an excessively "strong" intellectual property regime may actually inhibit the pace of innovation', and slow the pace of economic development. Such a conclusion hinges, of course, on the correct interpretation of the effects of developments in IPRs in terms of communication costs on innovative activity.

A knowledge-based economy needs a welfare theory that is able to grasp and evaluate its dynamics. I have taken suggestions from Schumpeter for a dynamic welfare economics and developed some ideas for a dynamic (Schumpeterian) welfare economics. These ideas acknowledge the role of (increases in the) knowledge (base) for an economy. Distinguishing storage, decoding and transmission costs related to communication of knowledge I indicate that an increase in one will lower social welfare. Recent developments in IPR can be evaluated in such dynamic welfare terms, suggesting that the strengthening of IPRs is debatable from the perspective of the public interest. As knowledge develops cumulatively in direct interactions between people, and is not simply available off the shelf where it winds up like manna from heaven to be put to use freely, the costs of communication have a strong impact on the diffusion of knowledge and the social welfare of a country. The changes in IPRs we are experiencing now increase the costs of communication and could therefore be a potential impediment for the dynamics of the economy and for social welfare. The conclusion drawn by Romer (1993: 66) that an economics of ideas requires 'a policy of openness with few distortions' would thus find support in the analysis staged here.

Economists would be interested in the effects of such developments on competition in a market too (Boldrin and Levine 2002; Romer 2002). These effects are not always clear, and can perhaps be illustrated best by referring to the case of the music industry and the role copyrights play.[27] A legal system's geographical boundaries are important to keep in mind – at least until a complete harmonization on all issues is realized across the globe. The geographical basis of copyright law is a de facto restriction of the relevant market, allowing firms to monitor each other's behaviour closely – indeed a game-theoretic analysis shows that collusion is likely to occur (Klaes 1997). In the oligopolistic market such as this one is, the outcome is an absence of competition on price (cf. Selten 1973).

It is Baumol (2002) who has argued forcefully that competition in a free market is to be regarded as the main cause for economic growth. His explanation is the creation, but most importantly the diffusion of, knowledge that is best facilitated by the free market (see also Mokyr 2002). According to calculations by Baumol (2002), eighty per cent of the economic benefits generated by innovations do not accrue to the parties directly or indirectly involved with the innovation. Extending the scope and duration of IPR should decrease that percentage in the conviction that creation of new knowledge is thus stimulated. This is premised on a number of beliefs that need not be true. These (often incorrect or incomplete) include:

- Innovators are motivated by monetary / material rewards only;[28]
- Creative individuals possess the rights in their creations and will thus receive the reward;
- IPRs are the best means to reward creative individuals materially;[29]

- It is always, or at least in most cases, in the best interests of rights holders to diffuse the knowledge (or the products which embody them) as much as possible once they have obtained IPR protection.

The latter issue about the inclination to diffuse newly developed knowledge, stimulated by the system of IPRs, relates to the matter of what circumstances stimulate economic growth. Does allowing innovators a larger share of the economic pie stimulate innovation and economic growth such that in absolute (even if not in relative) terms, everybody's pie is larger, or is it a zero-sum game? The matter relates directly to a governments' goal of the public good and if that is best served by enforcing IPRs. The argument as suggested above particularly is that the dynamic effects are more important in such considerations than the static, distributive ones.

How may one evaluate the developments in a set of institutions that may be considered among the more important for a knowledge economy from the perspective of a dynamic (Schumpeterian) welfare theory? As knowledge is often communicated as information, the characteristics of information goods are important to note. The well-known characteristics of such goods and the markets in which they are exchanged (Dolfsma 1998) entail that a full scale application of IPRs in a knowledge economy is itself a de facto strengthening of IPRs, and certainly to the extent that the knowledge economy is a digital one (Stiglitz 1999). Stiglitz (1999: 10) holds that information goods generate more positive externalities than physical goods. While the social returns to innovation are much bigger than the private ones in general (Jones and Williams 1998), the creation of new information goods (knowledge) would in this line of reasoning serve the public interest even more. In terms of the relation between the public and the private realm, the latter expands because of this.

9   Concluding remarks

The phenomenon of the 'knowledge economy' has drawn quite a bit of attention, from policy makers to scholars of different feathers. There is a broad understanding that knowledge has always played an important role in the economy and that Hayek's (1945) key insight in this respect is as valid as ever. One should remember, however, that Hayek saw his focus on the role of knowledge in light of what is now referred to as the Socialist Calculation Debate: is a central organization able to coordinate production such that the waste and duplication sometimes superficially association with a market economy can be prevented? Hayek's point was that no such organization could ever be able to do so. Rather, a market economy would most effectively use all the relevant knowledge available in an economy – summarized in the prices quoted in the market.

The most important contribution of this book is not to question this insight concerning the importance for knowledge development and diffusion of incentives by which private parties are led to act, or about the need for self-organizing coordination between actors: far from it. While the market economy may at times seem messy, the very nature of new knowledge implies that there may at times be some need for a visible hand of government, completely substituting the invisible hand, of the market by the visible hand of the government will however be disastrous. If, the conclusion drawn from Hayek's argument is that what economists call the perfect market – where there are an infinite number of suppliers, consumers and homogenous products at a given price – is best suited for the knowledge economy, this should immediately be qualified. While research reported upon by others and elsewhere (compare Dolfsma and Van der Panne 2008) does indicate that private firms, "small and large", may be in a good position to contribute to the knowledge economy, the concern I would like to raise here is a slightly different one. It is also a more general one, not merely restricted to the role of small firms and upstarts in the economy.

Primarily what this book seeks to argue and show is that a knowledge economy hinges crucially on the extent to which actors are willing and able to *cooperate* with each other. The creation of new knowledge, as well as the diffusion of existing knowledge, within the economy so that it may be put to good and productive use depends on cooperation. This insight applies at the level of individuals working in a specific organisation, at the level of firms, as well as at the level of an economy or a field of enquiry. Cooperation does not equal co-ordination, as it requires two or more autonomous and purposeful parties consensually joining forces. To someone who takes Hayek's primary intentions with this key article very seriously, cooperation may be perceived of as the kind of action that would hamper the free and unfettered operation of the market, a breach of anti-trust law perhaps. It is here that the argument of this book may depart from that of scholars thus inspired by Hayek.

Cooperation is essential for the development of new knowledge. For many, this insight is a self-evident truth. For them, the theoretical discussion underscoring this point will be valuable. In addition, they may use, complement and extend the empirical work reported upon here validating this point. Others may still need to be convinced of the importance of cooperation between agents for the knowledge economy. Indeed, there is a widely held popular belief that new knowledge develops due to unique individuals being struck by a sudden lightning of genius, emerging from the experience with ideas fully developed. What is sometimes believed to prevent successful application and subsequent commercial success is the geniuses' clumsy business view. This romantic idea is powerful and persistent, and is reflected not just in wider, popular views, as in the media, but is also reflected in the shape that institutions, directly involved in the knowledge economy, take. While agents involved in the development of new knowledge are certainly not always, or even primarily, concerned about material benefits accruing to them, it is important to consider the sometimes perverse effects that incentive structures, shaped by institutions, have on these agents.

It is true, cooperation may not be easy to reward or otherwise stimulate directly. As Chapter three argues, there is a mixed bag of motives involved in the relations that people entertain, certainly in a context of knowledge development. Self-interest, however, is one, and it is implicated in the kind of exchange of gifts that is at the core of cooperation for new knowledge development. In line with Bourdieu, it is important to emphasize that how gift exchange is institutionalized, what rituals surround it, the scripts of which need to be known and adherred to, matters. The institutions are not merely a fringe phenomenon readily abstracted from when modelling self-interested agents maximizing their material gains.

Chapter four indicates that the reason for cooperation to be central to new knowledge development and diffusion is the paradigmatic nature of its development. While the structure of knowledge paradigms ensure that, prima facie, agents involved in the game will know almost immediately that not all knowledge is relevant, and that they can thus focus on a subset of it, the paradigmatic organisation of knowledge also indicates another truth about knowledge development. Development of new knowledge is literally like standing on the shoulders of giants. Development of new knowledge is impossible without previously developed knowledge, for two reasons. Firstly, it would be inconceivable to imagine that a new piece of knowledge would be developed had previous, relevant knowledge not been developed. What is important, is that the newly developed knowledge builds on, and extends, the previously developed knowledge.

The metaphor of knowledge developing by the actions of agents standing on the shoulders of giants is, however, also important in an immediate and personal sense as chapters five and six in particular convey. In some circumstances, this applies especially, as we are starting to learn. Where knowledge development is rapid and the knowledge being developed is complex, close cooperation is a sine qua non. These two chapters, at a micro and at a meso or regional level, offer insights into *how* this is true, as much as Chapter seven shows how this leads to patterns at a macro level of a knowledge economy as a whole. Some of these patterns are to be expected, some are surprising. However, they relate to the collective expectations that have arisen over the years and they all warrant further explorations.

As the patterns in a knowledge economy are further explored, it becomes clear that the central theme of cooperation in a social community is inevitably, and necessarily, related to characteristics of knowledge that have been understood and analysed in disciplines other than economics. Through exchanges of both a gift and a market nature, and drawing on a shared, institutionalized – ritualized to a degree – past, a frame of reference emerges that allows parties to interact. When development of new knowledge is sought, uncertainty of a cognitive, as well as behavioural, nature may come into play. Such uncertainty may only be dealt with if a shared frame of reference, that is sufficiently 'thick', can be drawn upon. Such a frame of reference indicates how data or information is preferably interpreted and how framing is to occur in a community. By categorizing possible alternative interpretations, a shared frame of reference will allow for more rapid, trusting cooperation. Understanding a 'knowledge economy', as Chapter two has argued, thus requires the acknowledgement that *interpretation* is involved in knowing. Conceptually coming to grips with interpretation entails that economists must un-learn some of their theory of knowledge, and start learning from other disciplines, if some measure of realisticness is to be attained.

These second major propositions lead me to make explicit what the reader will undoubtedly have already understood about the title of this book. The title mentions Knowledge Economies, in the plural. Of course this relates to the different levels at which the knowledge economy can be studied, and is studied in this book. It also relates to the necessity of crossing disciplinary borders. Crossing such borders requires one to at least be able to understand that there can be another perspective of a single phenomenon, and it requires one to sensibly use the concepts offered, combining them fruitfully with other insights. Even a single phenomenon can thus be plural in a way. Finally, the actors studied need not all have the same view of their circumstances. Differing views held by the actors studied by a scholar effect their behaviour and thus may have to be taken into account.

Notes

1 Introduction

1 Intellectual capital protected under patent law or contract law, for instance, or the knowledge in the heads of personnel.

2 Knowledge and learning

1 Capital as a concept used in economics is not clear and unambiguous in its meaning, as for instance the Cambridge capital debates have shown (Harcourt 1969). Kiker (1966) traces historically how capital was used as the metaphor for knowledge in neoclassical economics.

2 Indeed, as Mosselmans (2002) shows, arguing for the beneficial effects of education was a common thing to do in Jevons' time and before. Such arguments, however, sit uneasily within the theoretical framework scholars such as Jevons have developed.

3 See Albert and Ramstad (1997) for a perception of individuals and their behaviour that has inspired institutional type thinking. For a discussion of how institutional economics might theoretically relate 'knowledge' to 'institutions', see Boland (1979).

4 'Noise' is presented in Figure 2.1 by forkings in the different learning paths.

5 Machlup (1980, 1984) does assume the returns to a stock of knowledge to be measurable in terms of money. His point is that different concepts of capital should be used to address different matters. Rather than illuminating the concept of knowledge, however, Machlup seems to undermine the strength of that of capital by making this argument.

6 This distinction does not coincide with the distinction between complete versus incomplete, or perfect versus imperfect knowledge. These distinctions imply that somehow, objectively the full and true nature of knowledge can be determined. What I take as a starting point here is the knowledge people actually have, and how they use it.

7 Cognitive psychology need not be in conflict with a position that leans more towards social psychology. Cognitive psychologists Holland *et al.* (1989), for example, are strongly influenced by developments in artificial intelligence, but nevertheless develop ideas that are compatible with the ones advocated here.

8 See Hansen (1999), for instance, but also chapter 5 below, and similar research.

9 See Saxenian (1994), for instance, but also chapter 6 below.

3 Creating knowledge: Transfer exchange and gifts

1 Cf. proverbs 'never look a gift horse in the mouth', 'never criticize or express displeasure at a gift'.

2 Some have argued that gift exchange may be the only type of exchange to create a commercial product that can be used – open source software being a case in point (Zeitlyn 2003).

3 In line with the discussion in the appendix, generalized reciprocity is a situation in which individual A presents a gift or favour to individual B but is reciprocated by a third individual C making reciprocity indirect or mediated.
4 In line with the discussion in the appendix, direct reciprocity is a situation in which individual A gives to, and is reciprocated by, individual B; in contrast to generalized reciprocity individual B is now personally indebted to individual A (Levi-Strauss 1996, 1969; Ekeh 1974).
5 Appendix I presents a more formalized discussion on this, based on Boulding (1981).
6 The discussion presupposes cardinal utility or an objective determination of value, but, according to Boulding (1962), one can reformulate in terms of ordinal utility or (inter-)subjective value.

4 Development of economic knowledge: Paradigms and new ideas

1 Here, as others do, the concepts of paradigm and regime are used interchangeably. The two may, however, be distinguished (Van den Ende and Dolfsma 2005; Van de Poel *et al.* 2002).
2 See Nelson and Winter (1982) and Rip and Kemp (1998) for examples of the productive use of this approach.
3 Van den Ende and Kemp (1999) on computing technology.
4 All emphases in quotations are in the original unless otherwise noted.
5 Strassman (1993), and Strassman and Polanyi (1995) also argue that the audience of economists is culturally endowed in a particular fashion. Weir (1989) further underscores this point by analyzing the differential acceptance of Keynes' economic views in two contemporary cultures.
6 The 1543 English Act for the Advancement of True Religion forbade reading from the Bible by prentices, husbandmen, labourers, and others. (See Kastan, nd.: 16.)
7 See Leviticus, 25: 8–17, 23–28; Deuteronomy, 23: 20–21.
8 The elements used in defining 'poetic' are drawn from White's (pp. 82–83) discussion of Frye's (1957) views on the relationship of history to myth. McCloskey (1990: 12) speaks of models as the poetics of economics. For more on mathematics and form in economics see McCloskey (1985: 53; 1994: Ch.13), and Knorr Cetina (1991: 108).
9 In this quote Hexter is referring to the comparison of explanation in history to that in the science of physics.
10 Varley *et al.* (2005) even suggest that a different part of the brain is used in mathematical reasoning.
11 Out-of-equilibrium mathematical modeling is undertaken in fields that are, for instance, inspired by systems theory to analyze the 'entropy' that arises in such fields (see Leydesdorff and Fritsch 2006, and references therein).
12 Weintraub (1991: 5) describes this as the attitude that economics has progressed '. . . from a dark and uninformed past to an enlightened and scientifically sophisticated present'.
13 It is found that individuals who are unable to remember past events well are 'markedly impaired relative to matched control subjects at imagining new experiences' (Hassabis *et al.* 2007: 1746).
14 The expression owes to Brush (1974). As Alvin Gardner writes: 'The task of the historian of social theory is not, as is commonly thought, either to celebrate, to bury – or even to merely understand – the past; its task is to discomfort the present' (quoted in Lowry 1991: 136).

5 Knowledge exchange in networks: Within-firm analysis

1 The most accurate way to test H2 and H3 would be on the basis of effect size estimates. As the intra-unit and inter-unit networks are of unequal sizes, effect sizes in

network regression models cannot be calculated. Standardized beta-coefficients are thus compared.

2 In line with Freeman (1979) the degree centrality, C'd, for person i, mediating between persons j and k, is: C'd (n$_i$) = Σ_i a(n$_j$, n$_k$); where i ≠ k, and a(n$_j$, n$_k$) = 1 only if i and p are connected, and 0 otherwise. See also Marsden (2002).

3 Calculated as r = Z/√N (Rosenthal, 1991).

4 Strictly speaking, the category 'No tie' should be included as well as there are 9 ties in the knowledge transfer network without a corresponding tie in the informal or formal network. However, this is likely to be an artefact of the data collection methodology. These ties mostly involve individuals ranked highly in the organization as recipient, who have an extensive network and hence may not report all the ties they entertain in the (in)formal network surveyed.

6 Knowledge exchange between firms: Economic geography of high-tech firms

1 Survey Labour Force / Enquête beroepsbevolking (CBS 1999).

2 Variance Inflation Factors are well below critical levels, indicating that multi-collinearity is absent.

3 As the aggregated level of the Corop region can be assumed to be more economically homogeneous relative to more disaggregated levels of analysis, one would expect agglom-eration effects to show up as a significant factor more strongly when measured on the aggregated Corop level than if a more disaggregated level were chosen. The fact that agglomeration proves not to be a factor even under these circumstances indicates the robustness of these findings.

4 The Gauss-Markov theorem suggests that, under the circumstances, the ordinary-least-squares-method is the most appropriate (best linear unbiased estimator). The detailed nature of the data available – where every Corop region, for instance, has at least one high-tech firm – means that the tobit model estimated earlier on the basis of data provided by Statistics Netherlands (Van der Panne and Dolfsma 2001), does not have to be replicated here.

5 See Kleinknecht (2000) for a discussion of the advantages and disadvantages of dif-ferent ways of measuring innovation.

6 Dutch policy to stimulate innovation is mostly of the generic type, with tax measures playing a significant role (Ministry of Economic Affairs 2002).

7 The knowledge base of an economy: What contributes to its entropy

1 The so-called interaction or configurational information is defined by these authors as the mutual information in three dimensions, but with the opposite sign (McGill 1954; Han 1980).

2 Theil and Fiebig (1984: 12; cf. Frenken 2000: 263; Sahal 1979: 129) defined the mutual information in more dimensions as a straightforward extension of the mutual informa-tion in two dimensions. However, the decomposition of the mutual information in two and three dimensions enables us to account for the configuration of bilateral and trilateral relations in triple helix configurations (Leydesdorff 2003).

3 NACE stands for Nomenclature générale des Activités économiques dans les Communautés Européennes. The NACE code can be translated into the International Standard Industrial Classificiation (ISIC) and in the Dutch national SBI (Standaard Bedrijfsindeling) developed by Statistics Netherlands. The Chambers of Commerce have elaborated this classification into the so-called BIK code (Bedrijfsindeling Kamers van Koophandel). However, these various codes can be translated unambiguously into one another.

4 NUTS stands for Nomenclature des Unités Territoriales Statistiques (Nomenclature of Territorial Units for Statistics). COROP is the abbreviation of the Dutch 'Coordinatiecommissie Regionaal Onderzoeksprogramma'.

5 Laafia (1999) provides maps of Europe with indications of employment rates in high-tech manufacturing sectors and high-tech service sectors respectively. Laafia (2002a) adds relevant figures.

6 Flevoland is the only Dutch province amenable for EU support through the structural funds.

7 The relation between the geometrical metaphor of overlap or overlay and the algorithmic measure of mutual information is not strictly one-to-one, but the metaphor is helpful for the understanding.

8 The standard deviation of this distribution is 80,027.04 with a means of 94,305.7.

9 The value of H for the country corresponds to the mean of the values for the provinces in these dimensions: $\bar{H}_T = 4.088 \pm 0.097$ and $\bar{H}_O = 2.196 \pm 0.065$.

10 These are the regions Delfzijl and Zeeuwsch-Vlaanderen (COROP / NUTS-3 regions 2 and 31).

11 The formula is equally valid for the transmissions because these are based on the probability distributions in the mutual information between two or more probability distributions. The probability distribution in the transmission T_{ab} can be written as the intersect between the distributions for a and b, or in formula format as $\Sigma\, p_T = \Sigma(p_a \text{ AND } p_b)$.

12 More detailed analysis teaches that the provincial structure reduces the uncertainty in the mutual information between the sectoral and the size distribution as two dimensions with −7.79 mbits, while this uncertainty is reduced with − 20.06 mbits by the finer-grained structure of COROP regions. Unlike the effect on the mutual information in three dimensions, these reductions of the uncertainty at the NUTS-2 and the NUTS-3 levels are independent of the distribution of postal codes (since specified at these higher levels of aggregation).

13 The correlation between the contributions ΔT and the number of firms is high and significant both in the case of analysis at the NUTS-2 level ($r = 0.872$; $p < 0.01$) and the NUTS-3 level ($r = 0.801$; $p < 0.01$).

14 Only in COROP / NUTS-3 region 18 (North-Holland North) the value of the mutual information in three dimensions is more negative when zooming in on the knowledge-intensive services. However, this region is predominantly rural.

15 at http://www.europarl.eu.int/summits/lis1_en.htm#b

8 A dynamic welfare perspective for the knowledge economy

1 Casson (1997: 279) argues that transaction costs are a special case of communication costs. His is a plausible argument that needs to be pursued further, but will not be undertaken here.

2 Mokyr (2002) seems to combine these in his category of 'access costs'.

3 In addition, as Levinthal (1998) has argued, technologies (knowledge) are often perceived as radically new when introduced in a certain context (community) from another context where it had been developing incrementally.

4 For the sake of clarity, I assume that communication costs is a binary variable; it is either 'high' or 'low'.

5 A community need not be country, and is perceived here as relatively homogenous in terms of the cognitive distance (Nooteboom 2000) of its members towards each other and in terms of the knowledge that is tacit.

6 Therefore, this production function is strictly quasi-concave, while its isoquants are negatively sloped and strictly convex.

7 This rationale is founded in John Locke's argument for property rights in general. In his view, a person establishes a right of property in that with which she 'mixes her

labor', provided that 'enough and as good [is] left in common for others'. The later proviso has, as might be expected, provoked discussion.

8 The product of the mind is part of the self, so to speak. A result of this is that copyrights in a European context include so-called 'moral' rights. These are inalienable, non-transferable. Even when a piece protected under copyright law is sold, the new owner may not alter it without the consent of the author.

9 This would hold particularly in the case of patents as they protect the idea itself (and not the particular way in which an idea is expressed as is the case for copyrights) from being used without the permission of, and possible payment to, the rights holder. Copyright protection does tend to last longer (life of the author plus seventy years) than the protection patents offer (Twenty years in most cases).

10 See Raskind (1998) and Kitch (1998). For a broad overview, see Towse and Holzhauer (2002). For a theoretical economic justification for copyrights, see Landes and Posner (1989); Hettinger (1989) provides a broader discussion of the rationales for copyrights.

11 In 1998 in the US the duration copyrights last has increased from life of the author plus fifty years to life of the author plus seventy years, effective immediate. In that same year, again following Europe's example, the duration of patents has increased to twenty years, from seventeen years, in the US.

12 OECD (1997) discusses some of the differences in the way in which patents are administered in the US versus Europe, as well as their implications.

13 His is not a unique position among legal scholars (see Netanel 1996 a.o.) or among economists see the collection edited by Towse and Holzhauer 2002; in addition, see Stiglitz (1999) and Schmidt *et al.* (2007).

14 There are 6 regions (Dunt *et al.* 2002). These are: (1) USA, Canada and US territories; (2) Japan, Europe, South Africa and Middle East; (3) South-East Asia; (4) Autralia, New Zealand, PNG, Pacific Islands, Central and South America; (5) Africa, Russia, Former Russian States, North Korea, East Asia; (6) China & Tibet.

15 Court of Appeals for the Ninth Circuit, A&M records, INC. vs. Napster, INC; see Dolfsma (2002).

16 For a discussion of the US 'fair use' principle (fair dealing in the UK), and its relation to similar limitations in continental European law – in the Roman Law tradition – see Alberdingk Thijm (1998). In brief, where the US proposes a procedure in continental Europe (the Netherlands) an exhaustive list of uses that copyright does not prohibit is drawn up. How computer codes (software) can have effects on use that are in fact legal is discussed by Lessig (1999). Guibault (2002) discusses how contract law is used to obviate the limitations present in copyright so as to allow for an extended legal protection.

17 Intellectual Property Rights include patents (utility, design and plant), copyrights, and trademarks. 'Intellectual property rights are the rights given to persons over the creations of their minds'.

18 Legal scholars are clear on this as well. Oddi (1987) offers an early discussion on the effects of IPRs on the prospects for development of Third World countries.

19 Some firms, including Merck & Co, Bristol-Myers Squibb Co, GlaxoSmithKline PLC and Abbott Laboratories have reduced prices in Africa and Brazil for medication against HIV/AIDS. These firms may be genuinely concerned by the toll of this disease for these countries. They may also be concerned about their reputation, as well as by threats to produce generic variants of the drugs after invoking a compulsory license clause. It is likely that these firms are equally keen to prevent parallel import, in breach of stipulations about national exhaustion in IP law. The WTO-TRIPS agreement places significant restrictions on the ability of developing countries to impose compulsory licenses (Oddi 1987), the bilateral agreements that the US has made with several countries is even more restrictive (Hubbard & Love 2004). Contrast the discussion about HIV/AIDS drugs with the much more mooted discussion about patents on drugs that prevent or cure anthrax or avian influenza. In the former case the USA threatened

to invoke the compulsory license clause against the German manufacturer Bayer who had the patent on the drug to cure anthrax. In the latter case, a larger number of predominantly developed countries are worried about their populations being affected. The Swiss pharmaceutical company Roche owns the patent for, and produces, Tamiflu.

20 The number of patents granted to developing countries, especially to countries in Asia such as India and China, increases rapidly, albeit from a small base (UNCTAD 2005).

21 Including establishment of 'prior art', and bio-prospecting.

22 From the perspective of a legal scholar Oddi (1987: 839) has crucially argued that: 'Patent statutes do not distinguish, and appear to be incapable of distinguishing, those inventions that are patent induced from those that are nonpatent induced'. He holds that there are far less inventions in developing countries that are patent induced.

23 Some of that imitation will result in the creation of new processes and new products, even if only incremental improvements. It is shown that when supply of new innovations is elastic, the best way to induce innovation is through contracts and not through patents. As Wright (1983: 702) argues: 'contracts are best when the research process is most like activities routinely undertaken'.

24 In one of the few studies that can shed some empirical light on this issue, Bittlingmayer (1988) claims that the setting up of a patent pool for the aircraft industry, at the behest of the US government as it was drawn into WWI, certainly ended a paralyzing patent dispute. Bittlingmayer (1988: 248) found no evidence that this patent pool suppressed innovation and provided consumers with an inferior product. What is significant is that the board overseeing the patent pool would not allow any patent granted by the USPTO to enter the pool. Given that patent stacking is an often used strategy, opening up the possibility of creating a patent pool does decrease the possibility of negotiations breaking down (Levin *et al.* 1987).

25 The United States did not allow foreigners to obtain copyrights for a long time (Henn 1954). The first US Copyright Act expressly stated that nothing in the Act should be read to 'prohibit importation or vending, reprinting, or publishing within the United States of any map, chart, book, or books, written, printed or published by any person not a citizen of the United States, in foreign parts' (Post 1998). A similar situation hold for patent law (Oddi 1987).

26 Wright (1983: 704) has shown that contracts, rather than patents, work best to induce innovation when researchers are highly responsive to incentives!

27 Indeed, the existing business model of firms in the music industry is predicated on the existence of copyrights (Huygens *et al.* 2001 and Dolfsma 2000).

28 Hui and Png (2002), or Frey (1997) and Le Grand (2003) for a critical discussion.

29 However, see Shavell and van Ypersele (2001); see Dolfsma (2000) for some information on the actual highly skewed nature of the distribution of royalties among musicians.

References

Abernathy, W. J. and Clark, K. B., 'Innovation: Mapping the Winds of Creative Destruction', *Research Policy*, 14, 1, 1985, pp. 3–22.

Abramowitz, M. and David, P. A., Measuring Performance of Knowledge-Based Economy. In *Employment and Growth in the Knowledge-Based Economy*, OECD Paris 1996, pp. 35–60.

Abramson, N., *Information Theory and Coding*. New York 1963.

Abreu, D., 'On the Theory of Infinitely Repeated Games with Discounting', *Econometrica*, 56, 2, 1988, pp. 383–396.

Adam, F. and Roncevic, B., 'Social Capital: recent debates and research trends', *Social Science Information*, 42, 2, 2003, pp. 155–183.

Adams, J. S., 'Inequity in social exchange', in Berkowitz, L. (ed.), *Advances in experimental social psychology*. New York 1965.

Adams, W. J. and Encaoua, D., 'Distorting the direction of technological change', *European Economic Review*, 38, 1994, pp. 663–673.

Adler, P. and Kwon, S. W., 'Social Capital: The Good, the Bad and the Ugly' in Lesser, E. L. (ed.), *Knowledge and Social Capital: foundations and applications*. Boston 2000.

Adler, P. and Kwon, S. W., 'Social capital: prospects for a new concept', *Academy of Management Review*, 27, 1, 2002, pp. 17–40.

Adler, P. S., 'Market, Hierarchy, and Trust: The Knowledge Economy, and the Future of Capitalism' *Organization Science*, 12, 2, 2001, pp. 215–234.

Adler, P. S. and Borys, B., 'Two types of bureaucracy: Enabling and coercive', *Administrative Science Quarterly*, 41, 1996, pp. 61–89.

Agassi, J., *Science in Flux*. Dordrecht 1975.

Albert, A. and Ramstad, Y., 'The Social Psychological Underpinnings of Commons's Institutional Economics: The Signi. cance of Dewey's *Human Nature and Conduct*', *Journal of Economic Issues*, 31, 4, 1997, pp. 881–916.

Albrecht, T. L. and Ropp, V. A., 'Communicating about Innovation in Networks in Three U.S. Organizations', *Journal of Communication*, 61, 1984, pp. 12–28.

Alchian, A. A., 'Uncertainty, Evolution, and Economic Theory', *Journal of Political Economy*, 58, 1950, pp. 211–221.

Allen, T. J., *Managing the flow of technology*. Cambridge MA 1977.

Allen, T. J., and Cohen, S. I., 'Information Flows in Research and Development Laboratories' *Administrative Science Quarterly*, 14, 1969, pp. 12–19.

Amabile, T., Conti, R., Coon, H., Lazenby, J. and Herron, M., 'Assessing the work environment for creativity', *Academy of Management Journal*, 39, 5, 1996, pp. 1154–1184.

Anderson, P. and Tushman, M. L., 'Managing through cycles of technological change', *Research-Technology Management*, 34, 3, 1991, pp. 26–31.

Anselin, L. and Varga, 'Local Geographic Spillovers between University Research and High Technology Innovations', *Journal of Urban Economics*, 42, 1997, pp. 422–448.

Aquinas, T., *Summa Theologica*, Vol. 2. New York [1270] 1947.

Argote, L., McEvily, W. and Reagans, R., 'Managing Knowledge in Organizations: An Integrative Framework and Review of Emerging Themes', *Management Science*, 49, 2003, pp. 571–582.

Aristotle. *The Works of Aristotle*, in Ross, W. D. (ed.), 'Politica', Vol. X. Oxford 1908, pp. 1256^b25–1257^b20.

Arrow, K. J., 'Methodological Individualism and Social Knowledge', *American Economic Review*, 84, 2, 1994, pp. 1–9.

Arundel, A., 'The relative effectiveness of patents and secrecy for appropriation', *Research Policy*, 30, 2001, pp. 611–624.

Atzema, O. A. L. C., 'Location and local networks of ICT firms in the Netherlands', *Tijdschrift voor Economische en Sociale Geografie*, 92, 3, 2001, pp. 369–378.

Audretsch, D. B., 'Agglomeration and the Location of Innovative Activity', *Oxford Review of Economic Policy*, 14, 2, 1998, pp. 18–29.

Audretsch, D. B. and Feldman, 'R&D spillovers and the geography of innovation and production', *American Economic Review*, 86, 3, 1996, pp. 630–639.

Axelrod, R., *The Evolution of Cooperation*. New York 1984.

Backhouse, R., 'How Should We Approach the History of Economic Thought, Fact, Fiction or Moral Tale?', *Journal of the History of Economic Thought*, 14, 1992, pp. 18–35.

Bandura, A., *Social Learning Theory*. Englewood Cliffs, NJ 1977.

Bandura, A., *Social Foundations of Thought and Action – A Social Cognitive Theory*. Englewood Cliffs, NJ 1986.

Baptista, R. and Swann, 'Do firms in clusters innovate more?', *Research Policy*, 27, 1998, pp. 525–540.

Barton, J. H., 'Reforming the Patent System', *Science*, 287, 5460, 2000, pp. 1933–1934.

Bathelt, H., 'Growth Regimes in Spatial Perspective 1: Innovation, Institutions and Social Systems', *Progress in Human Geography*, 27, 6, 2003, pp. 789–804.

Bathelt, H. and Glückler, J., 'Towards a Relational Economic Geography', *Journal of Economic Geography*, 3, 2, 2003, pp. 117–144.

Baumol, W. J., *The free-market innovation machine: analyzing the growth miracle of capitalism*. Princeton, NJ 2002.

Baumol, W. J. and Quandt, R. E., 'Rules of Thumb and Optimally Imperfect Decisions', *American Economic Review*, 71, 1964, pp. 23–46.

Beals, R., 'Gifting, Reciprocity, Savings and Credit in Peasant Oaxaca', *Southwestern Journal of Anthropology*, 265, 3, 1970, pp. 231–241.

Becker, G. S., *Accounting for Tastes*. Cambridge, MA 1996.

Becker, G. S. and Murphy, K. M., 'A Theory of Rational Addiction', *Journal of Political Economy*, 96, 4, 1988, pp. 675–700.

Belk, R., 'Gift-Giving behavior', in Sheth, J. (ed.), *Research in Marketing Volume 2*. Greenwich, CT 1979.

Belk, R. W. and Coon, G. S., 'Gift Giving as Agapic Love: An Alternative to the exchange paradigm based on dating experiences', *Journal of Consumer Research*, 20, 1993, pp. 393–417.

Bell, M., ' "Learning" and the Accumulation of Industrial Technology Capacity in Developing Countries', in Fransman, M. and King, K. (eds), *Technological Capabilities in the Third World*. Hong Kong 1984, pp. 187–209.

Biddle, J. E., 'Purpose and Evolution in Common's Institutionalism', *History of Political Economy*, 22, 1, 1990, pp. 19–47.

Bilderbeek, R., Den Hertog, P., Marklund, G. and Miles, I., *Services in Innovation: Knowledge Intensive Business Services (KIBS) as C-producers of innovation*, STEP report no. S14S, 1998.

Bittlingmayer, G., 'Property rights, progress, and the aircraft patent agreement', *Journal of Law and Economics*, 31, 1, 1988, pp. 227–248.

Blau, P., *Exchange and Power in Social Life*. New York 1964.

Blau, P., 'Social Exchange', in Sills, D. S. (ed.), *International Encyclopedia of the Social Sciences vol. 7*. New York 1968.

Blau, P. and Scott, W., Formal Organizations. San Francisco, CA 1962.

Blau P. M. and Schoenherr, R., *The Structure of Organizations*. New York 1971.

Blaug, M., *Economic Theory in Retrospect*. Homewood, IL 1968.

Blaug, M., *The Methodology of Economics*. Cambridge 1980.

Blaug, M., 'No History of Ideas, Please, We're Economists', *Journal of Economic Perspectives*, 15, 1, 2001a, pp. 145–164.

Blaug, M., 'Is Competition Such a Good Thing? Static versus Dynamic Efficiency', *Review of Industrial Organization*, 19, 2001b, pp. 37–48.

Blehr, O., 'Social Drinking in the Faroe Islands: The Ritual Aspect of Token Prestations', *Ethnos*, 39, 1, 1974, pp. 53–62.

Blindenback-Driesen, F. and van den Ende, J., 'Innovation in project-based firms: The context dependency of success factors', *Research Policy*, 35, 2006, pp. 545–561.

Bodemann, Y. M. (1988), 'Relations of Production and Class Rule: The Hidden Basis of Patron-Clientage', in Wellmann, B. and Berkowitz, S. D. (eds), *Social Structures: A Network Approach*. Cambridge 1988.

Boettke, Peter J., 'Analysis and Vision in Economic Discourse', *Journal of the History of Economic Thought*, 14, 1, 1992, pp. 84–95.

Boland, L. A., 'Knowledge and the Role of Institutions in Economic Theory', *Journal of Economic Issues*, 13, 4, 1979, pp. 957–972.

Boldrin, M. and Levine, D., 'The case against intellectual property', *American Economic Review*, 92, 2, 2002, pp. 209–212.

Borgatti, S., Everett, M. G. and Freeman, L. C., 'Ucinet 6 for Windows'. Harvard 2002.

Boulding, K. E., 'Notes on a Theory of Philanthropy', in Dickinson, F. G. (ed.), *Philanthropy and Public Policy*. New York 1962, pp. 57–71.

Boulding, K. E., 'Notes on Goods, Services, and Cultural Economics', *Journal of Cultural Economics*, 1, 1, 1977, pp. 1–14.

Boulding, K. E., *A Preface to Grants Economics – The Economics of Love and Fear*. New York 1981.

Bourdieu, P., *Outline of a Theory in Practice*. Cambridge 1977.

Bourdieu, P., *Distinction – A Social Critique of the Judgment of Taste*. Cambridge, MA 1984.

Bourdieu, P., 'Forms of Capital', in Richardson, J. G. (ed.), *Handbook of Theory and Research for the Sociology of Education*. New York 1986.

Bourdieu, P. (1993), "The Production of Belief: Contribution to an Economy of Symbolic Goods" in: P. Bourdieu, *The Field of Cultural Production*. Cambridge: Polity Press, pp. 74–111.

Braczyk, H. J., Cooke, P. and Heidenreich, M. (eds), *Regional Innovation Systems*. London/Bristol, PA 1988.

Bradach, J. L. and Eccles, R. G., 'Market versus Hierarchies: From ideal types to plural forms', in Leenders, R. Th. A. J. and Gabbay, S. M. (eds), *Corporate Social Capital and Liability*. Dordrecht 1989, pp. 97–118.

Brahmananda, P. R., 'Jevons's "Theory of Political Economy" – A Centennial Appraisal', in Wood, J. C. (ed.), *William Stanley Jevons: Critical Assessments*, Vol. II. London 1988 {1971}.

Brass, D. J., 'Being in the Right Place: A structural Analysis of Individual Influence in an Organization', *Administrative Science Quarterly*, 29, 4, 1984, pp. 518–539.

Brouwer, E., Budil-Nadvornikova and Kleinknecht, A., 'Are urban agglomerations a better breeding place for product innovation? An analysis of new product announcements', *Regional Studies*, 33, 6, 1999, pp. 541–549.

Brush, S. G., 'Should the History of Science Be Rated X?', *Science*, 183, 1974, pp. 1164–1172.

Burgess, R. and Nielsen, J., 'An experimental analysis of some structural determinants of equitable and inequitable exchange relations', *American Sociological Review*, 39, 1974, pp. 427–443.

Burt, R. S., *Structural holes: The social structure of competition*. Cambridge, MA 1992.

Burt, R. S., 'Structural Holes and Good Ideas', *American Journal of Sociology*, 110, 2, 2004, pp. 349–399.

Carlile, P. R., 'Transferring, Translating, and Transforming: An integrative framework for managing knowledge across boundaries', *Organization Science*, 15, 5, 2004, pp. 555–568.

Carlsson, B. 2004. Innovation Systems: A Survey of the Literature from a Schumpeterian Perspective. Paper presented at the *10th Annual Meeting of the International Joseph A. Schumpeter Society*. Milan, 10–12 June 2004, at http://www.schumpeter2004.uni-bocconi.it/papers.php?tric=carl&cric=author&Invia=SEARCH.

Carlsson, B. and Stankiewicz, R., 'On the Nature, Function, and Composition of Technological Systems', *Journal of Evolutionary Economics*, 1, 2, 1991, pp. 93–118.

Carrier, J., 'Gifts, Commodities, and Social Relations: A Maussian View of Exchange', *Sociological Forum*, 6, 1, 1991, pp. 119–136.

Carrincazeaux, C., Lung & Rallet, 'Proximity and localisation of corporate R&D activities', *Research Policy*, 30, 2001, pp. 777–789.

Carter, A. P., 'Measuring the Performance of a Knowledge-Based Economy', in Foray, D. And Lundvall, B. A. (eds), *Employment and Growth in the Knowledge-Based Economy*. Paris 1996.

Casson, M., *Information and Organization – A new perspective on the theory of the firm*. Oxford 1997.

CBS, *Kennis en Economie 2003: Onderzoek en innovatie in Nederland*. Voorburg/Heerlen 2003.

CBS/Statistics Netherlands, Survey Labour Force/Enquête Beroepsbenolking. Central Bureau voor de Statistiek; Retrieved From www.cbs.nl, 1999.

Cheal, D., *The Gift Economy*. London and New York 1988.

Child, J. and Faulkner, D., *Strategies of Cooperation: Managing alliances, networks and joint ventures*. Oxford 1998.

Cicourel, A., *Cognitive sociology: Language and meaning in social interaction*. England 1973.

Clark, N., Juma, C. (1987), Long Run Economics – An Evolutionary Approach to Economic Growth, Pinter Publishers, London.

Coats, A. W., 'The Interpretation of Mercantilist Economics: Some Historiographical Problems', *History of Political Economy*, 5, 2, 1973, pp. 485–495.

Cohen, J., 'A power primer', *Psychological Bulletin*, 112, 1992, pp. 155–159.

Cohen, J., 'The March of Paradigms', *Science*, 283, 26 March 1999, pp. 1998–1999.

Cohen, W. M. and Levinthal, D. A., 'Innovation and Learning: The two faces of R&D', *The Economic Journal*, 99, 1989, pp. 569–596.

Cohen, W. M. and Levinthal, D. A., 'Absorptive capacity: a new perspective on learning and innovation', *Administrative Science Quarterly*, 35, 1990, pp. 128–152.

Coleman, J. S., 'Social Capital: in the creation of Human Capital', *American Journal of Sociology*, 94 Supplement, S95–S120, 1988.

Coleman, J. C. (1990), *Foundations of social theory*. The Belknap Press of Harvard University Press, Cambridge, Mass and London.

Coleman, J. S., *Foundations of Social Theory*. Cambridge, MA 1994.

Cook, K. and Emerson, R., 'Exchange Networks and the Analysis of Complex Organizations', in Bacharach, S. and Lawler, E. (eds), *Research on the sociology of organizations*. Greenwich, CT 1984.

Cooke, P., *Knowledge Economies: clusters, learning and cooperative advantage*. London 2002.

Cooke, P. and Leydesdorff, L., 'Regional Development in the Knowledge-Based Economy: The Construction of Advantages', *Journal of Technology Transfer*, 31, 1, 2006, pp. 1–15.

Cowan, R., David, P. and Foray, D. 'The Explicit Economics of Knowledge Codification and Tacitness', *Industrial and Corporate Change*, 9, 2, 2000, pp. 211–253.

Cowen, T., 'Introduction', in Cowen, T. (ed.), *Economic Welfare*. Cheltenham, 2000, pp. xiii–xviii.

Cross, R., Borgatti, S. and Parker, A., 'Making Invisible Work Visible: Using Social Network Analysis to Support Human Networks', *California Management Review*, 44, 2, 2002, pp. 25–46.

Cross, R., Parker, A., Prusak, L. and Borgatti, S., 'Knowing what we know: Supporting knowledge creation and sharing in social networks', *Organizational Dynamics*, 30, 2, 2001, pp. 100–120.

Cross, R. and Prusak, L., 'The People Who Make organizations Go- or Stop', *Harvard Business Review*, 80, 6, 2002, pp. 104–112.

Cummings, J. N., 'Work Groups, Structural Diversity, and Knowledge Sharing in a Global Organization', *Management Science*, 50, 3, 2004, pp. 352–364.

Dahl, M. S. and Pedersen, C. Ø. R., 'Knowledge Flows through Informal Contacts in Industrial Clusters: myth or reality?', *Research Policy*, 33, 2004, pp. 1673–1686.

Darr, A., 'Gifting Practices and Inter-organizational Relations: Constructing Obligations Networks in the Electronics Sector', *Sociological Forum*, 18, 1, 2003, pp. 31–51.

Dasgupta, P. and David, P., 'Towards a New Economics of Science', *Research Policy*, 23, 5, 1994, pp. 487–522.

Davenport, T. H. and Prusak, L., *Working Knowledge: How Organizations Manage What They Know*. Cambridge, MA 1998.

David, P. and Foray, D., 'Assessing and Expanding the Science and Technology Knowledge Base', *STI Review*, 16, 1995, pp. 13–68.

David, P. and Foray, D, 'An Introduction to the Economy of the Knowledge Society', *International Social Science Journal*, 54, 171, 2002, pp. 9–23.

Davis, J. B., 'Personal Identity and Standard Economic Theory', *Journal of Economic Methodology*, 2, 1995.

Davis, J. B., *The Theory of the Individual in Economics: Identity and Value*. London 2003.

De Vlieghere, M., 'A Reappraisal of Friedrich A. Hayek's Cultural Evolutionism', *Economics and Philosophy*, 10, 2, 1994, pp. 285–304.

Deal, T. E. and Kennedy, A. A., *Corporate Cultures: the rites and rituals of corporate life*. Reading, Mass. 1982.

Deckop, J. R., Cirka, C. C. and Andersson, L. M., 'Doing Unto Others: The Reciprocity of Helping Behavior in Organizations', *Journal of Business Ethics*, 47, 2003, pp. 101–113.

Denison, E. F., *Why Growth Rates Differ*. Washington, DC 1967.

Denzau, A. T. and North, D. C., 'Shared Mental Models: Ideologies and Institutions', *Kyklos*, 47, 1994, pp. 3–31.

Deutsch, M., 'Trust and Suspicion', *Journal of Conflict Resolution*, 2, 4, 1958, pp. 265–279.

Dika, S. and Singh, K., 'Applications of Social Capital in Educational Literature: A Critical Synthesis', *Review of Educational Research*, 72, 1, 2002, pp. 31–60.

Dolfsma, W., *The Origin of Evolutionary Theory in Economics: Learning*. Rotterdam 1994, unpublished mimeo.

Dolfsma, W., 'Internet: An Economist's Utopia?', *Review of International Political Economy*, 5, 4, 1998.

Dolfsma, W., 'How Will the Music Industry Weather the Globalization Storm?', *First Monday*, 5, 5, May 2000, www.firstmonday.org.

Dolfsma, W., 'Napster & KaZaA: Copyright & Competion', *IER – Intellectueel Eigendom en Reclamerecht*, 18, 4, 2002, pp. 178–180.

Dolfsma, W., 'The mountain of experience: how people learn in a complex, evolving environment', *International Journal of Social Economics*, 29, 8, 2002b, pp. 675–684.

Dolfsma, W., 'The Logic of Collective Consuming: Consumers as Subcontractors on Electronic Markets', *International Journal of Social Economics*, 31, 8, 2004.

Dolfsma, W. and Dannreuther, C. (2003) 'Subjects and Boundaries: Contesting social capital-based policies', *Journal of Economic Issues*, 37, 2, 2003, pp. 405–413.

Dolfsma, W., Finch, J. and McMaster, R., 'Market and Society: (how) do they relate, and contribute to welfare?', *Journal of Economic Issues*, 39, 2, 2005, pp. 347–356.

Dolfsma, W. and Soete, L. (eds), *Understanding the Dynamics of the Knowledge Economy*. Cheltenham 2006.

Dolfsma, W. and Panne, G. van der, Innovations from SMEs or Large Firms? Sector Structure and Dynamics Paper presented at the American Economic Association meetings, New Orleans, January 2008.

Dore, R., 'Goodwill and the spirit of market capitalism', *British Journal of Sociology*, 34, 4, 1983, pp. 459–482.

Dosi, G., 'Technologial Paradigms and Technological Trajectories: a Suggested Inter-pretation of the Determinants and Directions of Technical Change', *Research Policy*, 11, 1982, pp. 147–162.

Douglas, M., *How Institutions Think*. London 1986.

Douglas, M. and Isherwood, B., *The World of Goods*. New York 1979.

Dow, S. C., 'Knowledge, Information and Credit Creation', in Rotheim, R. (ed.), *New Keynesian Economics/Post Keynesian Alternatives*. London & New York 1998, pp. 214–226.

Dudley, L., 'Communication and Economic Growth', *European Economic Review*, 43, 1999.

Dunt, E., Gans, J. S. and King, S. P., 'The economic consequences of DVD regional restrictions', *Economic Papers*, 21, 1, 2002, pp. 32–45.

The Economist, *The business of giving – a survey of wealth and philanthropy*. 25 February 2006.

Ekeh, P. P., *Social Exchange Theory: The Two Traditions*. Cambridge, Mass 1974.

Ekelund, R. B., Hébert, R. F., Tollison, R. D., Anderson, G. M. and Davidson, A. B., *Sacred Trust – The Medieval Church as an Economic Firm*. New York 1996.

Elangovan, A. K. and Shapiro, D. L., 'Betrayal of Trust in Organization', *Academy of Management Review*, 23, 3, 1998, pp. 547–566.

Elster, J., 'Introduction', in Elster, J. (ed.), *Rational Choice*. Oxford 1986, pp. 1–33.

Emerson, R. M., 'Social Exchange Theory', In Rosenberg, M. and Turner, R. (eds), *Social Psychology: Sociological Perspective*. New York 1981.

Encaoua, D. and Hollander, A., 'Competition Policy and Innovation', *Oxford Review of Economic Policy*, 18, 1, 2002, pp. 63–79.

Engel, D. and Fier, 'Does R&D-infrastructure attract high-tech start-ups?', Discussion paper n. 00-30, Zentrum für Europäische Wirtschaftsforschung. 2000.

Etzkowitz, H. and Leydesdorff, L., 'The Dynamics of Innovation: From National Systems and "Mode 2" to a Triple Helix of University-Industry-Government Relations', *Research Policy*, 29, 2, 2000, pp. 109–123.

Etzkowitz, H., Webster, A., Gebhardt, C. and Terra, B. R. C., 'The Future of the University and the University of the Future: Evolution of Ivory Tower to Entrepreneurial Paradigm', *Research Policy*, 29, 2, 2000, pp. 313–330.

European Commission, *Towards a European research area*. Brussels, 18 January 2000, at http://europa.eu.int/comm/research/era/pdf/com2000-6-en.pdf.

European Commission, *Working together for growth and jobs. A new start for the Lisbon Strategy*, 2005, at http://europa.eu.int/growthandjobs/pdf/COM2005_024_en.pdf

Farace, R. V., Monge, P. R. and Russell, H. M., *Communicating and organizing*. Reading, MA 1977.

Feiner, S. and Roberts, B., 'Using Alternative Paradigms to Teach About Race and Gender: A Critical Thinking Approach to Introductory Economics', *American Economic Review*, 85, 2, 1995, pp. 367–371.

Fernandez, R. and Gould, R. V., 'A Dilemma of State Power in the National Health Policy Domain', *American Journal of Sociology*, 99, 6, 1994, pp. 1455–1491.

Fernandez, R. M., 'Structural Bases of Leadership in Intraorganizational Networks', *Social Psychological Quarterly*, 54, 1, 1991, pp. 36–53.

Ferrary, M., 'The Gift Exchange in the Social Networks of Silicon Valley', *California Management Review*, 45, 4, 2003, pp. 120–138.

Fetter, F. W., 'The Relation of the History of Economic Thought to Economic History', *American Economic Review*, 65, 2, 1965, pp. 136–142.

Field, J., *Social Capital*. London and New York 2004.

Fine, B., *Social Capital versus Social Theory. Political Economy and Social Science at the Turn of the Millennium*. London and New York 2000.

Fisher, W., 'Intellectual Property and Innovation: Theoretical, Empirical, and Historical Perspectives', in *Industrial Property, Innovation, and the Knowledge-based Economy, Beleidsstudies Technologie Economie*, 37, 2001.

Florax, R., *The University, a regional booster? Economic impacts of academic knowledge infrastructure*. Aldershot 1992.

Flynn, F. J., 'How much should I give and how often? The effects of generosity and frequency of favor exchange on social status and productivity', *Academy of Management Journal*, 46, 5, 2003, pp. 539–553.

Foley, M. and Edwards, B., 'Escape from politics? Social Theory and the Social Capital Debate', *American Behavioral Scientist*, 40, 5, 1997, pp. 550–561.

Foley, M. and Edwards, B., 'Is it time to Divest in Social Capital?', *Journal of Public Policy*, 19, 2, 1999, pp. 141–173.

Foray, D., *The Economics of Knowledge*. Cambridge, MA/London 2004.

Foray, D. and Lundvall, B. A., 'The Knowledge-Based Economy: From the Economics of Knowledge to the Learning Economy', in *Employment and Growth in the Knowledge-Based Economy*. Paris 1996, pp. 11–32.

Foss, N., *Strategy, Economic Organization and the Knowledge Economy*. Oxford 2005.

Frank, R. H., *Passions Within Reason, the Strategic Role of the Emotions*. New York 1988.

Freeman, C., 'Networks of innovators: A synthesis of research issues', *Research Policy*, 20, 1991, pp. 499–514.

Freeman, C. and Perez, C., 'Structural Crises of Adjustment, Business Cycles and Investment Behaviour', in Dosi, G., Freeman, C., Silverberg R. N. G. and Soete, L. (eds), *Technical Change and Economic Theory*. London 1988, pp. 38–66.

Freeman, L. C., 'Centrality in Social Networks: Conceptual Clarification', *Social Networks*, 1, 1979, pp. 215–239.

Frenken, K., 'A Complexity Approach to Innovation Networks. The Case of the Aircraft Industry (1909–1997)', *Research Policy*, 29, 2, 2000, pp. 257–272.

Frey, B. S., *Not Just for the Money – An Economic Theory of Personal Motivation*. Cheltenham 1997.

Friedman, A. F. and Podolny, J., 'Differentiation of boudary spanning roles: Labor negotiations and implications for role conflict', *Administrative Science Quarterly*, 37, 1993, pp. 28–47.

Friedman, M., 'The Methodology of Positive Economics', in Friedman, M. (ed.), *Essays in Positive Economics*. Chicago 1953, pp. 3–43.

Fritsch, M., 'Cooperation and the Efficiency of Regional R&D Activities', *Cambridge Journal of Economics*, 28, 2004, pp. 829–846.

Fritsch, M. and Schwirten, 'Enterprise-university co-operation and the role of public research institutions in regional innovation systems', *Industry and Innovation*, 6, 1, 1999, pp. 69–83.

Frye, N., *Anatomy of Criticism*. Princeton 1957.

Fudenberg, D. and Maskin, E., 'The Folk Theorem in Repeated Games with Discounting or with Incomplete Information', *Econometrica*, 54, 3, 1986, pp. 533–554.

Gabarro, J. J., 'The development of working relationships', in Galegher, J., Kraut, R. E. and Egido, C. (eds), *Intellectual Teamwork: Social and Technological Foundations of Cooperative Work*. Hillsdale 1990, pp. 79–110.

Geertz, C., *The Interpretation of Cultures*. New York 1973.

Geroski, P., Machin and van Reenen, J., 'The profitability of innovating firms', *The Rand Journal of Economics*, 24, 2, 1993, pp. 198–211.

Gilbert, R. J. and Newbery, D. M. G., 'Preemptive Patenting and the Persistence of Monopoly', *American Economic Review*, 72, 3, 1982, pp. 514–526.

Godin, B., 'The Knowledge-Based Economy: Conceptual Framework or Buzzword', *Journal of Technology Transfer*, 31, 1, 2006, pp. 17–30, at http://www.csiic.ca/Pubs_Histoire.html.

Gordon, D. F., 'The Role of the History of Economic Thought in the Understanding of Modern Economics', *American Economic Review*, LV, 2, 1965, pp. 119–127.

Gould, R.V. and Fernandez, R., 'Structures of mediation: A formal approach to brokerage in transaction networks', *Sociological Methodology*, 19, 1989, pp. 89–126.

Gouldner, A. W., 'The Norm of Reciprocity: A preliminary statement', *American Sociological Review*, 25, 1960, pp. 161–178.

Granovetter, M., 'The strength of weak ties', *American Journal of Sociology*, 78, 1973, pp. 1360–1380.

Granovetter, M., 'Economic Action and Social Structure: The Problem of Embeddedness', *American Journal of Sociology*, 91, November 1985, pp. 481–510.

Granovetter, M., 'Problems of explanations in economic sociology', in Nohria, N. and Eccles, R. (eds), *Networks and organizations: Structure, form and action*. Boston 1992.

Granstrand, O., *The Economics and Management of Intellectual Property*. Cheltenham 1999.

Grant, R. M., 'Toward a Knowledge-Based Theory of the Firm', *Strategic Management Journal*, 17, 1996, pp. 109–122.

Greenberg, M. S. and Frisch, D. M., 'Effect of Intentionality on Willingness to Reciprocate a Favor', *Journal of Experimental Social Psychology*, 8, 1972, pp. 99–111.

Grip, A. de and Willems, 'Opleidingsniveau en hoogwaardige werkgelegenheid; over het regionale belang van een succesfactor', in Atzema, O. A. L. C. And van Dijk, J. (eds), *Technologie en de regionale arbeidsmarkt*. Assen 1996, pp. 102–116.

de Groot, A. D., *Thought and Choice in Chess*. The Hague 1965.

Guibault, L., *Copyright Limitations and Contract*. Amsterdam 2002.

Gurbaxani, V., Melville, N. and Kraemer, K., 'The production of Information Services: a firm-level analysis of information systems budgets', *Information Systems Research*, 11, 2, 2000, pp. 159–176.

Hägerstrand, T., *Innovation diffusion as a spatial process*. Chicago 1967.

Hamouda, O. F. (ed.), *Controversies in Political Economy – Selected Essays of G. C. Harcourt.*, New York 1986 {1969}, pp. 145–206 {Reprinted from: *Journal of Economic Literature*, 1969(June): 369–405}.

Han, T. S., 'Multiple Mutual Information and Multiple Interactions in Frequency Data', *Informaiton and Control*, 46, 1, 1980, pp. 26–45.

Hansen, M., 'The search-transfer problem: The role of weak ties in sharing knowledge across organization subunits', *Administrative Science Quarterly*, 44, 1999, pp. 82–111.

Hansen, M., 'Knowledge networks: Explaining effective knowledge sharing in multiunit companies', *Organization Science*, 13, 3, 2002, pp. 232–248.

Hansen, M. and Lovas, B., 'How do Multinational Companies Leverage Technological Competencies? Moving from single to interdependent explanations', *Strategic Management Journal*, 25, 2004, pp. 801–822.

Hansen, M., Mors, M. L. and Lovas, B., 'Knowledge Sharing in Organizations: multiple networks, multiple phases', *Academy of Management Journal*, 48, 5, 2005, pp. 776–793.

Hansen, M. T. and Haas, M. R., 'Competing for Attention in Knowledge Markets: Electronic Document Dissemination in a Management Consulting Company', *Administrative Science Quarterly*, 46, 2001, pp. 1–28.

Harcourt, G. C., 'Some Cambridge Controversies in the Theory of Capital', in

Hargreaves Heap, S., 'Rationality', in Hollis, M., Hargreaves Heap, S., Lyons, B., Sugden, R. and Weale, A. (eds), *The Theory of Choice*. Oxford 1993, pp. 3–25.

Harris, C. and Vickers, J., 'Patent Races and the Persistence of Monopoly', *Journal of Industrial Economics*, 33, 4, 1985, pp. 461–481.

Harrison, B., 'Industrial districts: old wine in new bottles?', *Regional Studies*, 26, 1992, pp. 469–483.

Hassabis, D., Kumaran, D., Vann, S. D. and Maguire, E. A., 'Patients with hippocampal amnesia cannot imagine new experiences', *Proceedings of the National Academy of Sciences USA*, 104, 5, 2007, pp. 1726–1731.

Hatzichronoglou, T., *Revision of the High-Technology Sector and Product Classification*. Paris 1997, at http://www.olis.oecd.org/olis/1997doc.nsf/LinkTo/OCDE-GD(97)216.

Hayek, F. A., 'Economics and Knowledge', *Economica*, 1937, pp. 33–54.

Hayek, F. A., *The Pure Theory of Capital*. London 1941.

Hayek, F. A., 'The Use of Knowledge in Society', *American Economic Review*, 35, 4, 1945, pp. 519–530.

Hayek, F. A., *Studies in Philosophy, Politics and Economics*. New York 1969.

Heath, A. F., *Rational Choice and Social Exchange: A critique of Exchange Theory*. Cambridge 1976.

Heide, J. B. and Miner, A. S., 'The shadow of the future: Effects of anticipated interaction and frequency of contact on buyer-seller cooperation', *Academy of Management Review*, 35, 1992, pp. 265–291.

Heijs, J. B. M. and Schmitz, 'Clusters of concentraties', *Economisch Statistische Berichten*, 7 December 2001, pp. 943–945.

Heilbroner, R. L., 'Rhetoric and Ideology', in Klamer, A., McClosky, D. and Solow, R. (eds), *The consequences of economic rhetoric*. Cambridge 1988, pp. 38–43.

Heilbroner, R. L., 'Analysis and Vision in the History of Modern Economic Thought', *Journal of Economic Literature*, 28, 1990, pp. 1097–1114.

Helpman, E., Innovation, Imitation, and Intellectual Property Rights', *Econometrica*, 61, 6, 1993, pp. 1247–1280.

Henn, H. G., 'The Quest for International Copyright Protection', *Cornell Law Quarterly*, 43, 1954.

Hennings, K. H., 'Capital as a Factor of Production', in Milgate, M., Newman, P. and Eatwell, J. (eds), *The New Palgrave*. Hong Kong 1987, pp. 327–333.

Hettinger, E. C., 'Justifying Intellectual Property', *Philosophy and Public Affairs*, 18, 1, 1989, pp. 31–52.

Hexter, J. H., *The History Primer*. New York 1971.

Heyne, P., 'Theological Visions in Economics and Religion', *Forum for Social Economics*, 25, 2, 1996, pp. 1–7.

Hill, C. W. L., 'Cooperation, opportunism and the invisible hand: Implications for transaction cost theory', *Academy of Management Review*, 15, 3, 1990, pp. 500–513.

Hodgson, G. M., 'The Ubiquity of Habits and Rules', *Cambridge Journal of Economics*, 21, 6, 1997, pp. 663–684.

Hoen, A., *Clusters: determinants and effects*. The Hague 2001.

Holland, J. H., Holyoak, K. J., Nisbett, R. E. and Thagard, P. R., *Induction – Processes of Inference, Learning, and Discovery*. Cambridge, MA 1989.

Holt, C. A., *Psychology and Economics*. Paper presented at the ASSA meetings 1995.

Homans, G. C., *The human group*. London 1951.

Homans, G. C., *Social Behavior: Its elementary Forms*. New York 1974.

Houghton, J. W., 'Cultural Theory as Applied to the History of Economic Thought: A Case Study', *History of Political Economy*, 23, 3, 1991, pp. 497–518.

Hubbard, T. and Love, J., 'A new framework for global healthcare R&D', *PLoS Biology*, 2, 2, 2004, pp. 147–150.

Hubert, L. J. and Schulz, J., 'Quadratic assignment as a general data analysis strategy', *British Journal of Mathematical and Statistical Psychology*, 29, 1976, pp. 190–241.

Hui, K. L. and Png, I. P. L., 'On the Supply of Creative Work: Evidence from the movies', *American Economic Review*, 92, 2, 2002, pp. 217–220.

Humphrey, C. and Hugh-Jones, S., *Barter, Exchange and Value*. Cambridge 1992.

Huygens, M., Baden-Fuller, C., Van Den Bosch, F. A. J. and Volberda, H. W., 'Co-evolution of Firm Capabilities and Industry Competition: Investigating the Music Industry, 1877–1997', *Organisation Studies*, 22, 6, 2001, pp. 971–1011.

Ibarra, H., 'Network Centrality, Power and Innovation Involvement: Determinants of Technical and Administrative Roles', *Academy of Management Journal*, 36, 3, 1993, pp. 471–501.

Ingram, P. and Robert, P. W., 'Friendship among competitors in the Sydney Hotel Industry', *American Journal of Sociology*, 106, 2000, pp. 387–423.

Jablin, F. and Putnam, L. *The new handbook of organizational communication*. Thousand Oaks 2001.

Jackman, R. W. and Miller, R. A., 'Social Capital and Politics', *Annual Review of Political Science*, 1, 1998, pp. 47–73.

Jaffe, A., 'Real effects of academic research', *American Economic Review*, 79, 1989, pp. 957–970.

Jakulin, A. and Bratko, I., *Quantifying and Visualizing Attribute Interactions: An Approach Based on Entropy*, 2004, from http://arxiv.org/abs/cs.AI/0308002.

Jones, C. and Williams, J., 'Measuring the Social Returns to R&D', *Quarterly Journal of Economics*, 113, 3, 1998, pp. 1119–1135.

Kastan, D. S., 'The Noyse of the New Bible: Reform and Reaction in Henrician England'. Columbia nd, unpublished manuscript.

Keynes, J. M., *Essays in Biography*. London 1933.

Khalil, E., 'The Gift Paradox: Complex selves and symbolic goods', *Review of Social Economy*, 62, 3, 2004, pp. 379–392.

Khalil, E. L., 'The Three Laws of Thermodynamics and the Theory of Production', *Journal of Economic Issues*, 38, 1, 2004, pp. 201–226.

Kilduff, M. and Brass, D. J., 'The social network of high and low self-monitors: implications for workplace performance', *Administrative Science Quarterly*, 46, 1, 2001, pp. 121–146.

Kiker, B. F., 'The Historical Roots of the Concept of Human Capital', *Journal of Political Economy*, 74, 1966, pp. 481–499.

Kitch, E. W., 'Patents', in Newman, P. (ed.), *The New Palgrave Dictionary of Economics and Law*, Vol. 3. London 1998, pp. 13–17.

Klaes, M., 'Sociotechnical constituencies, game theory and the diffusion of the compact disc', *Research Policy*, 25, 1997, pp. 1221–1234.

Kleinknecht, A., 'Indicators of manufacturing and service innovation: Their strengths and weaknesses', in Metcalf, J. S. and Miles, I. (eds), *Innovation systems in the service economy*. Dordrecht, London 2000, pp. 169–186.

Kleinknecht, A. and Poot, T., 'Do regions matter for R&D?', *Regional Studies*, 26, 1992, pp. 221–232.

Knight, F. H., *Risk, Uncertainty and Profit*. Boston 1921 {1948}.

Knoke, D. and Kuklinski, J. H., *Network Analysis*. Beverly Hills 1982.

Knorr Cetina, K., 'Epistemic Cultures: Forms of Reason in Science', *History of Political Economy*, 23, 1, 1991, pp. 105–121.

Koelman, K., 'A Hard Nut to Crack: The Protection of Technological Measures', *European Intellectual Property Review*, 2000, pp. 272–288.

Kogut, B. and Zander, U., Knowledge of the Firm, Combinative Capabilities, and the Replication of Technology', *Organization Science*, 3, 1992, pp. 383–396.

Komter, A. E., *The Gift: An Interdisciplinary Approach*. Amsterdam 1996.

Krackhardt, D., 'QAP partialling as a test of spuriousness', *Social Networks*, 9, 1987, pp. 171–186.

Krackhardt, D. and Hanson, J., 'Informal Networks: The Company Behind the Chart', *Harvard Business Review*, 71, 1993, pp. 104–111.

Krackhardt, D. and Stern, K., 'Informal Networks and Organizational Crises: An Experimental Simulation', *Social Psychology Quarterly*, 51, 1988, pp. 123–140.

Kramer, R., Hanna, B. and Su., W., Collective Identity, Collective Trust and Social Capital" Linking Group Identification and Group Coordination, in Turner, M. E., *Groups at work: Theory and Research*. Lawrence Erlbaum Associates Inc. Publishers 2001.

Krebs, V., InFlow survey, 1999 at http://www.orgnet.com/INSNA/survey.html.

Kreps, D. M., 'Corporate culture and economic theory', in Alt, J. and Shepsel, K. (eds), *Perspectives on Political Economy*. Cambridge 1990.

Kreps, D., Milgrom, P. and Wilson, R., 'Rational Cooperation in the Finitely Repeated Prisoner's Dilemma', *Journal of Economic Theory*, 27, 1982, pp. 245–252.

von Krogh, G., 'Care in Knowledge Creation', *California Management Review*, 40, 3, 1998, pp. 133–153.

Krugman, P., *Development, Geography and Economic Theory*. Cambridge, MA 1995.

Kuhn, T., *The Structure of Scientific Revolutions*. Chicago 1962.

Laafia, I., *Regional Employment in High Technology*: Eurostat, 1999, at http://europa.eu.int/comm/eurostat/Public/datashop/print-product/EN?catalogue=Eurostat&product=CA-NS-99-001-_-I-EN&mode=download.

Laafia, I., 'Employment in High Tech and Knowledge Intensive Sectors in the EU Continued to Grow in 2001', *Statistics in Focus: Science and Technology*, Theme, 9, 4, 2002a, at http://europa.eu.int/comm/eurostat/Public/datashop/print-product/EN?catalogue=Eurostat&product=KS-NS-02-004-_-N-EN&mode=download.

Laafia, I., 'National and Regional Employment in High Tech and Knowledge Intensive Sectors in the EU – 1995–2000', *Statistics in Focus: Science and Technology*, Theme, 9, 3, 2002b, at http://europa.eu.int/comm/eurostat/Public/datashop/print-product/EN?catalogue=Eurostat&product=KS-NS-02-003-_-N-EN&mode=download.

Lakhani, K. R. and von Hippel, E., 'How Open Source Software Works: "Free" User-to-User Assistance', *Research Policy*, 32, 6, 2003, pp. 923–943.

Lakoff, G. and Johnson, M., *Metaphors We Live By*. Chicago 1980.

Landes, W. M. and Posner, R. A., 'An Economic Analysis of Copyright Law', *Journal of Legal Studies*, 18, June 1989, pp. 325–363.

Langford, J., 'Intellectual Property Rights: technology transfer and resource implication', *American Journal of Agricultural Economics*, 79, 5, 1997, pp. 1576–1583.

Langholm, O. 1979. *Price and Value in the Aristotelian Tradition*. Oslo: Unversitetsforlaget.

Lanjouw, J. O. and Schankermann, M., 'Protecting intellectual property rights: are small firms handicapped?', *Journal of Law and Economics*, 47, April 2004, pp. 45–74.

Larsen, D. and Watson, J. J., 'A guide map to the terrain of gift value', *Psychology & Marketing*, 18, 2001, pp. 889–906.

Laumann, E. O., Marsden, P. V. and Prensky. D., 'The boundary specification problem in network analysis', in Burt and Minor (eds), *Applied network analysis: A methodological introduction*, Beverly Hills 1983, pp. 18–34.

Lawler, E. J. and Yoon, J., 'Network Structure and Emotion in Exchange Relations', *American Sociological Review*, 63, 6, 1998, pp. 871–894.

Lawler, E. J., Yoon, J. and Thye, S. R., 'Emotion and Group Cohesion in Productive Exchange', *American Journal of Sociology*, 106, 2000, pp. 616–657.

Le Grand, J., *Motivation, Agency, and Public Policy*. New York 2003.

Lemley, M. A. and Shapiro, C., 'Probabilistic Patents', *Journal of Economic Perspectives*, 19, 2, 2005, pp. 75–98.

Lerner, J., 'Patenting in the shadow of competitors', *Journal of Law and Economics*, 38, 1995.

Lessig, L., *Code and other Laws of Cyberspace*. New York 1999.

Lessig, L., *The Future of Ideas – The fate of the commons in a connected world*. New York 2001.

Lev, B., *Intangibles – Management, Measurement and Reporting*. Washington, D.C. 2001.

Levinthal, D. A., 'The slow pace of rapid technological change. Gradualism and Punctuation in Technological Change', *Industrial and Corporate Change*, 7, 2, 1998, pp. 217–247.

Levi-Strauss, C., 'The principle of reciprocity', in Komter, A. E. (ed.), *The Gift: An Interdisciplinary Perspective*. Amsterdam 1996.

Levi-Strauss, C., *The Elementary Structures of Kinship*. Boston 1969.

Levin, R., Klevorick, A., Nelson, R. and Winter, S., 'Appropriating the Returns from Industrial Research and Development', *Brookings Papers on Economic Activity*, 3, 1987.

Levy, D. and Newborn, M., *How Computers Play Chess*. New York 1991.

Leydesdorff, L., 'Epilogue', in Leydesdorff, L. and Van den Besselaar, P. (eds), *Evolutionary Economics and Chaos Theory: New Directions for Technology Studies*. London/New York 1994, pp. 180–192.

Leydesdorff, L., *The Challenge of Scientometrics: The Development, Measurement, and Self-Organization of Scientific Communications*. Leiden 1995.

Leydesdorff, L., 'The New Communication Regime of University-Industry-Government Relations', in Etzkowitz, H. and Leydesdorff, L. (eds), *Universities and the Global Knowledge Economy*. London and Washington 1997, pp. 106–117.

Leydesdorff, L., *A Sociological Theory of Communication: The Self-Organization of the Knowledge-Based Society*. Parkland, FL 2001, at http://www.upublish.com/books/leydesdorff.htm.

Leydesdorff, L., 'The Mutual Information of University-Industry-Government Relations: An Indicator of the Triple Helix Dynamics', *Scientometrics*, 58, 2, 2003, pp. 445–467.

Leydesdorff, L., 'The University-Industry Knowledge Relationship: Analyzing Patents and the Science Base of Technologies', *Journal of the American Society for Information Science & Technology*, 55, 11, 2004, pp. 991–1001.

Leydesdorff, L., *The Knowledge-Based Economy – Modeled, Measured, Simulated*. Boca Raton, FL 2006.

Leydesdorff, L. and Etzkowitz, H., 'The Triple Helix as a Model for Innovation Studies', *Science and Public Policy*, 25, 3, 1998, pp. 195–203.

Leydesdorff, L. and Fritsch, M., 'Measuring the knowledge base of regional innovation systems in Germany in terms of a Triple Helix dynamics', *Research Policy*, 35, 10, 2006, pp. 1538–1553.

Li, T. Y. and Yorke, J. A., 'Period Three Implies Chaos', *American Mathematical Monthly*, 82, 1975, pp. 985–992.

Lin, N. and Dumin, M., 'Access to occupations through social ties', *Social Networks*, 25, 1986, pp. 467–487.

Locke, J. (1690), Second Treatise of Government. Edited, with an Introduction, by C. B. McPherson. Hacket publishing Company, Indianopolis and Cambridge, 1980.

Lowry, S. T., 'Are There Limits to the Past in the History of Economic Thought?', *Journal of the History of Economic Thought*, 13, 1991, pp. 134–143.

Lucas, R. E. Jr., 'Adaptive learning and economic theory', in Hogarth, R. M. and Reder, M. W. (eds), *Rational choice – the contrast between economics and psychology*. Chicago 1987.

Lundvall, B. Å., 'Innovation as an Interactive Process: From User-Producer Interaction to the National System of Innovation', in Dosi, G., Freeman, C., Nelson, R., Silverberg, G. and Soete, L. (eds), *Technical Change and Economic Theory*. London 1988, pp. 349–369.

Lundvall, B. Å. (ed.), *National Systems of Innovation*. London 1992.

Lyotard, J. F., *The Postmodern Condition: A Report on Knowledge*, Bennington, G. and Massumi and B. (trans.). Minneapolis 1984.

Maasen, S. and Weingart, P., *Metaphors and the Dynamics of Knowledge*. London & New York 2000.

Machlup, F., *An Economic Review of the Patent System*. Washington, DC 1958.

Machlup, F., *The Production and Distribution of Knowledge in the United States*. Princeton, NJ 1962.

Machlup, F., *Knowledge and Knowledge Production*. Princeton, NJ 1980.

Machlup, F., *The Economics of Information and Human Capital*. Princeton, NJ 1984.

Malecki, E. J., *Technology and Economic Development*. New York 1991.

Malinowski, B., The Principle of Give and Take, in Komter, A. E. (ed.), *The Gift: An Interdisciplinary Perspective*. Amsterdam 1996.

Malmbert, A. and Solvell, 'Localized innovation processes and the sustainable competitive advantage of firms: a conceptual model', in Taylor, M. and Conti, S. (eds), *Interdependent and uneven development. Global-Local perspectives*. Aldershot 1997, pp. 119–142.

Mansfield, E. and Lee, 'The modern university: contributor to industrial innovation and recipient of industrial R&D support', *Research Policy*, 25, 1996, pp. 1047–1058.

Manshanden, W., *Zakelijke diensten en regionaal-economische ontwikkeling*. (Ph.D. thesis, University of Amsterdam) 1996.

Madhaven, R. and Grover, R., 'From embedded knowledge to embodied Knowledge: New product development as knowledge management', *Journal of Marketing*, 62, 1998, pp. 1–12.

Manns, J., 'On Composing "by the Rules" ', *Journal of Aesthetics and Art Criticism*, 52, 1, 1994, pp. 83–91.

Mansfield, E., 'Patents and Innovation: an empirical study', *Management Science* 32, 2, 1986, pp. 173–181.

Marsden, P. V., 'Network Data and Measurement', *Annual Review of Sociology*, 16, 1990, pp. 435–463.

Marsden, P. V., 'Egocentric and sociocentric measures of network centrality', *Social Networks*, 24, 4, 2002, pp. 407–422.

Marshall, A., *Principles of Economics*, 8th edn. London 1920 [1891].

Martin, R., 'The New "Geographical Turn" In Economics: Some Critical Reflections', *Cambridge Journal of Economics*, 23, 1, 1999, pp. 65–91.

Maskell, P. and Malmberg, 'Localised learning and industrial competitiveness', *Cambridge Journal of Economics*, 23, 1999, pp. 167–183.

Maurer, S. M., Hugenholz, B. and Onsrud, en, H. J., 'Europe's Database Experiment', *Science*, 294, 26 October 2001, pp. 789–790.

Mauss, M., *The Gift: Forms and Functions of Exchange in Archaic Societies*. New York 1954 [2000].

Mayer, R. C., Davis J. H. and Schoorman, F. D., 'An integrative model of organizational trust', *Academy of Management Review*, 20, 3, 1995, pp. 709–734.

Mazzoleni, R. and Nelson, R. R., 'The benefits and costs of strong patent protection: a contribution to the current debate', *Research Policy*, 27, 1998, pp. 273–284.

McCloskey, D. N., 'Does the Past Have a Useful Economics', *Journal of Economic Literature*, 14, 2, 1976, pp. 434–461.

McCloskey, D. N., 'The Rhetoric of Economics', *Journal of Economic Literature*, 21, 2, 1983, pp. 481–517.

McCloskey, D. N., *The Rhetoric of Economics*. Madison 1985.

McCloskey, D. N., *If You're So Smart*. Chicago 1990.

McCloskey, D. N. *Knowledge and Persuasion in Economics*. New York: Cambridge University Press 1994.

McCloskey, D. N. L. and Ziliak, S. T., 'The Standard Error of Regression', *Journal of Economic Literature*, 34, 1, 1996, pp. 97–114.

McGill, W. J., 'Multivariate Information Transmission', *Psychometrika*, 19, 2, 1954, pp. 97–116.

McGrath, M. A. and Englis, B., 'Intergenerational Gift Giving in Sub-cultural Wedding Celebrations: The Ritual Audience As Cash Cow', in Otnes, C. and Beltramini, R. F. (ed.), *Gift Giving: A Research Anthology*. Bowling Green 1996.

Mehra, A., Kilduff, M. and Brass, D. J., 'The Social Networks of High and Low Self-monitors: Implications for Workplace Performance', *Administrative Science Quarterly*, 46, 2001, pp. 121–146.

Miles, I., Kastrinos, N., Flanagan, K., Bilderbeek, R., Den Hertog, P., Huitink, W. and Bouman, M., *Knowledge-Intensive Business Services: Users, Carriers and Sources of Innovation*. Luxembourg 1995.

Milgrom, P. and Roberts, J., 'Communication and Inventory as Substitutes in Organizing Production', *Scandinavian Journal of Economics*, 90, 3, 1988, pp. 275–289.

Mill, J. S., *Principles of Political Economy*. Fairchild, NJ [1848] 1987.

Ministry of Economic Affairs, *Innovatie in de Regio – Provinciale Innovatieprofielen*. The Hague/Amsterdam April 1997.

Ministry of Economic Affairs, *Samenwerken en Stroomlijnen: Optiesvoor een effectief innovatiebeleid*. The Hague 2002.

Mirowski, P., 'The When, the How and the Why of Mathematical Expression in the History of Economic Analysis', *Journal of Economic Perspectives*, 15, 1, 1991, pp. 145–157.

Mirowski, P., 'Economics, Science, and Knowledge: Polanyi vs. Hayek', paper presented at the EAEPE Conference, 19–21 October 1995, Cracow, Poland.

Mirowski, P. and Sent, E. M., *Science Bought and Sold: Essays in the Economics of Science*. Chicago 2001.

Mishan, E. J., 'A survey of welfare economics', *Economic Journal*, 70, 278, 1960, pp. 197–265.

Mitchell, W. C., *Types of Economic Theory*, Vol. I., Dorfman, R (ed.). New York 1967.

Mokyr, J., *The Gifts of Athena – Historical Origins of the Knowledge Economy*. Princeton, NJ 2002.

Molina, J., 'The informal organizational chart in organizations: An approach from the social network analysis', *Connections*, 24, 1, 2001, pp. 78–91.

Monge, R. and Contractor, N. S., 'Emergence of communication networks', in Jablin, F. M. and Putnam, L. L. (eds), *The new handbook of organizational communication*. Thousand Oaks, CA 2001, pp. 440–502.

Moorman, C. and Miner, A. S., 'Organizational Improvisation and Organizational Memory', *Academy of Management Review*, 23, 1998, pp. 698–723.

Moran, P. and Ghosal, S., 'Value creation by firms', in Keys, J. B. and Dosier, L. N. (eds), *Academy of Management Best Paper Proceedings*, 1996.

Mosselmans, B., 'The Role of Institutions in Jevons's Economics', *History of Economic Ideas*, X, 3, 2002, pp. 1–14.

Nahapiet, J. and Ghosal, S. 'Social capital, intellectual capital, and the organizational advantage', *Academy of Management Review*, 23, 20, 1998, pp. 242–266.

Neale, W. C., 'Technology as Social Process: A Commentary on Knowledge and Human Capital', *Journal of Economic Issues*, 28, 2, 1984, pp. 573–580.

Nelson, R. R., 'The simple economics of basic scientific research', *Journal of Political Economy*, 57, 1959, pp. 297–306.

Nelson, R. R., 'Assessing private enterprise: an exegesis of tangled doctrine', *The Bell Journal of Economics*, 12, 1, 1981, pp. 93–111.

Nelson, R. R., 'Research on Productivity Growth and Productivity Differences. Dead Ends and New Departures', *Journal of Economic Literature*, 19, 1981b, pp. 1029–1064.

Nelson, R. R., 'Capitalism as an engine of growth', *Research Policy*, 19, 1990, pp. 193–214.

Nelson, R. R., 'Gender, Metaphor, and the Definition of Economics', *Economics and Philosophy*, 8, 1992, pp. 103–125.

Nelson, R. R. (ed.), *National Innovation Systems: A Comparative Analysis*. New York 1993.

Nelson, R. R., 'Economic Growth via the Coevolution of Technology and Institutions', in Leydesdorff, L. and Van den Besselaar, P. (eds), *Evolutionary Economic and Chaos Theory: New Directions in Technology Studies*. London and New York 1994, pp. 21–32.

Nelson, R. R., 'The market economy, and the scientific commons', *Research Policy*, 33, 2004, pp. 455–471.

Nelson, R. R. and Winter, S. G., 'In Search for a Useful Theory of Innovation', *Research Policy*, 6, 1977, pp. 36–76.

Nelson, R. R. and Winter, S. G., *An Evolutionary Theory of Economic Change*. Cambridge, MA 1982.

Netanel, N. W., 'Copyright and a Democratic Civil Society', *Yale Law Review*, 106, 283, 1996.

Nonaka, I. and Takeuchi, H. *The Knowledge-Creating Company*. New York 1995.

Nooteboom, B., *Learning and Innovation in Organisations and Economies*. Oxford 2000.

Nooteboom, B., *Trust: Form, Foundations, Functions, Failures and Figures*. Cheltenham 2002.

North, D. C., *Instititutions, Institutional Change and Economic Performance*. New York 1990.

Nye, F. I., 'Choice, Exchange and the Family', in Burr, W. R. et al. (eds), *Contemporary Theories about the Family*. New York 1979.

Oddi, A. S. 'The international patent system and third world development: Reality of myth?', *Duke Law Journal*, 5 November 1987, pp. 831–877.

Organization for Economic Cooperation and Development (OECD), *OECD Science and Technology Indicators: R&D, Invention and Competitiveness*. Paris 1986.

Organization for Economic Cooperation and Development (OECD), *Employment and growth in the knowledge-based economy*. Paris 1996b.

Organization for Economic Cooperation and Development (OECD), *New Indicators for the Knowledge-Based Economy: Proposals for Future Work*. DSTI/STP/NESTI? GSS/TIP, 96, 6, 1996a.

Organization for Economic Cooperation and Development (OECD), *Patents and Innovation in the International Context*. Paris 1997.

Organization for Economic Cooperation and Development (OECD), *Promoting Innovation and Growth in Services*. Paris 2000.

Organization for Economic Cooperation and Development (OECD), *Science, Technology and Industry Scoreboard: Towards a Knowledge-based Economy*. Paris 2001.

Organization for Economic Cooperation and Development (OECD), *Science, Technology and Industry Scoreboard; 2003 Edition*. Paris 2003.

OECD/Eurostat, *Proposed Guidelines for Collecting and Interpreting Innovation Data, 'Oslo Manual'*. Paris 1997.

Offer, A., 'Between the Gift and the Market: The Economy of Regard', *The Economic History Review*, 50, 3, 1997, pp. 450–476.

Ortmann, A. and Gigerenzer, G. 'Reasoning in Economics and Psychology: Why Social Context Matters', *Journal of Institutional and Theoretical Economics*, 153, 4, 1997, pp. 700–710.

Ostrom, E. and Ahn, T. K. (eds), *Foundations of Social Capital*. Northampton 2003.

Ouwersloot, H. and Rietveld, P. 'The geography of R&D: tobit analysis and a Bayesian approach to mapping R&D activities in the Netherlands', *Environment and Planning A*, 32, 2000, pp. 1673–1688.

Paldam, M. and Svendsen, G. T., 'An Essay on Social Capital: Looking for the fire behind the smoke', *European Journal of Political Economy*, 16, 2000, pp. 339–366.

Parkhe, A., 'Strategic alliance structuring: A game theoretic and transaction cost examination of inter-firm cooperation', *Academy of Management Journal*, 36, 1993, pp. 794–829.

Pavitt, K., 'Sectoral Patterns of Technical Change: Towards a Theory and a Taxonomy', *Research Policy*, 13, 1984, pp. 343–373.

Perelman, M., 'The Political Economy of Intellectual Property', *Monthly Review*, 54, 8, 2003, pp. 29–37.

Perry-Smith, J. E. and Shalley, C. E., 'The social side of creativity: A static and dynamic social network perspective', *Academy of Management Review*, 28, 1, 2003, pp. 89–107.

Pigou, A. C., *The Economics of Welfare*. London: Macmillan 1924.

Pigou, A. C., *Memorials of Alfred Marshall*. London 1925.

Polanyi, M., *The Tacit Dimension*. Gloucester, MA 1983 {1966}.

Portes, A., 'Social capital: Its origins and applications in modern sociology', *Annual Review of Sociology*, 24, 1998, pp. 1–24.

Portes, A. and Sensenbrenner, J., 'Embeddedness and immigration: notes on the social determinants of economic action', *American Journal of Sociology*, 98, 1993, pp. 1320–1350.

Porter, S., *Rhythm and Harmony in the music of the Beatles*. Ann Arbor, MI 1979.

Post, D., *Some Thoughts on the Political Economy of Intellectual Property: A Brief Look at the International Copyright Relations of the United States*. Temple University Law School/ Cyberspace Law Institute 1998. *http://www.temple.edu/lawschool/dpost/Chinapaper.html*

Powell, W. W. and DiMaggio, P. J. (eds), *The New Institutionalism in Organizational Analysis*. Chicago 1991.

Powell, W. W., Koput, K. K. and Smith-Doerr, L., 'Inter-organizational collaboration and the locus of innovation: Network of learning in biotechnology', *Administrative Science Quarterly*, 41, 1996, pp. 116–145.

Pressman, S. and Holt, R., 'Teaching Post Keynesian Economics to Undergraduate Students', *Journal of Post Keynesian Economics*, 26, 1, 2003, pp. 169–186.

Pruitt, D. G., 'Reciprocity and credit building in a laboratory dyad', *Journal of Personality and Social Psychology*, 8, 1968, pp. 143–147.

Puddephatt, A. J., 'Chess Playing as Strategic Activity', *Symbolic Interaction*, 26, 2, 2003, pp. 263–284.

Pugh, D. S. and Hickson, D. J., 'The Context of Organization Structures', *Administrative Science Quarterly*, 14, 1, 1969a, pp. 91–114.

Pugh, D. S., Hickson, D. J. and Hinings, C. R., 'An empirical taxonomy of structures of work organizations', *Administrative Science Quarterly*, 14, 1969b, pp. 115–126.

Putnam, R. D., *Making Democracy Work: Civic Traditions in Modern Italy*. Princeton, NJ 1993.

Raskind, L. J., 'Copyright', in Newman, P. (ed.), *The New Palgrave Dictionary of Economics and Law*. London 1998, pp. 478–483.

Reagans, R. and McEvily, B. 'Network structure and knowledge transfer: The effects of cohesion and range', *Administrative Science Quarterly*, 48, 2, 2003, pp. 240–267.

Reder, M. W., *Economics: The Culture of a Controversial Science*. Chicago 1999.

Regan D. T., 'Effects of a Favor and Liking on Compliance', *Journal of Experimental Social Psychology*, 7, 1971, pp. 627–639.

Richardson, H. W., *The economics of urban size*. Westmead, Farnborough 1973.

Rip, A. and Kemp, R., 'Technological Change', in Rayner, S. and Malone, E. L. (eds), *Human Choice and Climate Change*, Vol. II. Columbus, OH 1998, pp. 327–399.

Rogers, E. M., *Diffusion of Innovations*, 3rd edn. New York 1983.

Rogers, E. M. and Kincaid, D. L., *Communication Networks*. New York 1981.

Romer, P., 'Increasing Returns and Long-Run Growth', *Journal of Political Economy*, 94, 5, 1987.

Romer, P., 'Two Strategies for Economic Development: Using Ideas and Producing Ideas', *Proceedings of the World Bank Annual Conference on Development Economics* 1992. IBRD/World Bank 1993.

Romer, P., 'New goods, old theory, and the welfare costs of trade restrictions', *Journal of Development Economics*, 43, 1994, pp. 5–38.

Romer, P., 'When should we use intellectual property rights?', *American Economic Review*, 92, 2, 2002, pp. 213–216.

Rooney, D., Hearn, G. and Ninan, A. (eds), *Handbook on the Knowledge Economy*. Cheltenham 2005.

Rose-Ackerman, S., 'Bribes and Gifts', in Ben-ner, A. and Putterman, L. (eds), *Economics, values and organization*. Cambridge 1998.

Rosenberg, N., 'Why do firms do basic research (with their own money)?', *Research Policy*, 19, 1990, pp. 165–174.

Rosenthal, R., *Meta-Analytic Procedures for Social Research*. Newbury Park, CA 1991.

Ruth, J. A., Otnes, C. C. and Brunel, F. F., 'Gift receipt and the reformulation of interpersonal Relationships', *Journal of Consumer Research*, 25, 4, 1999, pp. 385–402.

Ryle, G., *The Concept of Mind*. London 1966 {1949}.

Sahal, D., 'A Unified Theory of Self-Organization', *Journal of Cybernetics*, 9, 1979, pp. 127–142.

Sahlins, M. B., *Stone Age Economics*. Chicago 1972.

Sandefur, R. L. and Laumann, E. O., 'A paradigm for social capital', in Lesser, E. L. (ed.), *Knowledge and Social Capital: foundations and Applications*. Boston 1998.

Saxenian, A., *Regional Advantage*. Cambridge, MA 1994.

Schabas, M., 'Breaking Away: History of Economics as a History of Science', *History of Political Economy*, 24, 1, 1992, pp. 187–203.

Schein, E. H., *Organization Psychology*. New York 1965.

Schmalensee, R., 'Continuity and Change in the Economics Industry', *Economic Journal*, 101, 1991, pp. 115–121.

Schmidt, A., Dolfsma, W. and Keuvelaar, W., *Fighting the War on File Sharing*. The Hague 2002.

Schmitz, H., *Technology and employment practices in developing countries*. London 1985.

Schulz, M., 'The Uncertain Relevance of Newness: Organizational Learning and Knowledge Flows', *Academy of Management Journal*, 44, 4, 2001, pp. 661–681.

Schulz, M., 'Pathways of Relevance: Exploring inflows of knowledge into subunits of multinational corporations', *Organization Science*, 14, 4, 2003, pp. 440–459.

Schumpeter, J. A., *The Theory of Economic Development*. Cambridge, MA 1934 [1949].

Schumpeter, J. A., *Capitalism, Socialism and Democracy*. London 1943 [1952].

Schumpeter, J. A., *History of Economic Analysis*. New York 1954.

Schumpeter, J. A., *Business Cycles: A Theoretical, Historical and Statistical Analysis of Capitalist Process*. New York [1939] 1964.

Schwartz, B., 'The Social Psychology of the Gift', in Komter, A. E. (ed.), *The Gift: An Interdisciplinary Perspective*. Amsterdam 1996.

Schwartz, D., 'The Regional Location of Knowledge-Based Economy Activities in Israel', *Journal of Technology Transfer*, 31, 1, 2006, pp. 31–44.

Scotchmer, S. and Green, J., 'Novelty and disclosure in patent law', *RAND Journal of Economics*, 21, 1990, pp. 131–146.

Scott, J., *Social network analysis*. London 1991.

Selten, R. 'A simple model of imperfect competition', *International Journal of Game Theory*, 1973.

Sen, A., *Resources, Values and Development*. Cambridge, MA 1984.

Shaikh, A., 'Humbug Production Function', *The New Palgrave*, 1990.

Shannon, C. E., 'A Mathematical Theory of Communication', *Bell System Technical Journal*, 27, 1948, pp. 379–423 and 623–356.

Shapiro, C. and Varian, H., *Information Rules*. Boston, MA 1999.

Shapiro, S. P., 'The social control of impersonal trust', *American Journal of Sociology*, 93, 1987, pp. 623–658.

Shavell, S. and van Ypersele, T., 'Rewards versus intellectual property rights', *Journal of Law and Economics*, 44, 2001, pp. 525–547.

Sherry, J. F., 'Gift Giving in Anthropological Perspective', *Journal of Consumer Research*, 10, 2, 1983, pp. 157–168.

Simmel, G., 'Faithfulness and Gratitude', in Komter, A. E. (ed.), *The Gift: An Interdisciplinary Perspective*. Amsterdam 1996.

Simon, H. A., *Administrative Behavior*. New York 1976.

Simon, H. A. and Schaeffer, J., 'The Game of Chess', Aumann, A. and Hart, S. (eds), *Handbook of Game Theory, With Economic Applications*. Amsterdam 1992.

Skolnikoff, E. B., *The Elusive Transformation: Science, technology and the evolution of international politics*. Princeton 1993.

Smart, A., 'Gifts, Bribes, and Guanxi: A reconsideration of Bourdieu's Social Capital', *Cultural Anthropology*, 8, 3, 1993, pp. 388–408.

Smith, A., in R. H. Campbell and A. S. Skinner (eds), *An Inquiry into the Nature and the Causes of the Wealth of Nations*, 2 vols, Indianapolis 1981 {1776}.

Stark, W., *The Sociology of Knowledge*. London 1958.

Sternberg, R., 'Innovative linkages and proximity: empirical results from recent surveys of small and medium sized firms in German regions', *Regional Studies*, 33, 6, 1999, pp. 529–540.

Stevenson, W. B., 'Formal Structure and Networks of Interaction within Organizations', *Social Science Research*, 19, 1990, pp. 113–131.

Stevenson, W. B. and Gilly, M. C., 'Information processing and problem solving: The migration of problems through formal positions and networks of ties', *Academy of Management Journal*, 34, 1991, pp. 918–928.

Stigler, G. J., *Essays in the History of Economics*. Chicago 1965.

Stigler, G. J. and Becker, G. S., 'De Gustibus non est Disputandum', *American Economic Review*, 67, 2, 1977, pp. 76–90.

Stiglitz, J. E., *Public Policy for a Knowledge Economy*. London 1999.

Stiglitz, J. E., 'Information and the Change in the Paradigm in Economics', *American Economic Review*, 92, 3, 2002, pp. 460–501.

Storper, M., *The Regional World – Territorial Development in a Global Economy*. New York 1997.

Strassman, D., 'The Stories of Economics and the Power of the Storyteller', *History of PoliticalEconomy*, 25, 1, 1993, pp. 147–165.

Strassman, D. and Polanyi, L., 'The Economist as Storyteller', in Kuiper, E. and Sap, J. (eds), *Out of the Margin: Feminist Perspectives on Economics*. London 1995, pp. 129–150.

Suárez, F. F. and Utterback, J. M., 'Dominant design and the survival of firms', *Strategic Management Journal*, 16, 1995, pp. 415–430.

Swann, P., 'Innovation and the Size of Industrial Clusters in Europe', in Gambardella, A. and Malerba, F. (eds), *The Organization of Economic Innovation in Europe*. Cambridge 1999, pp. 103–124.

Szulanski, G., 'Exploring internal stickiness: Impediments to the transfer of best practice within the firm', *Strategic Management Journal*, 17, 1996, pp. 27–43.

Szulanski, G., *Sticky knowledge*. London and Thousand Oaks, CA 2003.

Szulanski, G., Cappetta, R. and Jensen, R. J., 'When and How Trustworthiness Matters: Knowledge Transfer and the Moderating Effect of Causal Ambiguity', *Organization Science*, 15, 5, 2004, pp. 600–613.

Takalo T. and Kanniainen, V., 'Do patents slow down technological progress? Real options in research, patenting, and market introduction', *International Journal of Industrial Organization*, 18, 2000, pp. 1105–1127.

Takeyama, L. N., 'The welfare implications of unauthorized reproduction of intellectual property in the presence of demand network externalities', *Journal of Industrial Economics*, 42, 2, 1994, pp. 155–166.

Teece, D., 'Capturing Value from Knowledge Assets: The New Economy, Markets for Know-How, and Intangible Assets', *California Management Review*, 40, 3, 1998, pp. 55–79.

Teece, D., Pisano, G. and Shuen, A., 'Dynamic Capabilities and Strategic Management', *Strategic Management Journal*, 18, 7, 1997, pp. 509–533.

Teitel, S. and Westphal, L. E. (eds), 'Symposium on Technological Change and Industrial Development', *Journal of Development Economics*, 16, 1 and 2, 1984.

Telser, L. G., 'A theory of self-enforcing agreements', *Journal of Business*, 53, 1980, pp. 27–44.

Theil, H., *Statistical Decomposition Analysis*. Amsterdam/London 1972.

Theil, H. and Fiebig, D. G., *Exploiting Continuity: Maximum Entropy Estimation of Continuous Distributions*. Cambridge, MA 1984.

Thijm, Chr. Alberdingk, *Fair use: het auteursrechtelijk evenwight hersteld, Informatierecht/ AMI*, 1988, vol. 9, pp. 145–154.

Thrift, N., *Knowing Capitalism*. London 2005.

Tillekens, G., *Het Geluid van de Beatles*. Amsterdam 1998.

Towse, R. and Holzhauer, R. (eds), *The Economics of Intellectual Property*. Cheltenham 2002, 4 volumes.

Tsai, W., 'Knowledge transfer in intra-organizational networks: Effects of network position and absorptive capacity on business unit innovation and performance', *Academy of Management Journal*, 44, 2001, pp. 996–1004.

Tsai, W. and Ghosal, S., 'Social Capital and Value Creation: The role of intra firm networks', *Academy of Management Journal*, 41, 4, 1998, pp. 464–476.

Tushman, M., 'Special boundary roles in the innovation process', *Administrative Science Quarterly*, 22, 4, 1977, pp. 587–605.

Tushman, M. and Scanlan. T. J., 'Boundary Spanning Individuals: Their role in information transfer and their antecedents', *Academy of Management Journal*, 24, 2, 1981, pp. 289–305.

Uehara, E., 'Dual Exchange Theory, Social Networks, and Informational Support', *American Journal of Sociology*, 96, 1990, pp. 521–557.

Ulanowicz, R. E., *Growth and Development: Ecosystems Phenomenology*. San Jose 1986.

Ullman-Margalit, E., 'Invisible-hand explanations', *Synthesis*, 39, 1978, pp. 263–291.

UNCTAD, *World Investment Report*. United Nations Conference on Trade and Development, 2005.

Utterback, J. M. and Suárez, F. F., 'Innovation, Competition, and Industry Structure', *Research Policy*, 22, 1993, pp. 1–21.

Van de Poel, I., Fransen, M. and Dolfsma, W., 'Technological Regimes: Taking Stock, Looking Ahead', *International Journal of Technology, Policy and Management*, 2, 4, 2002, pp. 482–495.

Van den Ende, J. and Dolfsma, W., 'Technology-Push, Demand-Pull and the Shaping of Technological Paradigms – The Development of Computing Technology', *Journal of Evolutionary Economics*, 15, 1, 2005, pp. 83–99.

Van den Ende, J. and Kemp, R., 'Technological Transformation in History: How the Computer Regime Grew out of Existing Computing Regimes', *Research Policy*, 28, 1999, pp. 833–851.

Van der Panne, G. *Entrepreneurship and Localized Knowledge Spillovers*. Unpublishe Ph. D. Thesis, Technical University Delft, Delft 2004.

Van der Panne, G. and Dolfsma, W., 'Hightech door Nederland', *Economisch Statistische Berichten*, 86, 4318, 2001, pp. 584–586.

Van der Panne, G. and Dolfsma, W., 'The Odd Role of Proximity in Knowledge Relations: High-Tech in the Netherlands', *Journal of Economic and Social Geography*, 94, 4, 2003, pp. 451–460.

Van der Panne, G. and Dolfsma, W., 'Currents and Subcurrents in the River of Innovations: Explaining innovativeness using new product announcements', *Research Policy*, 2008.

Van der Vegt, C., Muskens and Manshanden, *Groei, Arbeid en Ruimte – scenario's van hoge groei in de regio Amsterdam*. Amsterdam 2000.

Van der Vegt, C., Lambooy, J., Van Esterik, Poot, T., Webbing, *Economie en Arbeidsmarkt in de economische regio Amsterdam*. Amsterdam 1995.

Van Lente, H. and Rip, A., 'Expectations in Technological Developments: An Example of Prospective Structure to Be Filled in by Agency', in Disco, C. and van de Meulen, B. (eds), *Getting New Technologies Together. Studies in Making Sociotechnical Order*. Berlin 1998, pp. 203–230.

Van Oort, F., Innovation and agglomeration economies in the Netherlands. *Tijdschrift voor Economische en Sociale Geografie*, 93, 3, 2002, pp. 344–360.

Varley, R. A., Klessinger, N. J. C., Romanowski, C. A. J. and Siegal, M., 'Agramatic but Numerate', *Proceedings of the National Academy of Sciences*, 102, 9, 2005, pp. 3519–3524.

Veblen, T. B., 'On the nature of capital: Investment, intangible assets, and the pecuniary magnate', *Quarterly Journal of Economics*, 23, 1, 1908, 104–136.

Veblen, T. B., *The Place of Science in Modern Civilisation and other Essays*. New York 1961 [1898].

Vickers, J., 'Concepts of competition', *Oxford Economic Papers*, 47, 1, 1995, pp. 1–23.

Vonortas, N. S., 'Multimarket Contact and Inter-firm Cooperation in R&D', *Journal of Evolutionary Economics*, 10, 1–2, 2000, pp. 243–271.

Vroon, P. and Draaisma, D., *De Mens als Metafoor {Man as a Metaphor}*. Baarn 1985.

Walsh, J. R., 'Capital Concept Applied to Man', *Quarterly Journal of Economics*, 49, 1935, pp. 255–285.

Walster, E., Berscheid, E. and Walster, G. W., 'New Directions in Equity Research', in Berkowitz, L. and Walster, E. (eds), *Equity Theory: Towards a General Theory of Social Interaction*. New York 1976.

Wasserman, S. and Faust, K., *Social network analysis*. New York, NY 1994.

Watts, R. J. and Porter, A. L., 'R&D cluster quality measures and technology maturity', *Technological Forecasting & Social Change*, 70, 2003, pp. 735–758.

Weigelt, K. and Camerer, C., 'Reputation and corporate strategy: A review of recent theory and applications', *Strategic Management Journal*, 9, 1988, pp. 443–454.

Weintraub, E. R., *Stabilizing Dynamics*. Cambridge 1991.

Weir, M., 'Ideas and Politics: The Acceptance of Keynesianism in Britain and the United States', in Hall, P. A. (ed.), *The Political Power of Economic Ideas*. Princeton 1989, pp. 53–86.

Weiss, M. A., 'High-technology industries and the future of employment', in Bertuglia, C. S., Fischer, M. M. and Preto, G. (eds), *Technological change, economic development and space*. Heidelberg 1995, pp. 80–143.

Wever, E. and Stam, E., 'Clusters of High Technology SMEs: the Dutch case', *Regional Studies*, 33, 1999, pp. 391–400.

White, H., 'The Historical Text as Literary Artifact', *Tropics of Discourse*. Baltimore 1978, pp. 81–100.

Whitehead, A. N., *Modes of Thought*. New York 1968 {1938}.

Whitley, R. D., *The Intellectual and Social Organization of the Sciences*. Oxford 1984.

Whitley, R. D., 'National Innovation Systems', in Smelser, N. J. and Baltes, P. B. (eds), *International Encyclopedia of the Social and Behavioral Sciences*. Oxford 2001, pp. 10303–10309.

Wilke, H. and Lanzetta, J. T., 'The Obligation to Help: The Effects of the Amount of Prior Help on Subsequent Helping Behavior', *Journal of Experimental Social Psychology*, 6, 1970, pp. 488–493.

Williamson, O. E., *The Economic Institutions of Capitalism: Firm Markets, Relational Contracting*. New York 1985.

Williamson, O. E., 'Calculativeness, Trust, And Economic Organization', *Journal of Law and Economics*, 36, 1993, pp. 159–502.

Windrum, P. and Tomlinson, M., 'Knowledge-Intensive Services and International Competitiveness: A Four Country Comparison', *Technology Analysis and Strategic Management*, 11, 3, 1999, pp. 391–408.

Winter, S. G., 'Schumpeterian Competition in Alternative Technological Regimes', *Journal of Economic Behavior and Organization*, 5, 1984, pp. 287–320.

Winter, S. G. and Szulanski, G., 'Replication as Strategy', *Organization Science*, 12, 6, 2001, pp. 730–743.

Wintjes, R., *Regionaal-economische effecten van buitenlandse bedrijven*. (Ph.D. thesis, University of Utrecht) 2001.

Wintjes, R. and Cobbenhagen, J., 'Knowledge intensive Industrial Clustering around Océ; Embedding a vertical disintegrated codification process into the Eindhoven-Venlo region', *MERIT Research Memorandum*, nr. 00-06, MERIT, University of Maastricht, Maastricht, 2000.

Woolcock, M., 'Social Capital and Economic Development: towards a Theoretical synthesis and policy framework', *Theory and Society*, 27, 2, 1998, pp. 151–208.

Wright, B. D., 'The economics of invention incentives: Patents, prizes, and research contracts', *American Economic Review*, 73, 4, 1983, pp. 691–707.

Zeitlyn, D., 'Gift economies in the development of open source software', *Research Policy*, 32, 7, 2003, pp. 1287–1291.

Zelizer, V. A., *The Social Meaning of Money*. Princeton, NJ 1997.

Zucker, L. G., 'Production of trust: Institutional sources of economic structure, 1840–1920.' *Research in Organizational Behavior*, 8, 1986, pp. 53–111.

Index

Printed in the United States
by Baker & Taylor Publisher Services